THE PRESIDENCY

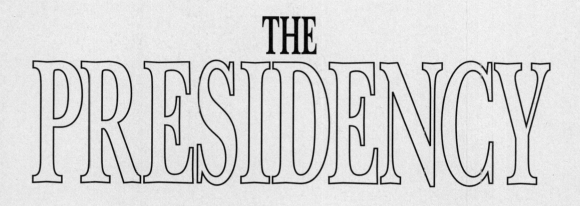

THE
PRESIDENCY

A history of the office of the President of the United States from 1789 to the present

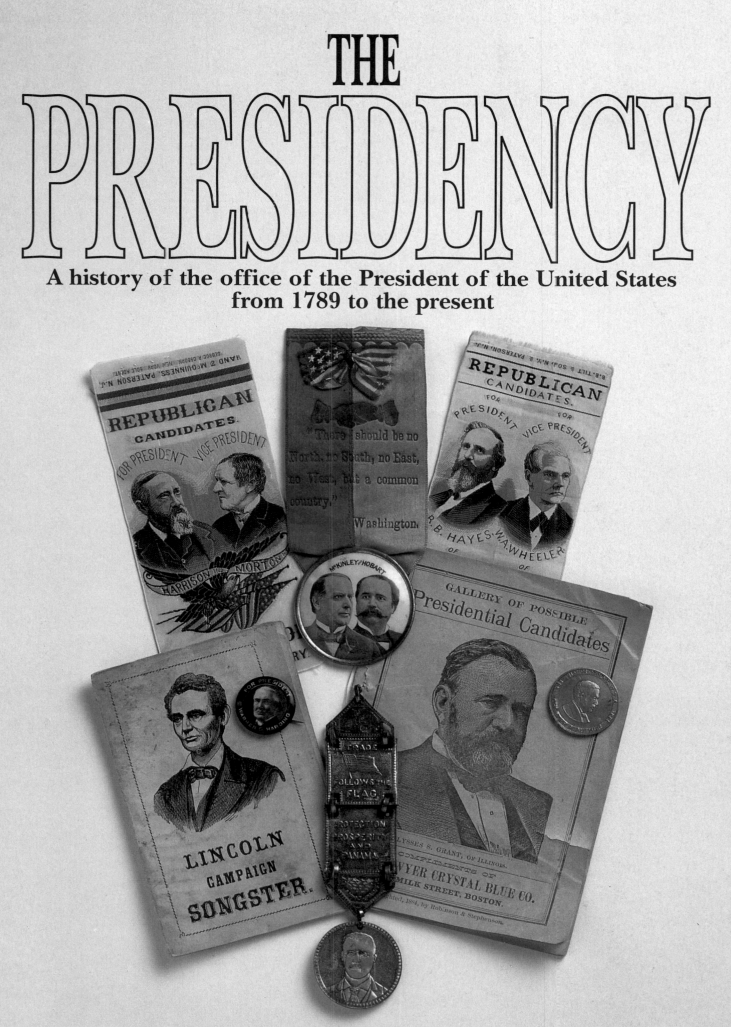

Editor: Michael Nelson
Professor of Political Science, Rhodes College, Memphis, Tennessee

a Salamander book
Published by Salamander Books Limited
LONDON

A Salamander Book

Published by Salamander Books Ltd
129-137 York Way
London N7 9LG
United Kingdom

© Salamander Books Ltd 1996

ISBN 0 86101 810 9

All correspondence concerning the content of this volume should be addressed to Salamander Books Ltd.

CREDITS
Project Editors: Christopher Westhorp and Tony Hall
Designer: Paul Johnson
Copy Editor: Nick Brock
Commissioned photography: Don Eiler's Custom Photography, Richmond, Virginia, USA
Technical Consultant: Russ A. Pritchard
Filmset: SX DTP Ltd, England
Colour reproduction: P & W Graphics PTE, Singapore

9 8 7 6 5 4 3 2 1

Printed and bound in Italy

EDITOR
MICHAEL NELSON (Foreword, The Constitutional Presidency, The Vice Presidency, The Changing Office) is professor of political science at Rhodes College in Memphis, Tennessee. A former editor of the *Washington Monthly*, he is the author of numerous books and articles on the presidency, presidential elections, and other subjects. One of those books, *The American Presidency: Origins and Development, 1776-1993*, won the Benjamin Franklin Award in the category of history, politics, and philosophy.

Front jacket: The Presidential Seal, courtesy The White House (supplied by Folio).
Back jacket: A selection of items reproduced from the various chapters of the book; the exception is the 50-star Presidential Seal flag (bottom left) with gold and silver fringe that was used in President Eisenhower's office after the admission of Alaska and Hawaii as the 49th and 50th states, respectively. (Courtesy Dwight D. Eisenhower Library and Museum.)

Prelim captions:
Endpapers: The monumental sculpture of the heads of Washington, Jefferson, Lincoln, and Theodore Roosevelt carved in the granite of Mount Rushmore, South Dakota.
Page 1: Presidential campaign buttons, from left to right: Franklin D. Roosevelt, Richard Nixon, Harry S. Truman, Ronald Reagan, and Dwight D. Eisenhower.
Page 3: Miscellaneous campaign material: (top, from left to right) ribbon for Benjamin Harrison in the 1888 election, ribbon and button for William McKinley in 1896, and a ribbon for Rutherford B. Hayes in 1876; (bottom, from left to right) a songster for the Abraham Lincoln campaign, a button for Warren Harding, a double luck medal for Theodore Roosevelt, a campaign booklet for Ulysses S. Grant, and a medallion for Chester A. Arthur.
Page 4: This is the actual sign (not the museum displayed duplicate) that sat on President Truman's desk from October 2, 1945, onward. Wood and glass, it was made at the United States Southwest Reformatory in El Reno, Oklahoma. A similar one sat on the desk of the warden L. Clark Schilder. It was designed by the head of the printshop, Buford Earl Tressider, who made and patented the upright glass portion. The wood base was made by Dave Morgan.
Page 5: Cartier-made President's Seal die belonging to Woodrow Wilson, with its original storage case. It became obsolete in 1945 when Harry S. Truman revised the design. The die was used with sealing wax on envelopes containing official presidential messages to Congress.

CONTRIBUTING AUTHORS
HAROLD F. BASS, Jr., (Electing the President) is professor of political science and director of the Maddox Public Affairs Center at Ouachita Baptist University in Arkadelphia, Arkansas. He is the author of several articles and book chapters on the American presidency and political parties.

MARK BYRNES (The Jacksonian Era, The Civil War Presidents) is assistant professor of political science at Middle Tennessee State University in Murfreesboro, Tennessee. He is the author of *Politics and Space*, 'The Presidency and the Bureaucracy' in *Guide to the Presidency*, and 'Tennessee Government and Politics' in *United States Government*.

BURTON I. KAUFMAN (The Modern Presidency Emerges, The Modern Presidency, The Contemporary Presidency) is professor of history and humanities and director of the Center for Interdisciplinary Studies at Virginia Polytechnic Institute and State University in Blacksburg, Virginia. A specialist on the American presidency and foreign policy, his most recent books are *The Presidency of James Earl Carter, Jr.*, and *The Arab World and the United States*.

JOHN A. MALTESE (The American System) is assistant professor of political science at the University of Georgia in Athens, Georgia. He has written extensively on the presidency and the judiciary, and his books include *The Selling of Supreme Court Nominees*, *Spin Control: The White House Office of Communications and the Management of Presidential News* (which won the Frank Luther Mott Award), and *Selecting the President*.

STEPHEN L. ROBERTSON (The Seat of Presidential Power, The First Ladies) teaches political science at Middle Tennessee State University. He has contributed articles to *Guide to the Presidency* and is coauthor of *Cabinets and Counselors: The President and the Executive Branch* and *The Presidents, First Ladies, and Vice Presidents*.

JOHN R. VILE (The Early Presidents) is professor and chair of political science at Middle Tennessee State University. He is the author of several books about the U.S. Constitution and is a contributor to the *Oxford Companion to the Supreme Court* and *Guide to the Presidency*. His most recent book is *Amending the Constitution*.

STEPHEN H. WIRLS (The 'Gilded' Age) is assistant professor of political science at Rhodes College. He is the author of several articles on American political institutions in *Presidential Studies Quarterly* and other journals and has coauthored two chapters for *Guide to the Presidency*.

Contents

Michael Nelson

FOREWORD

The dawn scene in Washington, D.C., with the Lincoln Memorial,
the Washington Monument, and the Capitol.

Henry Jones Ford, in his classic 1898 work, *The Rise and Growth of American Government*, quoted Alexander Hamilton's prediction to a friend that the time would 'assuredly come when every vital question of the state will be merged in the question, "Who shall be the next president?"' Ford cited this remark to support his argument that, in creating the presidency, the Constitutional Convention of 1787 had 'revived the oldest political institution of the race, the elective kingship.'

Although there is much truth in Ford's evaluation of the presidency, it also displays a certain measure of ambivalence on a fundamental issue. Is the presidency best understood as primarily a person ('Who shall be the next president?') or an office (an 'elective kingship')?

Presidential scholars in the 20th century have continued to grapple with Ford's conundrum but have not resolved it. Most of them probably would agree that the best answer to the person-or-office question is both: person *and* office, president *and* presidency. The office has become important mostly because its constitutional design suited it well for national leadership in the changing circumstances of history. But because the Constitution invested so much responsibility in the person who is the president, that person's background, personality, and leadership skills are also consequential.

THE PRESIDENCY AS OFFICE

The Constitutional Convention created a government marked not by separation of powers (the traditional formulation) but rather, in the political scientist Richard Neustadt's apt phrase, by 'separated institutions sharing powers.' Institutional separation meant, for example, that in stark contrast to parliamentary governments, which draw their executive leadership from the legislature, the president was forbidden by Article I, Section 6 of the Constitution to appoint any sitting member of Congress to the cabinet or White House staff. These severely separated branches were, however, constitutionally enjoined to share in the exercise of virtually all the powers of the national government – the president is 'Commander in Chief of the Army and Navy,' but Congress has the power to 'declare war'; the Senate may (or may choose not to) give 'Advice and Consent' concerning presidential appointments to the executive branch and the judiciary; and so on.

Powers, of course, do not define power – through history, the presidency has become increasingly powerful even though the formal powers of the office have remained the same. A second cluster of constitutional decisions, those concerning the number and selection of the executive, provides much of the explanation for the presidency's expanding influence. The Framers of the Constitution, after much debate, created the presidency as a one-person, not a plural or committee-style, office and provided that the president would be elected by the entire nation, independent of Congress and the state governments. In doing so, they made the president the only national officer who can plausibly claim both a political mandate to speak for the people and their government and an institutional capacity to lead with what the Pennsylvania delegate James Wilson described as 'energy, unity, and responsibility.'

Lead, that is, when national leadership is sought, which, during the 19th century, it usually was not. Historically, it took a century and a quarter – from 1789, when George Washington was inaugurated as the first president, to 1913, Woodrow Wilson's first year in office – for parchment to become practice, that is, for all of the constitutionally enumerated powers of the presidency to come to life. During the 19th century the country, then a congeries of local economies and cultures, was not seeking the energetic leadership on behalf of national initiatives that the presidency was constitutionally designed to provide. But the broad extension of railroads and telegraph lines made all but inevitable the development of a national economy and society, and with this transformation came demands that the national government take measures variously to facilitate the spread and to tame the excesses of massive corporations.

With all eyes turned to Washington, the presidency was in business. Early 20th-century presidents Theodore Roosevelt and Wilson roused a popular mandate for the president to make full use of the office's constitutional powers to lead Congress and the executive branch. Franklin D. Roosevelt, during the Great Depression of the 1930s, and more recent presidents such as Lyndon B. Johnson and Ronald Reagan have also played the role of chief legislator on a grand scale. The post-World War II rise of the United States to superpower status in a then-bipolar, now unipolar international system lifted the presidency to center stage not just at home but in the world.

THE PRESIDENCY AS PERSON

Because the presidency is important, so is the person who at any moment is the president. What background characteristics do presidents typically acquire before taking office? What manner of personality? What skills of leadership?

As to background, presidents almost always have been drawn from the ranks of white, male, married, Christians who already have held high governmental office. Women, African Americans, Jews, bachelors, even nationally prominent leaders from the realms of business, education, and elsewhere in the private sector have found it hard to rouse serious interest in their potential presidential candidacies. Recent historical trends indicate both an expansion (in social terms) and a contraction (in occupational terms) of the talent pool from which Americans choose their presidents. Until John F. Kennedy's election in 1960, for example, Roman Catholics were effectively excluded from consideration; so, until Reagan was elected in 1980, were divorced men. Public opinion surveys indicate a growing willingness among voters to select a black, female, or Jewish president. Yet the rosters of presidential candidates in recent elections have included few cabinet officers, members of the House of Representatives, generals, or other government officials who were not either a senator, a governor, or the vice president.

The personality, or psychological character, that a president brings to the White House is, considering the power of the office and the pressures that weigh upon its occupant, of obvious importance. Public interest in the moral and psychological character flaws of candidates in recent presidential elections illustrates the widespread concern about presidential character. So do the efforts of political scientists to develop behavioral models that relate presidential character to presidential performance. Regrettably, however, scholarly understanding of this matter has not kept pace with public concern. Personality theory is still too undefined a field to explain, much less to predict, the presidential character.

The skills of leadership that a president requires may be more confidently described. In relations with the rest of the executive branch, the president is called upon to be a talented manager of authority, both of lieutenants on the White House staff (whose chronic sycophancy toward the president and hostility toward the president's critics perennially threaten to overwhelm the good effects of their loyalty, talent, and hard work) and of the massive departments and agencies of the bureaucracy, whose activities lie at the heart of the president's role as chief executive.

Presidential leadership of Congress requires different, more tactical political skills. Senators and representatives, no less than the president, are politically independent and self-interested. No one has described the challenge of leading them more precisely and pithily than Neustadt: to lead is to persuade, to persuade is to bargain, and to bargain is to convince individual members of Congress that their interests and the president's are (or can be made to be) the same.

Ultimately, a president's standing with Congress and the bureaucracy rests on the bedrock of public opinion, which makes the 'presentation of self' (a phrase invented by the sociologist Erving Goffman) to the American people an important aspect of leadership skill. 'Presentation of self' involves not just speechmaking, press conferences, and other forms of rhetoric, but dramaturgy as well. During Richard Nixon's first term, for example, he effectively reinforced a televised speech appealing for the support of the 'silent majority' of blue-collar workers and their families by dramatically donning a hard hat before a cheering crowd (and a battery of observing cameras) at a New York construction site.

Perhaps a president's most important leadership skills involve a strategic sense of the historical possibilities of the time. These possibilities are defined both by objective conditions (the international situation, the budget, the health of the economy, and so on) and by the public mood. Above all, the president must have a highly developed aptitude for what Woodrow Wilson called 'interpretation' – that is, the ability to understand and articulate the varying, vaguely expressed desires of the American people for change or quiescence, material prosperity or moral challenge, isolation from or intervention in the problems of the world, and so on.

In the end, the background, personality, and leadership skills of the president are important because of the ways in which the Constitution and changing historical circumstances have made the presidency important. Person and office, although defined and often discussed separately, are in essence one.

MICHAEL NELSON
PROFESSOR OF POLITICAL SCIENCE
RHODES COLLEGE

Michael Nelson

1

THE CONSTITUTIONAL PRESIDENCY

The delegates to the Constitutional Convention arrived in Philadelphia in May 1787 with few ideas about how to design an executive that would be strong enough to be effective but no so strong as to be oppressive. They completed their work successfully, but with consequences for the presidency as a living institution that have often been surprising.

The Liberty Bell superimposed over the United States' flag and the Declaration of Independence.

The genetic code of the American presidency, conceived at the Constitutional Convention of 1787, is written in the Constitution.[1] In this chapter, the constitution-makers' decisions and their longterm consequences are examined in three clusters: *number and selection*, the series of choices that made the presidency a single-person office elected by an independent national constituency; *term and removal*, the former fixed in length, the latter difficult to achieve; and *institutional separation and powers*, which made the presidency, in the political scientist Richard Neustadt's phrase, one of three 'separated institutions sharing powers.'[2]

THE CONSTITUTIONAL CONVENTION

As the political scientist John Roche has suggested, the Convention that assembled in Philadelphia's Independence Hall in late May 1787 can usefully be described as a 'nationalist reform caucus,' a meeting of relatively like-minded political leaders whose major objective was to develop a plan of government that 'would bolster the "National interest"' by being strong but not oppressive and 'be acceptable to the people,' who would have to ratify and live under it.[3] Most of the great battles among the delegates were not about the powers of the new government but rather about how power within that government should be allocated. More often than not, the issues in dispute lent themselves to compromise solutions, as when small states split the difference with larger states and provided for a bicameral legislature – a House of Representatives apportioned by population and a Senate by state.

But when it came to the nature and powers of the executive, the Convention labored in a realm of such intellectual and political uncertainty that the politics of compromise was largely irrelevant. It was unclear to all groups of delegates how either of their primary goals could be met. An executive that was strong but not oppressive? They had several models of what they did not want but few that they found attractive. The British king and his royal governors, under whom Americans had lived until 1776, had been, in the delegates' eyes, tramplers of liberty. The state constitutions that were written after independence provided for nonoppressive governors, but also rendered them weak to the point of impotence. The national government of the Articles of Confederation, such as it was, had no chief executive at all.

Nor was it clear what the people would accept. Hatred for monarchy existed side by side with a longing to make George Washington king. As the political scientist Seymour Martin Lipset has shown, Washington was a classic example of Max Weber's charismatic leader, a man 'treated as if endowed with supernatural, superhuman, or at least specifically exceptional powers or qualities.'[4] But the people's longing for Washington, who was appalled by such anti-republican adulation, was just that: longing for Washington, not for a hereditary monarchy.

The lessons the delegates drew from these observations and experiences varied widely. To Roger Sherman of Connecticut, history taught that the best executive for the new national government would be 'nothing more than an institution for carrying out the will of the legislature.'[5] Alexander Hamilton of New York wanted a powerful 'Governor' selected for life by 'electors chosen by the people.' Other delegates

Above: This satirical cartoon dates from February 16, 1776, and is titled 'The Wise Men of Gotham and their Goose'. It is a comment on the folly of the British government's approach to its colonies.

had ideas of their own or no firm ideas at all. But, as shown by their ready acceptance of the Virginia Plan, a working draft of the Constitution that was written on the eve of the Convention by James Madison of Virginia, a plurality of delegates began their work determined to hem in executive power. They were ready for a strong national government (the Virginia Plan would even have empowered the federal government to veto state laws), but not for a strong executive within that government. Madison's president would have been elected by Congress for no more than a single term.

NUMBER: SHOULD THE EXECUTIVE BE UNITARY OR PLURAL?

So controversial was the question of whether the executive should be unitary or plural that the Virginia Plan left it literally blank. The practical wisdom of this decision became clear on June 1, 1787, when the Convention considered the motion of James Wilson of Pennsylvania that the executive be a single person. After an awkward silence, several delegates rose to attack the proposed 'foetus of monarchy' and to suggest ideas as different as a three-person committee (one from each region of the country), a variable executive whose number could be set and changed by Congress, and a single person sharing power with a council of judges.

Wilson's list of purported single-executive virtues – energy, dispatch, and responsibility – demonstrates the political shrewdness that he, fellow Pennsylvanian Gouverneur Morris, and their allies displayed throughout the Convention. Their own desire was for as powerful an executive as possible, a vigorous national leader. But, realizing that they held a minority position at the outset of the Convention, the presidentialists advanced their ideas on number in terms that their reluctant colleagues could accept.

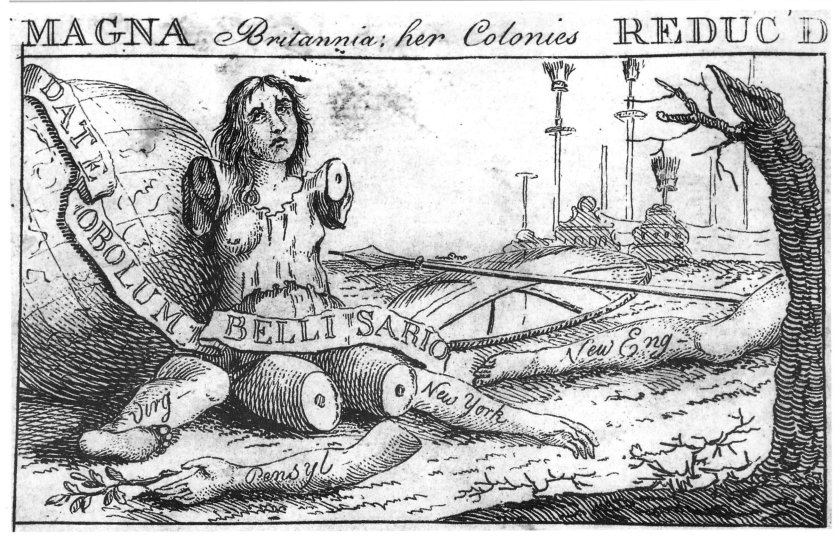

MAGNA *Britannia: her Colonies* REDUC'D

Responsibility could be fixed to a single executive, Wilson argued. Corrupt or incompetent actions by a president, but not by an executive committee, could be checked and punished.

SELECTION: HOW IS THE EXECUTIVE TO BE CHOSEN?

The Convention's deliberations concerning selection also were influenced by the political shrewdness of the presidentialist delegates. In June, July and again in August 1787 the delegates reaffirmed the Virginia Plan's initial proposal for selection of the executive by the legislature, parliamentary-style. Wilson and Morris saw this as a serious problem: a president who owed the job to Congress, they felt, would be the legislature's subordinate. But their efforts on behalf of direct election by the people were unavailing. To most of the delegates, democracy was a synonym for mob rule. George Mason of Virginia said that to allow the people to choose the president would be 'to refer a trial of colours to a blind man.' Failing popular election, Wilson and his colleagues still wanted to secure a provision for selection that would make the president the only person in government who could claim a mandate from the entire nation.

The Electoral College

The electoral college, which was proposed on September 4 (two weeks before the end of the Convention) along with a recommendation that no restriction be placed on the president's eligibility for re-election, was the delegates' jerry-rigged compromise solution to the selection stalemate. The electoral college entrusted the selection of the president to a group of electors chosen by the states, with each state receiving a number of electoral votes equal to its representa-

Above: Benjamin Franklin devised this cartoon prior to the 1766 debate on the repeal of the Stamp Act. He warned that unless it changed its policies Britain would end up like the Roman general Belisarius, reduced to beggary. Note the dismembered Britannia speared by New England.

tion in Congress. The presumption was that most states would turn the choice of their electors over to the voters. Thus, after months of struggle, the presidentialists had won all that they had wanted short of direct popular election. The president would have an independent political base, the only national constituency in the government.

Interestingly, many delegates who still favored legislative selection went along with the electoral college idea. One reason was that the Convention had spun off supplementary proposals to prevent voters from selecting as president anyone younger than thirty-five, fewer than 'fourteen Years a Resident within the United States,' or not a 'natural born Citizen.' The age requirement, it was felt, would limit the choice to candidates old enough to have demonstrated their character and ability, not just 'those brilliant appearances of genius and patriotism which, like transient meteors, sometimes mislead as well as dazzle.' The apparently xenophobic citizenship and residency requirements were also designed in part to prevent rash popular choices, namely of foreign princes (the name of George III's second son, Frederick, Duke of York, somehow entered the public rumor mill) or of popular foreign military leaders like Baron Frederick von Steuben of Prussia, who had emigrated to the United States to fight in the revolution.

A more important reason that legislative-selection proponents suffered defeat gladly on

the electoral college was that many thought they actually had won a victory. Their assurance was based on the constitutional provision that if no candidate received a majority of electoral votes, the House would pick the president from among the leading candidates. George Mason predicted that the House would end up making the choice in 19 elections out of every 20.

Mason's prediction has not stood up well: as of 1996, the House has chosen the president in only two of 51 elections, the most recent being in 1824. The early organization of American politics into a two-party system, which the delegates had not anticipated, helped to assure that in almost every election a major party candidate would win a majority of electoral votes.

Selection by Vice Presidential Succession

The vice presidency came into being at the Convention as a constitutional residue of the electoral college. As Hugh Williamson of North Carolina, a member of the committee that invented the electoral college, told his fellow delegates, 'Such an office as Vice-President was not wanted. It was introduced only for the sake of a valuable mode of election which required two to be chosen at the same time.' The constitutional task assigned to the vice presidency was relatively unimportant – to preside, voting only to break ties, over the Senate – and the reason for allowing it even this power seems to have been the one offered by Roger Sherman: otherwise 'he would be without employment.'

One side-effect of bringing into the government the person whom electors presumably had judged the second most qualified to be president was that it solved the problem of presidential succession. In the event of the president's death, resignation, disability, or impeachment and removal, the vice president would automatically assume the powers and duties of the presidency. The delegates seem to have wanted the succession to be temporary, until a special election could be held to choose a new president. But they neglected to stipulate this clearly in the Constitution.[6] Thus, when President William Henry Harrison died in 1841, Vice President John Tyler's claim to serve as president until the end of Harrison's term in 1845 not only went unchallenged, but set the pattern for future successions. Eventually, the Tyler precedent received explicit constitutional sanction. Section 1 of the Twenty-fifth Amendment, which was added to the Constitution in 1967, states: 'In case of the removal of the president from office or of his death or resignation, the Vice President shall become President.'

NUMBER AND SELECTION: CONSEQUENCES

The Constitutional Convention's most important decisions concerning number and selection, unaltered by subsequent amendments, were those that made the executive a unitary office whose occupant is chosen by an independent national constituency of voters.

The consequences of this cluster of decisions have not always been those foreseen by the convention delegates, but they are real and enduring nonetheless. The number and selection provisions combined the roles of *chief of state and chief of government* into one office. They injected a powerful element of *psychological character* into an otherwise mechanistic plan of government. And they placed *prerogative* power – that is, the power to defy the law in the national interest – in the hands of the president.

Chief of State, Chief of Government

The executive function includes both a symbolic role (chief of state or, in the British case, monarch) and a political one (chief of government, or prime minister). As the political scientist Clinton Rossiter has argued, the significance of the president's chief of state role lies not in the insignificant, formal powers that accompany it or in the activities the role requires: to 'make proclamations of thanksgiving and commemoration, bestow medals on flustered pilots, hold state dinners for the diplomatic corps and the Supreme Court, light the nation's Christmas tree,' and so on.[7] Rather, the importance of the chieftainship of state derives from the emotions the role arouses in citizens.

Research by the political scientist Fred Greenstein is conclusive on the emotional ties that bind the American people to the presidency. He found that, long before they have any real knowledge of what the president actually does, children already think in terms of almost limitless power and benevolence. The president, as seen by elementary school students, 'gives us freedom . . . worries about all the problems of all the states . . . makes peace with every country but bad.' The death of a president causes adults to react in an equally emotional way. Surveys taken shortly after the Kennedy assassination found that Americans displayed symptoms of grief that otherwise arise only at the death of a close friend or relative. They 'didn't feel like eating' (43 percent), 'cried' (53 percent), 'felt very nervous or tense' (68 percent), and 'felt sort of dazed and numb' (57 percent). Similar emotional outpourings seem to have accompanied the deaths in office, whether by assassination or natural causes, of all presidents, whether popular or not.[8] In Great Britain, it is the monarch's death that occasions such deep emotions, not the prime minister's. It is the monarch whom children conceive of as powerful and good: 62 percent offer images of the queen that suggest she 'rules, governs, commands'; only 24 percent offer similar images of the prime minister.[9]

Traditional views of the presidency hold that the chief of state role buttresses the more important political functions that the president performs as chief of government. 'No president,' wrote Rossiter, 'can fail to realize that all his powers are invigorated, indeed are given a new dimension of authority, because he is the symbol of our sovereignty, continuity, and grandeur.'[10]

Much evidence exists to support this view. The 'honeymoon' that every president enjoys with the people at the start of the term is, in a sense, an affirmation of faith in the office. New presidents invariably receive the initial approval of millions of citizens who voted against them; vice presidents who succeed to the office, for whom no one voted, actually fare better. Even after experiencing, in consecutive order, the highly unpopular presidencies of Lyndon Johnson and Richard Nixon, Americans initially rallied to President Gerald Ford's support by a margin of nearly 25 to one.

Presidents are especially able to trade on their chief of state role when dealing with foreign policy. Citizens 'rally round the flag' to sustain the president in all sorts of international circumstances. Support for Nixon's Vietnam policies jumped in 12 days from 58 to 77 percent among those who heard his November 1969 'Vietnamization' speech. Ford's approval rating was 11 points higher after he 'rescued' the merchant ship *Mayaguez* from its Cambodian captors in 1975. Jimmy Carter added 12 points to his rating as a result of the 1978 Camp David summit that brought Israel and Egypt together. Ronald Reagan scored politically with his 1983 invasion

Below: Alexander Hamilton by John Trumbull. An important political figure in the devising of the American system, Hamilton also served as Treasury Secretary, creating economic order for Washington but a growing conflict with Jefferson.

Right: This evocative painting by Howard Pyle depicts Thomas Jefferson writing the Declaration of Independence in Graff House, Philadelphia, while a Virginia delegate to the Continental Congress during the summer of 1776.

nation's chieftainship of state. The political scientist Bruce Buchanan argues that this exposes incumbents to excessive 'deference' that 'nurtures systemic distortion in the perceptions of self and of external events,' as well as to 'dissonance,' which encourages 'the use of secrecy, misrepresentation, and lying as weapons in the struggle for political success and survival.'[12]

Oddly enough, veneration-rooted failures in office seem most likely to occur when things are going best for a president. The consequences can be serious. It seems more than coincidental that each of the four 20th-century presidents who won the largest election victories (thus demonstrating their political skills and sensitivity) instantly breached the bounds of permissible presidential power in a way that brought down the public's wrath: Franklin D. Roosevelt's plan to 'pack' the Supreme Court with additional justices in 1937, Johnson's unilateral escalation of the Vietnam War in 1965, Nixon's cover-up of the Watergate scandal in 1973, and Reagan's involvement in the Iran-Contra affair in 1985. Ironically, the same veneration for the office that encourages such self-destructive acts then allows presidents who are temperamentally so disposed, as were Johnson and Nixon, to 'circle up the wagons,' all of them armed by deferential White House staffers, and thus seal out political reality when things go badly. Such isolation readily becomes yet another wellspring of the sort of politically foolish or dangerous actions that eventually can bring a president down.

The Importance of Presidential Character

A basic tenet of the Constitutional Convention delegates' political philosophy was that, whatever its institutional form, the strong but nonoppressive government they were seeking to create

Below: James Wilson of Pennsylvania was one of the most influential delegates at the Convention in 1787, arguing for a powerful and vigorous national leader and strong central government.

of Grenada and 1986 bombing of Libya. George Bush's approval rating zoomed to around 90 percent after the Gulf War. The 'rally-round the flag' phenomenon is not confined to presidential successes. The public rallied, at least temporarily, to Kennedy's support after the disastrous Bay of Pigs invasion of Cuba in 1961, to Carter's when American embassy officials were taken hostage in Iran in 1979, and to Bill Clinton's when terrorists bombed the federal building in Oklahoma City in 1995.

Presidents are not always popular. Following Watergate Nixon ultimately was forced by public opinion to leave office. So, in less dramatic and thus more significant ways, have most postwar presidents. The roster of political failures – Truman, Johnson, Nixon, Ford, Carter, and Bush – is considerably longer than the list of political successes – Eisenhower, Kennedy, and Reagan. One reason is that in several less than obvious ways, the joining of the roles of chief of government and chief of state can burden presidents politically.

Part of the problem has to do with the public

Above: This painting on glass dates from the 1802-1810 period and depicts George Washington rising from his tomb with angels. It reflects a revered status that it is difficult to imagine a modern American politician attaining.

expectations that each role generates, which the president is supposed to meet even though they seem contradictory. The political scientist Thomas Cronin's list of ten 'paradoxes' of presidential leadership is rooted in these expectations. Americans want the president to be, for example, 'gentle and decent but forceful and decisive,' to be 'inspirational' but not to promise too much, and to be a 'national unifier–national divider.'[11] At base, most of these paradoxes are one: citizens want the president to be both a chief of state who represents the things that unite them and a chief of government who will take the political initiative and thus divide them.

A problem equal to but perhaps more avoidable than such contradictory expectations is that of public veneration. Each president inherits the public's adulation for the presidency as the

should be a 'government of laws and not of men.' They associated liberty with law and tyranny with rulers who departed from law, as George III and his colonial governors were thought to have done. George Mason bespoke this sentiment when, after the Convention's decisions on presidential number and selection were made, he said: 'We are not indeed constituting a British Government but a more dangerous monarchy, an elective one.' All the more remarkable, then, that Mason's fellow delegates did not agree.

Several reasons seem to explain the Convention's decision to inject such a powerful dose of character, both in the moral and psychological senses of the word, into their plan of government. First was the assurance that Washington would be the nation's first president. Just as his charismatic 'gift of grace' would legitimize the new government, so would his personal character assure its republican nature. The constitutional powers of the president 'are full great,' wrote South Carolina delegate Pierce Butler to a British kinsman, 'and greater than I was disposed to make them. Nor, entre nous, do I believe they would have been so great had not many of the delegates cast their eyes toward General Washington as President; and shaped their Ideas of the Powers to be given to a President, by their

Left: This engraving and etching of the Declaration of Independence that the Continental Congress had voted for on July 2 was produced in about 1816. The 13 original states can be seen, as can three of the principals involved: the wealthy Bostonian John Hancock, and Virginians Thomas Jefferson and George Washington.

opinions of his Virtue.' The presidency would continue to function well after Washington, it was felt, because the election of presidents, whether by electors or members of the House, would involve selection by peers, personal acquaintances of the candidates who would screen out those of defective character.

Still, faith in Washington and in electors was faith in human beings. Could not someone of low character slip through the net and become president? If so, the delegates felt that they had structured the office so as to keep the nation from harm. 'The founders' deliberation over the provision for indefinite reeligibility,' writes Jeffrey Tulis, 'illustrates how they believed self-interest could sometimes be elevated.' Even if motivated by 'avarice,' 'ambition,' or 'the love of fame,' presidents would do their best in order to secure the re-election that enabled them to fulfill that desire.[13] Underlying this confidence was the assurance that in a relatively slow-paced world a mad or wicked president could do only so much damage before being impeached.

The delegates' decision to inject character into the Constitution, then, was a conscious one. But it was made for reasons that no longer pertain. 'Peer review,' which never really took hold in the electoral college, has been absent from the voter-dominated nominating process since the parties reformed their rules in the late 1960s. The destructive powers at a president's disposal are ultimate and swift in the nuclear age; the impeachment process now seems uncertain and slow. In sum, the delegates' carefully conceived defenses against a president of defective character are gone. Public interest in various candidates'

Above: The Continental Congress formally approved the declaration in Pennsylvania State House (now Independence Hall), Philadelphia, on July 4, 1776. The ideas – by then well established – had never been so eloquently expressed.

erratic behavior, acts of deception, truthfulness, sexual promiscuity, and explosive temper in recent elections provides evidence of the voters' continuing concern about presidential character.

The Issue of Presidential Prerogative

Most of the delegates to the Constitutional Convention had read and were influenced by John Locke's 1690 work the *Second Treatise of Government*. In it Locke argued for the general superiority of governments of law and by legislatures, but in a chapter called 'Of Prerogative' he noted certain powerful exceptions to that rule. Legislatures are unable 'to foresee, and so by laws to provide for, all accidents and necessities,' Locke wrote. They are also, by virtue of their size, unwieldiness, and frequent absence, too slow to alter and adapt the law as circumstances may dictate in time of crisis. Thus, occasions may arise when existing, temporarily unsuitable laws should 'give way to the executive power, or rather to this fundamental law of nature and government, viz., that, as much as may be, all members of society are to be preserved.' Prerogative, according to Locke, is 'the people's permitting their rulers to do several things of their own free choice, where the law was silent, or sometimes, too, against the direct letter of the law, for the public good, and their acquiescing in it when so done.'

Madison was probably typical of most of the delegates in his response to Locke's argument. He agreed that 'it is in vain to oppose constitutional barriers to the impulse of [national] self-preservation.' But he also realized that Americans would resist any proposed plan of government in which unbounded executive power, which they associated with British monarchs and ancient Roman dictators, was thought to lurk. For that reason, he told the Convention, it was politically necessary 'to fix the extent of the Executive authority,' to 'confine and define' it in the language of the Constitution.

Thus, to the extent that presidential prerogative may be found in the Constitution, it hides in the shadows. Does the president's oath (the only oath of office included in the Constitution) to 'preserve, protect, and defend the Constitution of the United States' include a Lockean responsibility to do whatever it takes – legal, extralegal, or illegal – to keep the nation free and the Constitution supreme? The vesting clause of Article I of the Constitution – the Congress article – says that 'All legislative Powers herein granted shall be vested in a Congress of the United States;' the vesting clause for Article II – the executive article – is identical but for the omission of the words 'herein granted.' It reads: 'The executive Power shall be vested in a President of the United States of America.' Does that omission mean that the framers envisioned an executive power greater than those specifically

granted in the Constitution?

Certainly some presidents have acted on the assumption that they have prerogative power. In 1861, for example, Abraham Lincoln, responding to the secession of the Southern states from the Union, ordered Southern ports to be blockaded, seized several newspapers, increased the size of the army, and spent unappropriated funds, all on his own authority.

Prerogative has been a mixed blessing for presidents. To be sure, some prerogatory responses to crises have had what the political scientist Richard Pious calls 'frontlash' effects – that is, successful crisis management by the president

Above: Lord Cornwallis and his force surrender at Yorktown on October 19, 1781, to the old tune of 'The World Turn'd Upside Down'. With the war resolved the United States' future independence was now a matter of diplomacy in Paris.

has been greeted by congressional, judicial, and public acquiescence. Most 'frontlash' effects have occurred in national security cases, including the Civil War and Franklin Roosevelt's unauthorized transfer of 50 US naval destroyers to Great Britain in 1941. But other prerogative-style actions have produced 'backlash' effects (the crisis was managed successfully, but the other

Right: George Washington resigning his army commission before Congress in Maryland in December 1783. Earlier that year his status with the army was needed when discontent threatened the new republic with military rule.

branches of government and the public severely challenged the president's authority) or even 'overshoot and collapse' (the president's actions were checked before they took effect, with severe political consequences). Such negative effects tend to greet presidential actions in response to situations that are essentially domestic but that the president perceives as having national security implications. Truman's seizure of the steel mills during the Korean War exemplifies the milder 'backlash' effect: it got the mills going but was flatly undone by the Supreme Court in the 1952 case of *Youngstown Sheet and Tube* v. *Sawyer*. 'Overshoot and collapse' followed Andrew Johnson's efforts to reconstruct the South after the Civil War in ways contrary to congressional desires. Not only was Johnson impeached and almost removed, but the presidency was weaker for his action.[14]

The problem for presidents is that although the constitutional system calls on them to do what needs to be done in times of crisis, it does not define either what a crisis is or which responses are suitable. Success can make presidents 'great' in the eyes of historians. But failure can doom them to short-term defeat and long-term ignominy. Locke foresaw all this, of course: as noted above, the final act in any drama of prerogative is whether 'the people . . . acquiesc[e] in it when so done.'

Below: 'Washington Addressing the Constitutional Convention' by Julius Brutus Stearns in 1856. The 1787 Convention devised and approved the Constitution and the picture shows Washington urging delegates to approve it.

THE TERM OF THE PRESIDENT

Questions of presidential term, re-eligibility, and selection were interwoven in the minds of the delegates to the Constitutional Convention. John Roche has compared their efforts to sort out these issues to a game of 'three-dimensional chess.' Underlying this complexity, however, was a basic choice: Which did the delegates care about more, legislative selection of the president or eligibility for re-election? As the historian Max Farrand summed up the controversy,

> If the executive were to be chosen by the legislature, he must not be eligible for reelection lest he should court the favor of the legislature in order to secure for himself another term. Accordingly, the single term of office should be long. But the possibility of reelection was regarded as the best incentive to faithful performance of duty, and if a short term and reeligibility were accepted, then choice by the legislature was inadvisable.[15]

At the start of the Convention, most delegates favored legislative selection of the president – and thus a long, single term. Later, when the relative virtues of re-eligibility rose in the delegates' esteem, they shortened the term and changed the mode of election. At various times, before the Convention settled on four years, proposals for terms of three, six, seven, eight, 11 and 15, or 20 years floated around.

The Two-Term Limit

After the Constitution was ratified, indefinite re-eligibility for the presidency took on a specific meaning, first in practice, then in constitutional law. Washington and Jefferson each retired voluntarily after two terms – Washington for personal reasons, but Jefferson with the argument that for any president to seek a third election would make the term 'in fact for life' and the office only 'nominally elective.' Few of Jefferson's successors as president seemed interested in challenging this precedent, and only Franklin D. Roosevelt, arguing that the conditions of wartime uncertainty that prevailed in 1940 and 1944 necessitated an exception to the general rule, succeeded. But Roosevelt's action brought down the wrath of the Republican Eightieth Congress, which in 1947 rushed through a constitutional amendment to limit future presidents to two terms. Although only one other amendment has required more time to be ratified by the states, the Twenty-second eventually entered the Constitution in 1951.

Ironically, the only presidents who have served long and, in political terms, successfully enough to feel the constraints of the two-term limit have been Republicans: Eisenhower in 1960 and Reagan in 1988. Eisenhower indicated to his son and deputy chief of staff, John, that he would have liked to run a third time; Reagan, during his second term, campaigned actively but in vain to repeal the two-term limit. In truth, few modern presidents have been happy with the current arrangement concerning term. Johnson and Carter endorsed a proposal to alter the president's tenure to a single, six-year term, arguing that with more time to address national problems and less need to pay attention to electoral politics, they could have served the country better when they were in office.

Starting the Term

A desire to strengthen, not weaken, the presidency underlay the enactment of the only other constitutional amendment bearing on term. The original Constitution had been silent on the question of when the president's four years was to begin. Congress passed a law in 1792 to establish the March 4 after the presidential election as inauguration day. But as time went by, the four-month hiatus between the election in November and the inauguration in March came to seem excessively long. For those four months, it was argued, the outgoing president was a 'lame duck,' unable to do anything of consequence, while the president-elect was forced to maintain a discreet silence even as the electoral mandate for action was most fresh. Section 1 of the Twentieth Amendment, enacted in 1933, established noon on January 20 (less than three months after the election) as the beginning of the president's term.

REMOVAL OF THE PRESIDENT

Although the Constitutional Convention fixed the president's term at four years, it also provided methods for emergency removal. But it did so in ways guaranteed to assure that removal would be difficult to effect and thus rare to occur.

Impeachment

Provision for presidential impeachment was a part of the Constitution in all its working drafts. Although Gouverneur Morris initially argued that impeachment would open the door to congressional encroachment on the presidency, most presidentialists at the Convention endorsed impeachment in full awareness that unless the Constitution included some means to remove a president who behaved badly, they would never be able to convince their fellow delegates to accept an otherwise strong presidency. Through-

Above: Vice President Richard Nixon is greeted by Senator Joseph R. McCarthy upon the former's arrival in Milwaukee, Wisconsin, as part of his campaign tour in 1956. As a Congressman Nixon was prominent in the notorious Alger Hiss case.

out the Convention, the delegates tinkered with both the mechanism and the grounds for impeachment. The mechanism became ever more political, changing during the course of debate and discussion from the Supreme Court alone to the Court and the House, then finally to the House and the Senate: the House to impeach by majority vote, and the Senate to try, with a two-thirds vote needed to convict. Simultaneously, the grounds for impeachment became less political. 'Malpractice or neglect of duty,' a broad standard, gave way to 'treason, bribery, and corruption' and, finally, to 'treason, bribery, or other High Crimes and Misdemeanors.' The latter term, which was borrowed from the British common law, referred to profound abuses of official power.

The extraordinary difficulty of impeaching and removing a president is revealed both by the minuscule number of presidents who have come close to being impeached (two of 41) and by the circumstances of their cases. Andrew Johnson, who was impeached in 1868, was spared removal when just 19 of 54 senators (the constitutionally required one-third plus one) voted in his favor. In contrast, Nixon almost certainly would have been banished from office in 1974 if he had not resigned. But Nixon's removal became possible only because a series of voice-activated tape recordings, which he alone among presidents had secretly ordered to be made in various executive offices, provided direct evidence that he had used the powers of the presidency to try to block an official investigation into the Watergate affair.

Disability

Although the delegates considered the grounds for and process of presidential impeachment thoroughly, they treated the matter of a disabled president in a most cavalier fashion. When the constitutional clause that reads 'In case of the . . . inability [of the President] to discharge the Powers and Duties of the said Office, the Same shall devolve on the Vice President . . . until the Disability be removed, or a President shall be elected' came before the Convention, John Dickinson of Delaware rose to ask, 'What is the extent of the term "disability" and who is to be the judge of it?' The Convention decided to deal with the matter later. In a historic case of oversight, it never did.

The lack of a definition or procedure for presidential removal effectively left the nation without a leader for parts of ten presidencies prior to the 1950s: no one could find a way to transfer authority to the vice president without appearing to be a usurper. Eisenhower's ailments – a heart attack in 1955, an ileitis attack in 1956, and a stroke in 1957 – prompted him to write an open letter to Vice President Nixon in 1958 saying that if he was ever disabled again, he would instruct Nixon to serve temporarily as acting president. (Nixon himself could make that decision if a disabled Eisenhower was unable to communicate.) The President's reason for writing the letter – that in the nuclear age the nation should not be even briefly 'without a Chief Executive, the armed forces without a Commander-in-Chief' – encouraged Congress to address the disability issue in a more formal, constitutional way.

Congress's solution was contained in Sections 3 and 4 of the Twenty-fifth Amendment. Interestingly, the Amendment includes no definition of disability. It is clear from the congressional debate that disability is not to be equated with incompetence, laziness, unpopularity, or impeachable conduct. But as to what disability is, Congress thought that any definition it might write into law would likely be rendered obsolete by changes in medical technology.

In place of a definition, the Twenty-fifth Amendment offers a set of procedures, which address three very different situations involving presidential disability. In the first, a president who is aware that he is 'unable to discharge the powers and duties of his office' signs over temporary custody of the presidency to the vice president, then reclaims power when the disability is ended. In the second situation the president is disabled but, perhaps having gone into a coma, is unable to say so. Should this happen, presidential power would flow temporarily to the vice president if both the vice president and a majority of the president's cabinet agreed on this course. Again, the president is empowered to decide when the disability is over and to reclaim the powers of the office.

The third situation covered by the disability procedures of the Twenty-fifth Amendment is the most troubling. It involves situations (such as questionable mental health or sudden physical disability) in which the president's ability to fulfill the office is in doubt – the president claims to be able but the vice president and cabinet disagree. The Amendment provides that should this happen, the vice president would become acting president pending a congressional resolution of the matter. Congress would have three weeks to decide whether or not the president were disabled, with a two-thirds vote of both the House and the Senate needed to overturn the president's judgment. But because the amendment only transfers power to the vice president for as long as the president is disabled, a subsequent claim of restored health by the president would set the whole process in motion again.

Three decades of experience with the Twenty-fifth Amendment confirm the difficulty of removing a president, even temporarily, before the expiration of the term. Use of the disability procedures has been grudging and infrequent. Although doubts have been raised about Nixon's mental health during the final days of his presidency, no obvious occasion of disability occurred until March 30, 1981, when Reagan was wounded by an assassin's bullet. Conscious and lucid before entering surgery, he nonetheless did not sign over his powers to Vice President Bush. Meanwhile, presidential aides stifled discussion at the White House about the possibility of a cabinet-initiated transfer. On July 13, 1985, before undergoing cancer surgery, Reagan did sign over his powers to the vice president for eight hours, but only after arguing that the Twenty-fifth Amendment was not meant to apply to such brief episodes of disability.

TERM AND REMOVAL: CONSEQUENCES

Removal of a president on grounds of disability is similar to removal by impeachment for reasons of 'treason, bribery, or other High Crimes and Misdemeanors' – it is constitutionally possible but politically near-impossible. The Constitution's provisions for term and removal make it extremely likely that, in contrast to a prime minister in a parliamentary government, a president who stays alive can count on serving at least four years in office.

One traditional benefit of the four-year, 'no cut' contract for presidents has been that they could take time to learn their job. As Richard Neustadt, among others, has argued, the first two years of a president's term are 'a learning time for the new president, who has to learn – or unlearn – many things about the job.'[16] This is a particular advantage for former state governors, like Carter, Reagan, and Clinton, who have not served in Washington before becoming president. A second benefit has been that presidents could bear temporary unpopularity for the sake of pursuing bold but initially unpopular policies. The long economic boom of the 1980s arose from the ashes of the 'Reagan recession' of 1981–2. Presidents would be less likely to take short-term political risks if they lived in fear that they would not be around to see the long term because of a vote of no confidence by the state legislatures, as was proposed at the Constitutional Convention, or by the national legislature, as in a parliamentary system.

But the value of these benefits for presidents is waning. The 'short' in short term is growing ever shorter in the modern era. Election-year politics has always forced presidents to try to get their popularity into good shape during the last six months of the fourth year of their term. But the president who wishes to be renominated by the party in the contemporary open primary process needs to have the approval ratings in good shape by not much later than halfway through the third year of the term, lest a battle occur like the one between Reagan (then the governor of California) and President Ford for the 1976 Republican nomination or, four years later, between Senator Edward Kennedy and President Carter for the Democratic nomination. If the president cares about the party's fortunes in the mid-term congressional and gubernatorial elections, as most presidents do, the administration's risk-taking period probably will not run very much past the middle of the second year. The political scientist Edward Tufte suggests that almost as much economic 'pump-priming' (the very opposite of long-term planning) occurs during the second year as during the fourth year of the typical president's term.[17]

That leaves the first year as the only time that presidents can afford to pursue wise but initially unpopular courses of action – the very time when they are least likely to know which courses of action are wise. For re-elected presidents, the first and second years of the second term may seem better suited to providing the traditional advantages of the fixed term. But presidents often forfeit these advantages by running re-election campaigns that celebrate the successes of the first term rather than offering an agenda for the second term, a strategy that allows no claim to a mandate after the election is over. During the final two years of the second term, the Twenty-second Amendment's two-term limit renders the president politically weak. Not surprisingly, no

Below: President George Bush takes lunch with American troops in the Persian Gulf in November 1990 during the build-up to the war with Iraq that culminated in Operation Desert Storm.

Left: The shooting of President Garfield on July 2, 1881, happened just four months after his taking office. It took a further 80 days before he died of his wounds, exposing Constitutional ambiguities over the issue of succession.

month stretch during the Clinton administration, the White House was assaulted by a Cessna airplane that crashed outside the president's bedroom, two incidents of gunfire, and several fence climbers who were apprehended by uniformed Secret Service agents.

INSTITUTIONAL SEPARATION AND SHARED POWERS

The Constitutional Convention created a government of separated institutions, a separation in which the membership of Congress may not overlap with that of the executive branch.

From the beginning, the delegates imposed two constitutional prohibitions to preserve institutional separation. The first, born of the fear that Congress might try to persuade or punish the president by raising or lowering the salary, forbids any change in compensation during an incumbent president's term. The second prohibition bars any member of one branch from serving simultaneously in the other. This requirement was imposed for the reason stated by Pierce Butler of South Carolina when he 'appealed to the example of G.B. where men got

modern president's second term has been as successful as the first term.

A final note on the subject of removal: of the constitutional provisions that deal with a president's premature departure from office, impeachment and disability have accounted for the removal of none, resignation for one (Nixon), and death by natural causes for four (William Henry Harrison in 1841, Zachary Taylor in 1850, Warren G. Harding in 1923, and Franklin D. Roosevelt in 1945). Distressingly, a final method of premature removal needs to be mentioned in any study of the presidency. Assassins have killed four presidents (Abraham Lincoln in 1865, James A. Garfield in 1881, William L. McKinley in 1901, and John F. Kennedy in 1963), and have come close to killing Andrew Jackson, Ford, Reagan, and others. In one ten-

Below: President Lincoln meeting with General McClellan and staff at Antietam in 1862. Lincoln used prerogative powers to prosecute the Civil War in the national interest as he saw it.

Above: President Carter joins hands with Anwar Sadat of Egypt and Menachem Begin of Israel after the signing of their peace treaty in March 1979.

into Parlt. that they might get offices for themselves or their friends. That was the source of corruption that ruined their Govt.' George III was regarded by Americans as an especially egregious dealer of executive patronage to buy support from members of Parliament.

As for powers, the Convention gave the executive its share – in both senses of the word – of all the new government's enumerated powers. Although Congress was empowered to 'make all laws,' the president still could report to the legislature on 'the state of the Union,' recommended to it 'such Measures as he shall judge necessary and expedient,' convene it on 'extraordinary Occasions,' and veto the laws it passed subject to override by a two-thirds vote of both the House and the Senate. Congress's charge to 'declare war' was tempered by the president's power as commander-in-chief of the armed forces. Congress was empowered to create and fund the administrative departments, but the president had the right to appoint the department heads and bore the responsibility to 'take Care that the Laws be faithfully executed.' Finally, the president was granted the power to 'make treaties' and to appoint all federal judges and ambassadors, subject to Senate approval.

Right: The 'Great Communicator' President Ronald Reagan receives rapturous applause at his State of the Union Address in February 1986.

Parchment became practice only slowly. Historically, as later chapters will show, it took a century and a quarter, from the start of the new government in 1789 to the first year of the Woodrow Wilson administration in 1913, for all of the enumerated powers of the presidency to come to life. Treaty-making and other matters of foreign affairs aside – who but the president could represent the United States to other nations or lead it into war? – Congress seized the lion's share of the government's shared powers nearly from the beginning, dominating even the executive appointment process. When it came to legislation, representatives and senators treated with scorn most presidential efforts to recommend or influence their consideration of bills. Indeed, until Andrew Jackson in the 1830s, presidents were reluctant to exercise the veto power for fear of the wrath and reprisal such an action would provoke on Capitol Hill.

Presidential disempowerment was, if long-lived, temporary, the logical consequence of the condition of weak national government that generally prevailed during the 19th century. The country, then an amalgam of mostly local economies and cultures, was not seeking what the presidency was institutionally designed to offer, namely, energetic leadership in behalf of new national initiatives. But the conditions that sustained weak government began to change around the turn of the century. The widespread dissemination of railroads and telegraph lines made a national economy and society not just possible but inevitable, and with this transformation came demands that the national government take measures to tame the massive corporations that were beginning to dominate the new order. Early 20th century presidents like Theodore Roosevelt (1901–09) and Wilson (1913–21) roused a popular mandate for the president to make full use of the office's constitutional powers to lead Congress and the executive branch. Franklin D. Roosevelt, during the Great Depression of the 1930s, and more recent presidents, such as Johnson and Reagan, have also played the role of chief legislator on a grand scale.

INSTITUTIONAL SEPARATION AND SHARED POWERS: CONSEQUENCES

As noted earlier, the Constitutional Convention designed a system of government that amounted not to separation of powers, but to 'separated institutions sharing powers.' This phrase of Neustadt's contains an important perception: namely, that because the responsibilities of government are shared by an institutionally separated president and Congress, powerful limits restrain what presidents can do to exercise their constitutionally enumerated powers without the acquiescence of the legislative branch that shares those powers with them.

During most of the 20th century, with the nation accustomed by Wilson and the two Roosevelts to vigorous presidential leadership, the political party has provided the strongest bridge joining Congress with the president. A common Democratic or Republican party affiliation between the president and a majority of legislators has helped to unite, at least to some extent, the branches that the Constitution made separate. When a Democrat was president, Democrats in Congress had a political stake in the president's success; the same rule applied to Republicans under a Republican presidency.

From 1900 to 1968, the party that controlled the White House also controlled both houses of Congress 79 percent of the time – that is, for all but eight years.

The post-1968 era has been sharply different: divided government, not party government, has been the norm. Since the elections of 1968, different parties have controlled the presidency and Congress more often than not – 16 of 28 years through 1996. In most cases the president has been Republican and Congress Democratic, but in 1994 the voters sent a Republican Congress to Washington (the first in 40 years) to oppose Democratic president Bill Clinton. The party that did not occupy the White House controlled one house of Congress for another six years in this period (the first six years of the Reagan administration, when Democrats had a majority in the House of Representatives). Same-party control of the presidency and Congress prevailed just 21 percent of the time – during the four years that Carter was president and the first two years of the Clinton administration.

The Consequences of Divided Government

As a pattern of politics, rather than as an occasional aberration, the new era of divided government is historically unprecedented in US history. At least three consequences for the presidency and the political system seem likely if the pattern

Above: President Theodore Roosevelt addressing an audience with all his customary fervor. He believed nations needed to fight to survive and termed the presidency 'the bully pulpit'.

continues: inter-branch hostility, inter-branch avoidance, and judicial warfare.[18]

Hostility first. The Constitution created 'an invitation to struggle,' in the political scientist Edward S. Corwin's phrase, between a constitutionally separate president and Congress.[19] In divided government, the constitutional fissures between the branches are reinforced by party. As each party comes to feel a stake in the branch of government that it controls, presidents may be expected to assault the constitutional powers and prerogatives of Congress and Congress to undermine the constitutional status of the presidency.

As for avoidance, difficult policy challenges, especially to eliminate the massive annual federal budget deficits, await the US government. Although no painless or popular solutions exist to address these problems, a party that controlled both the presidency and Congress would have a powerful political incentive to rise to the occasion, lest it be blamed for ineptness or policy failure. Divided government, however, creates a different set of political incentives. As during the Reagan–Bush years, for example, a Republican

Above: Presidential nominee Governor Bill Clinton and his vice presidential candidate Al Gore respond to the cheers of delegates at the Democratic National Convention in July 1992.

president and a Democratic Congress each do better politically to blame the other for the nation's woes than to call for the sacrifices that may be necessary to alleviate them.

The judiciary also suffers. Constitutionally, judges of the third branch of the federal government, the Supreme Court, must be nominated by the president and approved by the Senate. During most of the 20th century, the Senate deferred to the president on court appointments, as one would expect when the same party controlled both institutions: from 1900 to 1968, the Senate rejected only 3 of 45, or 7 percent, of all presidential nominations. Since 1968, 15 Supreme Court nominations have been made, all but five of them by Republican presidents to Democratic Senates. The rejection rate has risen

to 27 percent (or 40 percent when different parties control the presidency and Senate), including two Nixon nominees and two Reagan nominees.

SUMMARY AND CONCLUSION

The decisions of the Constitution's framers and amenders about the method of selecting the president and the president's powers, term of office, susceptibility to removal, and institutional separation from Congress have had important and enduring effects on the presidency. One understanding that grows from close examination of these decisions and their practical consequences concerns presidential power: almost every such decision raised high the power of the presidency and, simultaneously, made the office more vulnerable.

By making the presidency a unitary, nationally elected office, the delegates to the Convention combined the roles of chief of state and chief of government. In doing so, they placed at the disposal of the nation's political

leader the people's intense feelings of patriotism. But they also made the president the object of the excessive and often contradictory expectations that attend these two roles.

The term and removal provisions of the Constitution all but guarantee presidents a span of time in which they can try to succeed without fear of removal. The delegates' definition of that time as four years, however, has come to seem ever more brief, because of the protracted nature of the presidential electoral process.

Presidents from 1789 to 1913 struggled long and hard to invigorate the enumerated powers of their office. They eventually succeeded, to the extent that the president gained the initiative, if not the upper hand, over Congress. As a result, the public's expectations that presidents will exercise the powers of the federal government successfully have been raised. Under most circumstances, but especially in an era of divided government, those expectations may be as much a curse to presidents as a blessing.

Notes

1. Hargrove, E. C. and Nelson, M. *Presidents, Politics, and Policy*, Baltimore, 1984, ch. 2.
2. Neustadt, R. E. *Presidential Power*, New York, 1960.
3. Roche, J. P. 'The Founding Fathers: A Reform Caucus in Action,' in *American Political Science Review* December 1961, pp. 799–816. For a more extensive treatment, see Milkis, S. M. and Nelson, M. *The American Presidency: Origins and Development, 1776–1993* Washington, D.C.: 1994, chs. 1–2.
4. Lipset, S. M. *The First New Nation: The United States in Historical and Comparative Perspective*, New York, 1979.
5. All quotations from the Constitutional Convention are drawn from Farrand, M. (ed.), *The Records of the Federal Convention of 1787*, 4 vols, New Haven, 1966, 1987.

6. Nelson, M. *A Heartbeat Away*, 1988, ch. 5.
7. Rossiter, C. *The American Presidency*, Baltimore, 1984, p. 15.
8. Sheatsley, P. B. and Feldman, J. J. 'The Assassination of President Kennedy: Public Reactions,' *Public Opinion Quarterly* (Summer 1964), pp. 189–215.
9. Greenstein, F. 'The Benevolent Leader Revisited: Children's Images of Political Leaders in Three Democracies,' *American Political Science Review* (December 1975), pp. 1371–1398.
10. Rossiter, *American Presidency*, pp. 16–17.
11. Cronin, T. E. 'The Presidency and its Paradoxes' in H.A. Bailey (ed.), 1980, pp. 111–123.
12. Buchanan, B. *The Presidential Experience*, Englewood Cliffs, New Jersey, 1973, pp. 7, 23.
13. Tulis, J. K. 'On Presidential Character,' in Bessette, J. M.

and Tulis (eds), *The Presidency in the Constitution*, Baton Rouge, 1981, p. 21.
14. Pious, R. M. *The American Presidency*, New York, 1978, pp. 32–33.
15. Farrand, M. *The Framing of the Constitution of the United States*, New Haven, Connecticut, 1913, p. 78.
16. Neustadt, *Presidential Power*, p. 149.
17. Tufte, E. R. *Political Control of the Economy*, Princeton, New Jersey, 1978, p. 25.
18. For a fuller treatment, see Michael Nelson, 'Constitutional Aspects of the Elections,' in Nelson (ed.), *The Elections of 1988*, Washington, D.C., 1989, pp. 181–209.
19. Corwin, E. S. *The President: Office and Powers*, 4th edition, New York, 1957.

John A. Maltese

2

THE AMERICAN SYSTEM

In designing the presidency, the framers of the Constitution
rejected proposals for a plural, or committee-style,
executive in favor of a unitary, or one-person, office.
Yet the modern presidency has become so large and institutionalized
as to make one wonder whether the plural executive-advocates won
the argument after all. Presidents themselves have enlarged the
presidency in an effort to fulfill the responsibilities laid on them
by other actors in the American system – but at what cost ?

A snow-bound west front of the Capitol in Washington, D.C.,
during a recent winter.

Modern presidents are policy leaders. Among other things, they propose an annual federal budget, submit legislation to Congress, direct foreign policy, and wage war. Accomplishing these things requires not only the help of staff to formulate policy proposals, but the ability to persuade others to go along with those policies. This chapter looks at how the president interacts with other parts of the political system in his pursuit of policy leadership.

THE RISE OF THE MODERN PRESIDENCY

The modern White House contains a wide array of specialized staff units that advise the president on policy and serve as liaison with other political actors. This is a relatively recent development. Until the 1930s, presidents engaged in comestic policy leadership on a sporadic and largely unorganized basis.[1] There were, of course, strong presidents who exerted policy leadership before then, but White House staff support was meager and there was no legislation compelling presidents to act. Many presidents left primary responsibility for policy formulation to Congress.

The Constitution says little about presidential power in the domestic sphere. Article I, Section 7 gives the president the power to veto congressional legislation (which Congress can override by a two-thirds vote in both Houses). Article II, Section 2 gives the president the power to appoint (with the advice and consent of the Senate) high government officials in the executive and judicial branches of government. And Article II, Section 3 gives the president the power to convene special sessions of Congress, instructs that he 'from time to time give Congress Information of the State of the Union, and recommend to their Consideration such Measures as he shall judge necessary and expedient,' and says that 'he shall take Care that the Laws be faithfully executed.'

THE CABINET

Helping the president in all this are the heads of the executive departments, collectively known as the president's 'cabinet.' There is no direct mention of the cabinet in the Constitution, although

Article II, Section 2 says that the president 'may require the Opinion, in writing, of the principal Officer in each of the executive Departments, upon any Subject relating to the duties of their respective Offices.' At the outset there were only four cabinet secretaries (the Attorney General, plus the heads of the State, Treasury, and War departments), and the degree to which early presidents relied on the cabinet varied quite dramatically.

By the 1920s, the executive branch had grown much larger and considerably more complex than it had been at the time of George Washington. The number of cabinet departments had increased to ten, and as demands for services increased, individual departments created bureaus to perform specialized functions. In addition, Congress created powerful regulatory agencies, such as the Interstate Commerce

Above: President Kennedy addressing a joint session of Congress on Capitol Hill in May 1961. Seated immediately behind are Speaker of the House Sam Rayburn and Vice President Johnson.

Commission (1887), and placed them in the executive branch. Because of these developments, the approximate number of civil servants working in the executive branch had increased from 3,000 in 1800 to 550,000 in 1920.[2]

CONGRESS MAKES THE PRESIDENT A POLICY LEADER

Until the 20th century, departments and agencies negotiated directly with Congress for appropriations, and Congress appeared to be the chief policy-maker. But congressional legislation in 1921 expanded the president's role in domestic policy formulation and helped to make him the nation's 'Chief Legislator.' The Budget and Accounting Act of 1921 sought to bring about greater efficiency by requiring the president to present a unified executive budget to Congress. This meant that the president had to come up with a detailed program for all the departments and agencies and, based on that, prepare a comprehensive annual budget for congressional approval. Previously, no president had put together such an extensive program, and many presidents had played no direct role in overall fiscal policy. Now presidents were obliged to initiate programs. To offer the president advice on fiscal matters and help him prepare the budget, Congress created the Bureau of the Budget (BOB) as part of the Treasury Department.

The goal of the Budget and Accounting Act was to promote efficiency, not the aggrandizement of presidential power. The first three presidents affected by the Act – Warren Harding, Calvin Coolidge, and Herbert Hoover – duti-

Left: Nearly 33 years later, in January 1994, President Clinton stands at the same spot as Kennedy to deliver his State of the Union address, urging work on his health and welfare reforms.

fully submitted budgets to Congress but seldom exerted strong leadership to secure enactment.[3] This changed during the presidency of Franklin D. Roosevelt, who came into office in 1933 determined to lead the nation out of the Great Depression.

As panic spread and banks began to close around the country, Roosevelt used his inaugural address to try to instill confidence. He reminded his audience (including millions listening on radio) that 'the only thing we have to fear is fear itself.' He then used his constitutional authority to call Congress into a special emergency session. In the extraordinary 100 days that followed, Roosevelt introduced and Congress passed a wide array of programs, including the Emergency Banking Act, the National Industrial Recovery Act, and the Agricultural Adjustment Act. Legislation passed at Roosevelt's behest had the effect of dramatically increasing the size of government by creating new executive agencies, such as the National Recovery Administration, the Public Works Administration, and the Federal Emergency Relief Administration. Estimates suggest that the number of civil servants working in the federal government more than doubled in Roosevelt's first six years in office (from some 600,000 in 1933 to some 1,400,000 in 1938).[4]

THE GROWTH OF PRESIDENTIAL STAFF

The increased size and complexity of government put new demands on the president, and in 1936 Roosevelt appointed a committee of public administrators headed by Louis Brownlow to study the organization of the executive branch and make suggestions for reform. The Brownlow Committee concluded that 'the President needs help.' As the chief administrator of the executive branch, the president should have institutional staff support to help perform his managerial

Below: When Franklin D. Roosevelt took the oath on March 4, 1933, the economy was close to collapse. His optimistic tone and promised 'new deal' helped to alleviate the despair felt by many.

Above: The first cabinet had four members: from left to right, George Washington, Secretary of War Henry Knox, Secretary of the Treasury Alexander Hamilton, Secretary of State Thomas Jefferson, and Attorney General Edmund Randolph.

duties. Thus, the Committee recommended 'salvation by staff' through the creation of the Executive Office of the President (EOP).[5] Roosevelt submitted the recommendations for congressional approval in January 1938, but opposition to FDR's 'court-packing' plan bogged down the reorganization bill. Finally, in 1939, Congress passed a watered-down version of the Brownlow Committee recommendations.

The Reorganization Act of 1939 endorsed the enlargement of the president's personal staff and gave the president the power to create the EOP as an additional source of ongoing institutional staff support.[6] As originally envisaged, 'institutional' staff would constitute part of the EOP as a politically neutral organization consisting of civil servants who would serve as expert advisers to successive presidents. 'Personal' staff, on the other hand, would serve in the White House Office (a division of the EOP) as political aides dedicated to the particular president in office. Roosevelt quickly established the EOP, moving the Bureau of the Budget there from the Treasury Department, and created three new agencies to reside within the EOP. Since then, the composition of the EOP has changed a good deal. Congress has the power to create and dis-

Below: By the time of Franklin D. Roosevelt's second administration in 1938 there were ten cabinet positions in addition to the presidency and the vice-presidency.

"THE ONLY THING WE HAVE TO FEAR IS FEAR ITSELF—"

band units by statute, and presidents can do the same by executive order. Currently, the EOP contains twelve divisions, including the National Security Council, the Council of Economic Advisers, and the Office of Management and Budget (which used to be the BOB).[7]

Like the Budget and Accounting Act of 1921, the Reorganization Act of 1939 reinforced the president's leadership position. The Budget and Accounting Act had made him a policy manager, and the Reorganization Act expanded his staff resources to accomplish that function of management. Moreover, the Brownlow Committee recommendations were reaffirmed by a commission led by former Republican president Herbert Hoover in 1947. The result was a further expansion of presidential staff support with bipartisan endorsement.[8]

THE INSTITUTIONAL PRESIDENCY

The need for presidential staff support to help manage the executive branch becomes obvious once one realizes just how large the executive branch is. Currently, there are fourteen cabinet departments (including the Department of Defense, Department of Agriculture, and Department of Justice), and over sixty other divisions, including independent regulatory commissions (such as the Federal Communications Commission and the Interstate Commerce Commission), government corporations (such as the Tennessee Valley Authority and the Federal Deposit Insurance Corporation), and agencies (such as the Central Intelligence Agency and the Environmental Protection Agency). The president simply cannot oversee the programs and determine the budgets for all of these entities without expert advice.

Thus, by the 1950s, presidents of both political parties had increased their staff support and solidified their position as policy leader. Now the White House contained not just the president and his family, but also an extensive personal staff to advise the president. In fact, the staff grew so large that it soon spilled out from the White House into surrounding buildings, and the Republican president Eisenhower created the post of White House Chief of Staff to oversee the staff operation. White House staff, which had numbered only 47 in Franklin D. Roosevelt's first term, grew to some 250 by 1953, and over 500 by 1973. If one includes the EOP, presidential staff exceeded 5,000 by 1969.[9] As John P. Burke had noted, this led to a marked change in the character of the office. It was now an institution, a *presidency* rather than merely a *president*.[10] And this institution was now a policy-making body.

By the 1950s, the Bureau of the Budget exercised central legislative clearance of all legislative proposals from any part of the executive branch. Virtually every communication to Congress from this network of departments, agencies, and other divisions that dealt with pending legislation was cleared by BOB to be sure that it was in accord with presidential policy. (This is now done by the Office of Management and Budget, the BOB's successor.) The result was the assertion of presidential (rather than departmental) judgments, choices, and priorities in molding a legislative package.[11]

Right: Sherman Adams (center), first White House Chief of Staff, overseeing the appointment of a member of the Office of Legislative Affairs created during the Eisenhower administration.

THE OFFICE OF LEGISLATIVE AFFAIRS: DEALING WITH CONGRESS

The BOB was (as the OMB is now) part of the president's institutional staff in the EOP. Soon presidents began creating additional units as part of the president's personal staff in the White House Office. President Eisenhower, for example, created the White House Office of Legislative Affairs. Originally designed to inform members of Congress about presidential support or opposition to legislation, the Office of Legislative Affairs soon evolved into a tool to steer presidential initiatives through Congress.[12] It became, in short, a body for lobbying Congress to pass legislation that the president supports. Presidents were now aggressively seeking enactment of legislation as well as coordinating legislative proposals from the executive branch. Again, there had been strong presidents

Above: The grand Beaux-Arts style of the Old Executive Office Building makes it attractive, but its size also tells of the growth in presidential bureaucracy and the move toward institution.

in the past who had aggressively sought enactment of their policy proposals. What was new was the institutional support that presidents now enjoyed in this effort and the regularity with which presidents from both political parties sought to influence legislation.

Traditionally, presidents have relied on support from within their own political party to achieve legislative victories. But this is obviously more difficult when the opposition party controls one or both houses of Congress. The same party controlled the White House and both houses of Congress for all but eight years from 1897 to 1954. But recently 'divided government'

has prevailed. From 1969 to 1996, unified party control of the White House and both houses of Congress existed for only six of 28 years.[13] In addition, parties have become more decentralized, which has led to some breakdown of party unity.

In such an atmosphere, the president must rely on other means of persuasion besides the traditional rallying cry for party loyalty. Thus, a structure such as the Office of Legislative Affairs becomes an especially important tool to plot strategy and lobby members of Congress. The Office targets legislators whose support is needed by the president for an upcoming vote. Then it helps to orchestrate constituent mail to the targeted senators and House members, finds out what favors may help secure a favorable vote (ranging from a jog with the president to an assurance that the president will support that member's pet policy initiative), and directs personal lobbying by the president and other administration officials.

THE PUBLIC PRESIDENCY

Public support of the president is a particularly important resource for leading Congress. Legislators are acutely attuned to their 'electoral connection,' with public opinion in their state or district having an important effect on how they will vote. Thus, presidents actively seek to direct public opinion. In fact, the emergence of the president as an opinion leader correspond with his emergence as a policy leader. The development of the president as an opinion leader is often referred to as the rise of the 'public' presidency.[14]

The advent of new communications technologies, such as radio and television, made it easy for the president to speak directly to the American people and rally their support for his initiatives. Presidents used to rely on public support mainly to get elected. Now public support is a president's most visible source of political power in office and presidents routinely take their messages directly to the people in an attempt to mold mandates for policy initiatives. A strategy of presidential power based on such appeals is known as 'going public.'[15]

Above: Eisenhower's administration was notable for its business-oriented cabinet with lawyers and executives appointed to the key positions. It indicated his preference for the private sector.

Below: The president has to maintain a working relationship with both House and Senate. Here, President Clinton is meeting with Congressional leaders Daschle, Gingrich, and Dole.

Subsequent presidents used the new medium of television in a similar manner. Eisenhower successfully pioneered its use during his presidency in the 1950s, although John F. Kennedy refined the art and is often thought of as the first television president.[18] By then, presidents were no longer as dependent on reporters to filter their views to the public as they used to be. Radio and television were a direct way to reach the masses. Even presidential press conferences came to be used more to meet the people than to meet the press. As Nixon's Chief of Staff, H.R. Haldeman, bluntly put it in an internal White House memorandum in 1970: 'The President wants you to realize and emphasize to all appropriate members of your staff that a press conference is a TV operation and that the TV impression is really all that matters.'[19]

This new emphasis on bypassing reporters eroded the intimate professional relationship between the White House and reporters that earlier presidents had cultivated. FDR had formally created a White House Press Office as part of his effort to reach the people through the press. He also established an extraordinary repartee with reporters through informal biweekly press conferences. Unlike modern-day press conferences, Roosevelt maintained strict control over how

Jeffrey Tulis has argued that this strategy is very different from what the Framers expected. He points out that prior to the 20th century, popular presidential rhetoric was largely proscribed because it was thought to 'manifest demagoguery, impede deliberation, and subvert the routines of republican government.'[16] But by the time Franklin D. Roosevelt became president, those norms had changed. FDR used the new medium of radio to great effect during his presidency, delivering 31 informal 'fireside chats' aimed directly at the radio audience.[17] In addition, his inaugural addresses and some other public speeches were broadcast 'live' for the benefit of millions of listeners. Thus, the president became not just a symbol of leadership, but also a familiar, reassuring voice – a friend welcomed into living rooms across America.

reporters could use information from those private sessions. Nixon, on the other hand, distanced himself from reporters. During his entire presidency, Nixon held only 39 formal exchanges with reporters. This compared with 132 under Lyndon Johnson, 65 under Kennedy, 193 under Eisenhower, 160 under Truman, and 998 under Roosevelt.[20] By contrast, Nixon's use of prime-time television speeches rose to an all-time high. The number of prime-time appearances on national television by presidents during their first 19 months in office rose from four under Kennedy, to seven under Johnson, and fourteen under Nixon.[21]

Nixon explained his strategy in an extraordinary memo that he wrote in the third person (referring to himself as 'RN') in September 1970. 'Instead of trying to win the press, to cater to them, to have backgrounders with them, RN has ignored them and talked directly to the country by TV whenever possible,' Nixon wrote. 'He has used the press and not let the press use him.'[22] As part of his effort to 'use' the press, Nixon created the White House Office of Communications in 1969.[23] The Office not only institutionalized the tactic of 'going public,' but it also reinforced the concept of a White House-centered system of government.

THE OFFICE OF COMMUNICATIONS: DEALING WITH THE MEDIA

The Office of Communications, like the Office of Legislative Affairs that Eisenhower had created, is part of the president's personal staff in the White House Office. Used by every president

Above: President Eisenhower was the first to make extensive use of the medium of television – and not just for press conferences. Several times cabinet members were shown reporting to him.

Below: Franklin D. Roosevelt shown in relaxed, confident manner during one of his regular press conferences. His preference, however, lay with the radio, many newspapers being hostile to him.

since Nixon, the Office of Communications plans a long-range communications agenda, serves as liaison with local media outlets throughout the country (thus allowing the White House to target messages to specific media markets in congressional districts where the president needs support), plans the 'line-of-the-day' (the message that the White House wants everyone in the administration to repeat so that the media will pick it up and cover it), and coordinates the flow of news from the entire executive branch. The goal of the Office of Communications is to set the public agenda, to make sure that all parts of the executive branch adhere to that agenda, and to promote the public agenda through aggressive mass marketing.

Thus, just as the Bureau of the Budget became a central clearing house for legislative initiatives from the departments and agencies, the Office of Communications has provided – with admittedly variable success – central clearance of all public communications from the executive branch. Nixon was particularly eager to implement this sort of central clearance because of his distrust of the federal bureaucracy – 'damn government,' as he liked to call it.[24] He felt that many of the career bureaucrats serving in the executive branch were liberal Democrats opposed to his policies. Although the president was theoretically the policy leader and chief manager of the executive branch, Nixon felt thwarted by his own underlings.

Therefore, in addition to establishing central clearance of executive branch publicity, Nixon attempted to exert even more control over executive branch policy-making. Even the most powerful modern presidents had exerted legislative initiative only in areas that were particularly important or that they had a particular interest in. Otherwise, they gave considerable latitude to the departments and agencies to develop their own legislative recommendations. The White House maintained policy leadership by simply approving or disapproving those recommendations.[25]

Nixon, however, sought on a more routine basis to influence the actual development of legislative proposals coming out of the departments through the use of White House 'working groups' that were supervised by his chief domestic affairs adviser, John Ehrlichman.[26] Harold Seidman has written that Nixon's ultimate goal appeared to have been for the departments to 'wither away with the White House assuming direct operational responsibility.'[27] But Nixon's efforts were ultimately thwarted by the Watergate scandal and his forced resignation in August 1974. His immediate successors, Gerald Ford and Jimmy Carter, reverted to a more decentralized approach to policy-making. But Ronald Reagan later exerted considerable influence through a return to a more assertive White House-centered system.

Nixon's creation of the Office of Communications was also motivated by his distrust of the press. He felt that they, too, opposed his policies, and he saw the Office of Communications as a way to circumvent the negative coverage of the 'influential, opinion-making "Eastern Establishment" media.'[28] To achieve this for each president, the Office plans direct appeals (both by the president and his spokespersons) through television, radio, town meetings, speaking tours, and outreach to local media. In addition, the Office attempts to manipulate the 'establishment' media

through a combination of persuasion, access, and easy news. Background briefings, phone calls to reporters, and other forms of 'spin control' are used to try to influence what direction stories will take. In addition, the Office tries to make reporters' jobs easier by feeding them information and staging photo opportunities.

The result of the Office of Communications' efforts is a blatant (though not always successful) attempt to manage the news. 'Nixon had a fetish about [trying to] dominate the news,' according to his close aide Charles Colson. Colson says that the White House came 'as close to managing the news as you can do' in 1972, the year of Nixon's triumphant visits to China and the Soviet Union and his landslide re-election. Daily public opinion polls conducted for the White House helped to determine 'what issues were sensitive with the public' so that the White House 'could tell one night how people were reacting to things, and the next morning back off or intensify what [it] wanted to say with almost simultaneous polling.'[29]

More recently, the Reagan White House set up a tracking system of network television newscasts to see how many minutes each one devoted to the stories being peddled by the White House. Based on the results, the White House modified its efforts to communicate its stories more effectively.[30] in January 1993, Bill Clinton's first communications director, George Stephanopoulos, asked rhetorically, 'Do we want to control the message?' His answer: 'Of course we do.'[31] The reason is perhaps best summed up by Dick Cheney, who served as Defense Secretary under George Bush and as Gerald Ford's White House Chief of Staff. 'The most powerful tool you have [in the White House] is the ability to use the symbolic aspects of the presidency to promote your goals and objectives,' he said. 'You're never going to get anywhere if you let someone step on your lead, or if you step on your lead yourself.' That means controlling the agenda. 'You don't let the press set the agenda. The press is going to

Above: President Nixon was never comfortable with the press. This picture was taken at his first news conference in the East Room of the White House on January 27, 1969.

object to that. They like to set the agenda. They like to decide what's important and what isn't important. But if you let them do that, they're going to trash your presidency.'[32]

Bill Clinton learned that lesson the hard way in the first months of his presidency. Despite the best first-year record of any president since Eisenhower in securing congressional passage of legislation he supported, Clinton's early public relations was a disaster.[33] He alienated the White House press corps by cutting off their access and ignoring them. In return, press coverage of the new president tended to be harsh.

Clinton compounded his problems by appearing indecisive and quickly losing control of the agenda. Instead of immediately focusing on

Below: 'Controlling the message' is now an essential part of the political process. It is also vital to be seen to be in command. Here, Bill Clinton meets with George Stephanopoulos.

health care reform and other major initiatives, he lost steam through a series of troubled nominations, his handling of the proposal to allow gays in the military, his infamous $200 haircut on the runway at Los Angeles airport, and later the Whitewater scandal. When the president's health care reform proposal finally came to a vote in 1994, he lost – despite a majority of fellow Democrats in both houses of Congress. He then faced a stunning setback in the 1994 mid-term elections when Republicans seized control not only of the Senate, but also of the House of Representatives (which the Democrats had controlled since 1955). Divided government had returned after only two years of unified party rule.

Part of the trick of maintaining a successful public image (a trick that often eluded both Nixon and Clinton) is to strike a careful balance between courting the press and circumventing them. Among recent presidents, Ronald Reagan used the public presidency most effectively. Though facing divided government – with fellow Republicans holding only a slender majority in the Senate (53-47) and remaining heavily outnumbered in the House (191-244) – Reagan was able in his first year in office to push through Congress a sweeping economic program that included the largest tax cuts in American history.

In setting the new course, the Reagan team demonstrated a mastery of Congress not witnessed since the heyday of Lyndon Johnson and his 'Great Society' in the 1960s (when Johnson had solid majorities of fellow Democrats in both houses of Congress). Reagan enjoyed an unusual degree of Republican unity in Congress, successfully courted conservative Southern Democrats, and was able to turn an unsuccessful assassination attempt in March 1981 into a vehicle for building new political capital. But an unusual mastery of White House staff units also helped. As Reagan's former communications director, David Gergen, put it: 'For the first time in any presidency, we molded a communications policy around our legislative strategy.'[34]

Under Reagan, all the staff units that presidents had created over the years were aggressively used in tandem to promote legislative success. Reagan used the Office of Policy Development, with a staff of about forty, to help plan domestic

policy initiatives. He then used the Office of Public Liaison to build support for those initiatives among interest groups, the Office of Political Affairs to mobilize support within the Republican Party, and the Office of Intergovernmental Affairs to build support among elected officials at the state level. The Office of Communications planned public relations and used its Office of Public Affairs to coordinate public statements from executive branch officials, the Office of Media Affairs to target messages to local media in congressional districts where votes were needed, and the Speechwriting Office to draft speeches and talking points for administration spokespersons. The Office of Legislative Affairs worked closely with all these units while shepherding the initiatives through Congress and directing the lobbying of individual senators and representatives.

Below: David Gergen finessed communications during the Reagan and Clinton presidencies. He is pictured here at the National Press Club in April 1986 discussing the Soviet detention of a US journalist, held on suspicion of spying.

Above: The modern master of his public image was a former actor, President Reagan. He is seen here having an apparently cosy chat with Prime Minister Margaret Thatcher, his conservative ally.

THE PRESIDENT VERSUS CONGRESS

White House staff units are not miracle workers. They certainly do not guarantee presidential success. But they can help. When the votes just aren't there to secure legislative victories, presidents still have some fallback options. The most obvious is the constitutional power to veto legislation. If the president chooses this option, he returns the legislation to the house in which it originated, along with his objections. That house then reconsiders the bill. If, after reconsideration, two-thirds of that body votes to support the bill, it is sent on to the other house for its consideration. If two-thirds of that house also supports the bill, the president's veto is overridden and the bill becomes law. But a two-thirds vote of both houses of Congress is very difficult to muster, and historically more than 90 per cent of presidential vetoes have succeeded in killing legislation.

The Constitution also provides for what is called a 'pocket' veto. If Congress does not stay in session for at least ten days after the president receives a bill, he can veto it without returning it for reconsideration. Thus, the bill simply dies. Legislation passed at the very end of a session is subject to the pocket veto unless Congress chooses to extend its session in anticipation of such a veto.

In addition to the 'regular' and 'pocket' veto, which apply to a bill in its entirety, many have suggested that Congress should pass legislation allowing the president to make a 'line-item' veto. This would give the president the power to veto isolated sections of bills (such as one or more parts of a complex appropriations bill). Suggestions for a presidential line-item veto were made as early as the 1840s. It is a power that more than four-fifths of the state governors now have, and in the 1980s, President Reagan – who had enjoyed the power as governor of California – championed the idea of giving the power to the president. A promise to do just that was a major part of the Republican's 'Contract With America' in 1994. Once in power, however, the

Republican-controlled House and Senate backed down from the idea of giving the Democratic president Bill Clinton the power of a line-item veto. By the summer of 1995, the proposal seemed dead – at least for the time being.[35]

Presidents have also thwarted Congress by failing to spend money that Congress has appropriated for particular projects. This practice, known as 'impoundment,' can be an important money-saving tool, and it has been used by presidents since at least the time of Thomas Jefferson. If a project can be completed without spending all the money that Congress appropriated, few would object to the president withholding the additional funds. Some presidents, however, used impoundment as a policy-making rather than managerial tool. In other words, rather than simply saving left-over money, they withheld appropriations in their entirety to thwart the will of Congress. President Nixon, in particular, abused the practice of impoundment and provoked Congress to limit the president's

Above: House Banking Committee Chairman Henry Gonzalez opening the first hearings into the Whitewater affair, news of which raised questions about Bill Clinton's financial probity.

power to impound funds through its passage of the Impoundment Control Act of 1974. Now presidents can 'rescind' (or terminate) funds only with the approval of both houses of Congress. However, presidents may still temporarily 'defer' funds unilaterally.

THE PRESIDENT AND THE JUDICIARY

Even if Congress passes a president's legislative initiatives, it is still possible for the courts to strike down the legislation on the grounds that it violates the Constitution. This was a particular problem for Franklin D. Roosevelt. After securing remarkable legislative victories during his first 100 days in office, the conservative majority on the Supreme Court invalidated major provisions of the laws including the National Industrial Recovery Act, the Agricultural Adjustment Act, and the Bituminous Coal Act. Four justices (Butler, McReynolds, Sutherland, and Van Devanter) stood solidly opposed to most New Deal legislation, three justices (Brandeis, Cardozo, and Stone) almost always supported it, and two 'swing' voters (Hughes and Roberts) usually sided against the legislation. That meant a block of 6-3 or 5-4 that often opposed the president.

Roosevelt forged ahead with new legislative victories despite threats that the court would strike them down. During his first term, Roosevelt had no opportunity to appoint a new justice. After his landslide re-election in 1936, he proposed legislation to reorganize the federal judiciary and, in the process, to increase the size of the Supreme Court so he could 'pack' it with new members who would uphold his policies. The legislation was bitterly opposed as a political ploy.

The Constitution gives Congress the power to determine the size of the Supreme Court. Congress originally set the size of the court at six in the Judiciary Act of 1789, and has passed legislation changing the size seven times since then: to five in 1801, back to six in 1802, to seven in 1907, to nine in 1837, to ten in 1863, to seven in 1865, and back to nine in 1869.[36] Roosevelt's proposal would have allowed Congress to increase the size to as much as 15, but the proposal ultimately failed.

In the end it didn't matter. Just 20 days after Roosevelt's March 9, 1937, radio address tried to rouse public pressure on Congress to pass his bill, the court issued a 5-4 decision in *West Coast Hotel* v. *Parrish* in which Justice Roberts switched sides and voted with the pro-Roosevelt bloc to uphold a Washington state minimum wage law for women and children.[37] Two weeks later, Roberts was also the decisive vote in *National Labor Relations Board* v. *Jones & Laughlin Steel Corporation*, a 5-4 decision that upheld the National Labor Relations Act of 1935 (better known as the 'Wagner Act').[38] This 'switch in time that saved nine' led to a new 5-4 bloc that would vote to uphold New Deal legislation. The next month, one of the conservative stalwarts, Willis Van Devanter, resigned, giving FDR the opportunity to appoint a new justice. That turned out to be just the first of many opportunities for Roosevelt to change the composition of the court without Congress having to change its size.

JUDICIAL SELECTION

Clearly, the composition of the Supreme Court is important. In theory, impartial judges objectively applying the law should all reach the same 'correct' outcome in cases that come before them. But, in practice, that does not happen. Different judges have different views about how to interpret legal texts. In addition, judges are human beings who are influenced, at least in part, by their backgrounds and personal predilections. This is no small matter when one considers the profound effect that the Supreme Court can have on public policy. For example, it defines privacy rights (thereby determining abortion

Left: House Republican leader Newt Gingrich staged a ceremony in September 1994 at which his party contracted with the American people to enact reforms within 100 days of being elected.

policy), interprets the First Amendment (thereby determining policy on such diverse issues as prayer in the public schools and obscenity), and sets guidelines for the treatment of criminal defendants (thereby setting policy for law enforcement officials).

As White House aide Tom Charles Huston put it in a memo to President Nixon in 1969: '*In approaching the bench, it is necessary to remember that the decision as to who will make the decisions affects what decisions will be made.* That is, the role the judiciary will play in different historical eras depends as much on the type of men who become judges as it does on the constitutional rules which appear to [guide them].' Huston went on to urge Nixon to establish specific criteria for the type of judges to be appointed. The goal was to influence judicial policy-making. If the president 'establishes *his* criteria and establishes *his* machinery for insuring that the criteria are met, the appointments will be *his*, in fact, as in theory.' In response, Nixon wrote: 'RN *agrees*. Have this analysis in mind when making judicial nominations.'[39]

Under the Constitution, the president has the power to nominate Supreme Court Justices, with appointment coming only with the 'Advice and Consent of the Senate.' While dictating that the two branches share power, the Constitution is not clear about the precise scope of advice and consent. The Constitutional Convention of 1787 that drafted the 'advice and consent' clause was divided over who should have the power of judicial selection, and the resulting language was largely a compromise. Its ambiguity allowed for a degree of consensus that otherwise would have been impossible to achieve, since it allowed different framers to cling to differing interpretations of constitutional language.[40]

Below: The United States Supreme Court from the New Deal era pictured in 1934. The court had a conservative majority and Roosevelt sparked a political battle when he tried to alter its make-up.

The Senate has almost never given the president formal advice about whom to nominate (a rare exception came in 1874 when President Ulysses S. Grant sought the advice of Senate leaders before nominating Morrison Waite to be Chief Justice), but it has often exercised its consent function. From 1789 through 1994, the Senate blocked twenty-seven of the 149 nominations to the Supreme Court. It formally voted to reject 12 of those twenty-seven, and passively rejected ten others by voting to 'postpone' consideration of the nomination or by taking no action at all. Presidents withdrew the remaining five nominations in the face of certain Senate defeat. Indeed, the rate of unsuccessful Supreme Court nominations (19.5 percent) is the highest for any appointive post requiring Senate confirmation.[41] That failure rate shot up to 29 percent during the 25 year span from 1968 through 1993.

In 1789, President Washington suggested that the Senate has broad discretion to reject nominees. Just 'as the President has a right to nominate without assigning reasons,' he wrote, 'so has the Senate a right to dissent without giving theirs.'[42] Since then, the Senate has often done just that, although the precise amount of obstructive power exercised by the Senate has ebbed and flowed with changing political circumstances.[43] Divided government and a closely divided court in which single appointments had the potential to alter the direction of future court decisions on such controversial issues as abortion led to the increased number of contentious nominations in recent years. With important policies hanging in the balance, interest groups entered the fray, waging massive lobbying and public relations campaigns for and against Supreme Court nominees. In response, presidents turned to their staff units to mobilize public opinion, generate supportive interest group activity, and lobby senators as a way of combating opponents of their nominees.[44]

The tactics that these staff units use are similar to those associated with more traditional political battles, including the lure of patronage. 'Try to soften [Senator] Russell Long [a Democrat from Louisiana] on [the nomination] of Abe Fortas,' Johnson wrote to his congressional relations staff in 1968. 'He is interested in Camp Polk – I'm helping him; he wanted Buffalo NY building – I helped him; I need his quiet help.'[45] Similarly, a Nixon aide described the administration's efforts to secure confirmation of Clement Haynsworth, Jr., in 1969: 'We are gathering together the list of favors the target Senators have been asking the Administration for – jobs, projects, grants, etc., and are trying to use this as leverage with the Senators . . .'[46]

The White House may also attempt to bully support out of senators through threats. During the fights over Haynsworth in 1969 and G. Harrold Carswell in 1970, the Nixon administration leaked derogatory stories about Senate opponents to the press. It also enlisted corporate campaign contributors who threatened to stop funding senators who voted against Haynsworth. In the end, President Nixon 'froze out' Republican senators who did not support Haynsworth by ignoring them and denying them access to the White House.[47]

Judicial nominations – both at the Supreme Court and lower federal court level – are now part and parcel of a president's broader efforts to increase power over the policy-making agenda of government. Although the Supreme Court is far more visible, many more legal decisions are made by lower federal courts, making their composition just as important as that of the Supreme Court. When Ronald Reagan became president in 1981, he increased his control over the selection of federal judges by creating the President's Committee on Federal Judicial Selection as part of his personal staff in the White House Office. He also expanded the power of the Justice Department (which had assisted presidents in choosing judges since the 1800s) by giving its Office of Legal Policy broad responsibility for screening nominees. Thus, he

Above: Supreme Court nominee Robert Bork during his testimony in September 1987. Reagan's attempt to instal this conservative was rejected by the Senate by a vote of 58 to 42.

succeeded in creating the type of formal machinery that Tom Charles Huston had urged Nixon to create in 1969.

The efforts paid off. By the time Bill Clinton became president in 1993, Reagan and his Republican successor (and former vice president) George Bush had appointed more than 60 per-cent of the federal judges below the Supreme Court (389 of 645 district court judges in active service, and 102 of 167 courts of appeal judges in active service).[48] In addition, they had appointed six of the nine justices on the Supreme Court. Of the remaining three justices, only one – Byron White – had been appointed by a Democratic president (John F. Kennedy in 1962).

President Bush retained the Reagan-era screening units, and while President Clinton abolished the formal President's Committee on Federal Judicial Selection, an ad hoc version of the Committee continued to meet. Clinton gave White House responsibility for overseeing judicial nominations to the office of the White House Counsel. In the Justice Department, he gave responsibility for the screening of nominees to the Office of Policy Development.[49]

Just as Reagan and Bush had nominated judges who reflected their conservative ideolgy, Clinton began nominating judges with a more liberal bent. By July 1995, he had appointed over 150 lower federal court judges, with Senate action pending on an additional twenty nominations. In addition, he had appointed two Supreme Court justices, Ruth Bader Ginsburg in 1993 and Stephen Breyer in 1994. There are, of course, limits to a president's ability to influence judicial policy-making through the appointment process. The actions of appointees on the bench can be a surprise. Even the most careful selection and screening process is not an absolute guarantee of how nominees will eventually vote. But it minimizes the likelihood that they will be far off the mark.

CONCLUSION: THE PRESIDENT AS POLICY LEADER

As we have seen, presidents now enjoy consid-erable power in the development and implemen-tation of domestic policy. They have historically enjoyed even greater power in the arena of foreign policy. In both arenas, it is a power that is shared, and it is certainly not unlimited. But the president is the most visible figure in the modern American political system, and in his relations with other parts of government, one now thinks of the president as the leader.

Notes

1. Lester M. Salamon, 'The Presidency and Domestic Policy Formulation,' in Hugh Heclo and Lester M. Salamon (eds.), *The Illusion of Presidential Government,* Boulder, Colorado, 1981, p. 179.

2. Precise numbers are very difficult to calculate. This estimate comes from Robert Williams, 'The President and the Executive Branch,' in *The Modern Presidency,* New York, 1987, p. 120.

3. James L. Sundquist, *The Decline and Resurgence of Congress,* Washington, D.C., 1981, p. 33.

4. Williams, 'The President and the Executive Branch,' in *The Modern Presidency,* 1987, p. 20.

5. Erwin C. Hargrove and Michael Nelson, *Presidents, Politics, and Policy,* Baltimore, 1984, p. 175.

6. John Hart, *The Presidential Branch,* 2nd edition, Chatham, N.J., 1995, pp. 28-30.

7. John Hart, 'The Executive Office of the President,' in Leonard W. Levy and Louis Fisher (eds.), *Encyclopedia of the American Presidency,* New York, 1994, p. 576.

8. Matthew A. Crenson and Francis E. Rourke, 'By Way of Conclusion: American Bureaucracy since World War II,' in Louis Galambos (ed.), *The New American State,* Baltimore, 1987, p. 93.

9. Gary King and Lynn Ragsdale (eds.), *The Elusive Executive,* Washington, D.C., 1988, pp. 205, 208. For a discussion of the problems of counting White House staff, see Hart, *The Presidential Branch,* pp. 112-25.

10. John P. Burke, 'The Institutional Presidency,' in Michael Nelson (ed.), *The Presidency and the Political System,* 4th edn, Washington, D.C., 1995, p. 385.

11. Richard E. Neustadt, 'Presidency and Legislation: Planning the President's Program,' *American Political Science Review* December 1955, p. 980.

12. Stephen J. Wayne, 'White House Liaison with Congress,' in Levy and Fisher (eds.), *Encyclopedia of the American Presidency,* New York, 1994, p. 277.

13. James P. Pfiffner, *The Modern Presidency,* New York, 1994, p. 167.

14. George C. Edwards III, *The Public Presidency: The Pursuit of Popular Support,* New York, 1983.

15. Samuel Kernell, *Going Public: New Strategies of Presidential Leadership,* Washington, D.C., 1986.

16. Jeffrey K. Tulis, *The Rhetorical Presidency,* Princeton, New Jersey, 1987, p. 95.

17. William Lasser, 'Fireside Chats,' in Levy and Fisher (eds.), *The Encyclopedia of the American Presidency,* p. 629.

18. For an excellent account of Eisenhower's use of television, see Craig Allen, *Eisenhower and the Mass Media: Peace, Prosperity, and Prime-Time Television,* Chapel Hill, North Carolina, 1993.

19. 'Memo, H.R. Haldeman to Henry Kissinger and Patrick Buchanan, 14 January 1970,' quoted in Bruce Oudes (ed.), *From The President – Richard Nixon's Secret Files* New York, 1989, p. 88.

20. Figures for Truman through Nixon are provided in Table 5.4, 'Presidential News Conferences, 1949-1984,' in King and Ragsdale (eds.), *The Elusive Executive,* Washington, D.C., 1988, p. 268. Figures for Franklin Roosevelt are from Michael Baruch Grossman and Martha Joynt Kumar, *Portraying the President,* Baltimore, 1981, p. 245.

21. Newton N. Minow, John Bartlow Martin, and Lee N. Mitchell, *Presidential Television,* New York, 1973, p. 171.

22. 'Memo, Richard Nixon, "PR Points to Be Made," September 1970,' quoted in full in Herbert Klein, *Making It Perfectly Clear,* Garden City, N.Y., 1980, pp. 125-8.

23. For a full account of the office, see John Anthony Maltese, *Spin Control: The White House Office of Communications and the Management of Presidential News,* 2nd rev. edn, Chapel Hill, North Carolina, 1994.

24. William Safire, *Before the Fall,* New York, 1975, p. 247.

25. John Iglehart, 'Major HEW Legislation Tailored by White House "Working Groups",' *National Journal* 7 March 1970, p. 486.

26. For an account of these working groups, see Richard P. Nathan, *The Plot that Failed: Nixon and the Administrative Presidency,* New York, 1975.

27. Harold Seidman, *Politics, Position, and Power,* 3rd edn., New York, 1980, p. 115.

28. Safire, *Before the Fall,* p. 341.

29. Author's interview with Charles Colson conducted on 11 July 1989.

30. Author's interview with Frank Ursomarso, conducted on 26 June 1990.

31. Quoted in Burt Solomon, 'How a Leak-Loathing White House is Putting the Press in its Place,' *National Journal* 13 February 1993, p. 416.

32. Author's interview with Dick Cheney conducted on 10 March 1989.

33. Regarding Clinton's legislative success, see Mark A.

Peterson, 'The President and Congress,' in Michael Nelson (ed.), *The Presidency and the Political System,* 4th edn, Washington, D.C., 1995, p. 453.

34. Quoted in Mark Hertsgaard, *On Bended Knee: The Press and the Reagan Presidency,* New York, 1988, pp. 22-3.

35. David E. Rosenbaum's article entitled 'Push for Line-Item Veto Runs Out of G.O.P. Steam,' in the *New York Times,* 20 July 1995, B11.

36. Elder Witt (ed.), *Guide to the Supreme Court* Washington, D.C., 1979, pp. 664-5.

37. *West Coast Hotel* v. *Parrish,* 300 US 379 (1937).

38. *National Labor Relations Board* v. *Jones & Laughlin Steel Corporation,* 301 US 1 (1937). See Epstein and Walker, *Constitutional Law,* 301.

39. Quoted in John Anthony Maltese's article 'The Presidency and the Judiciary,' in Michael Nelson (ed.), *The Presidency and the Political System,* 4th edition, Washington, D.C., 1995, p. 469.

40. For a thorough discussion of the debate over judicial selection at the Constitutional Convention, see James E. Gauch's article 'The Intended Role of the Senate in Supreme Court Appointments,' *University of Chicago Law Review* (1989), p. 337.

41. P.S. Ruckman, Jr., 'The Supreme Court, Critical Nominations, and the Senate Confirmation Process,' *Journal of Politics* (1993), p. 794.

42. W.W. Abbot (ed.), *The Papers of George Washington* Charlottesville, Virginia, 1989, p. 401.

43. For a comprehensive discussion of this, see John Anthony Maltese, *The Selling of Supreme Court Nominees,* Baltimore, 1995.

44. See John Anthony Maltese, *The Selling of Supreme Court Nominees,* ch. 7.

45. Nigel Bowles, *The White House and Capitol Hill: The Politics of Presidential Persuasion,* Oxford, 1987, p. 166.

46. 'Memorandom, Harry Dent to Ken Belieu, 17 October 1969,' in folder 'Haynsworth (2 of 3),' Box 6, Harry Dent Files, Nixon Presidential Materials Project, College Park, Maryland.

47. See Maltese, *The Selling of Supreme Court Nominees,* chs 5 and 7.

48. Sheldon Goldman, 'Bush's Judicial Legacy: The Final Imprint,' 76 *Judicature* (1993), p. 295.

49. Author's interviews with White House and Justice Department officials, March 1994.

Michael Nelson

3

THE VICE PRESIDENCY

The vice presidency was an afterthought of the Constitutional
Convention of 1787, and has been an object of derisory humor
ever since. Yet historically more than a dozen vice presidents
have gone on to become president, including some of history's most
distinguished chief executives: John Adams, Thomas Jefferson,
Theodore Roosevelt, Harry S. Truman, and Lyndon B. Johnson.
And in modern times the office has grown dramatically in
responsibility, visibility, and influence.

Vice President Johnson takes the presidential oath
aboard Air Force One following Kennedy's assassination.

From the beginning, the vice presidency has been an easy and frequent target of political humor. Benjamin Franklin quipped that the vice president should be addressed as 'Your Superfluous Excellency.' Mr. Dooley, the invented character of the writer Finley Peter Dunne, described the office as 'not a crime exactly. Ye can't be sint to jail f'r it, but it's kind iv a disgrace. It's like writin' anonymous letters.' The popular 1930s Gershwin musical *Of Thee I Sing* featured a vice president whose name no one in the play could remember and who spent most of his time trying to find two people to serve as references so that he could obtain a library card.

Even vice presidents have poked fun at the office. Thomas R. Marshall, who was vice president in the Wilson administration, said that the vice president is like 'a man in a cataleptic fit: he cannot speak, he cannot move; he suffers no pain; he is perfectly conscious of all that goes on, but has no part in it.' Marshall also told the story of the two brothers: 'One ran away to sea; the other was elected vice president. And nothing was heard of either of them again.' The bowdlerized version of Vice President John Nance Garner's pithy assessment of the office is probably the most frequently quoted of all: 'The vice presidency isn't worth a pitcher of warm spit.'[1]

John Adams, the country's first vice president, began the practice of ridiculing the office. 'My country,' he wrote to his wife Abigail, 'has in its wisdom contrived for me the most insignificant office that ever the invention of man contrived or his imagination conceived.' Adams could not know that the vice presidency was actually at a peak of influence during the period he served. Because the Senate was small and relatively unorganized, Adams's position as Senate president (his only ongoing constitutional role) enabled him to break numerous tie votes and steer the legislative debate. More important, because the Constitution declared that the candidate who finished second in the presidential election was elected vice president, Adams was the heir apparent to the presidency. He and Thomas Jefferson, the nation's first and second vice presidents, became its second and third presidents.

The prestige associated with being (presumably) the second most qualified person in the country to be president was stripped from the vice presidency during the Jefferson administration, sending the office into a century-long tailspin. In response to a tied electoral vote in the 1800 presidential election, Congress and the states enacted the Twelfth Amendment in 1804 to separate the balloting for president and vice president. The amendment solved the immediate problem but created another. Because, as Massachusetts representative Samuel Taggart foresaw, 'the vice president will not stand on such high ground in the method proposed as he does in the present mode of a double ballot,' the nation could expect that 'great care will not be taken in the selection of a character to fill that office.'

Constitutionally weak from the beginning and now stripped of its political prestige, the vice presidency became an unattractive office to talented political leaders. The typical 19th-century vice president was an old or undistinguished politician who had been nominated to balance the party's ticket geographically or ideologically in the presidential election. After Martin Van Buren, who was President Andrew Jackson's vice president from 1833 to 1837, no

Above: Martin Van Buren in 1837 was the last incumbent vice president to be elected to the presidency – rather than obtain it through death in office – until George Bush.

vice president in that century ever was nominated to run for president, not even the four who succeeded to the presidency when the presidents whom they served died: John Tyler in 1841, Millard Fillmore in 1850, Andrew Johnson in 1865, and Chester A. Arthur in 1881. Whig party leader Daniel Webster, asked in 1848 to join the national ticket as a candidate for vice president, declined by saying, 'I do not propose to be buried until I am dead.'

Not surprisingly, the 19th-century vice presidents make up a virtual rogues' gallery of personal and political failures. Some became embroiled in financial scandals: Daniel D. Tompkins was charged with keeping inadequate records while serving as governor of New York during the War of 1812, and Schuyler Colfax and Henry Wilson were implicated in the notorious Credit Mobilier stock scandal of the 1870s. Other vice presidents fell prey to personal peccadilloes. Tompkins and Andrew Johnson were heavy drinkers. (Johnson's first address to the Senate was a drunken harangue.) Richard M. Johnson kept a series of slave mistresses, educating the children of one but selling another when she spurned his advances. George Clinton, John C. Calhoun, and Chester Arthur each publicly

expressed his dislike for the president. Arthur, for example, attacked President James A. Garfield over a patronage quarrel. 'Garfield has not been square, nor honorable, nor truthful,' he told a New York newspaper. Finally, some vice presidents did not even live in Washington – Richard Johnson left to run a tavern in his native Kentucky and William R. King took the oath of office in Cuba.

The early history of the vice presidency is not entirely bleak. When William Henry Harrison became the first president to die in office in 1841, the language of the Constitution was unclear about whether Vice President Tyler was to become president until the end of Harrison's four-year term, or merely acting president until a special election could be called. Tyler seized the day, taking the presidential oath of office and vowing to remain president for the balance of the term. Some members of Congress grumbled at the time, but a precedent had been set. When President Zachary Taylor died in 1850, no one

election, was that few presidents liked, trusted, or agreed on major issues with their vice presidents. In 1940 FDR, acting from a position of political strength, told the Democratic convention that if it did not nominate Secretary of Agriculture Henry A. Wallace for vice president he would decline its nomination to run for a third term as president. The convention acquiesced, establishing the precedent that presidential candidates choose their own running mates. One consequence of the new practice is that, after the election, the president has a personal stake in the vice president's success in office.

The most important turning point in the history of the vice presidency occurred in 1945, when Truman, who replaced Wallace in 1944, became president after FDR's death and discovered that he had been kept ignorant not only of the Allies' plans for the post-World War II era but of the very existence of the atomic bomb. The subsequent Cold War between the United States and the Soviet Union and the proliferation of missile-launched nuclear weapons heightened the sense, both within the government and among the general public, that the vice president should be ready and able to step into the presidency literally at a moment's notice.

The lessons of 1945 have had three important and beneficial consequences for the vice presidency.[2] First, all post-war presidents have kept their vice presidents privately well informed and

questioned Vice President Fillmore's right to succeed to the presidency.

Theodore Roosevelt, who was elected vice president in 1900, enhanced the prominence of his office through extensive political travel and a flair for publicity in the growing national media of mass-circulation magazines and newspaper chains. He shattered one historical pattern and established another. In 1904, after succeeding to the presidency when President William L. McKinley was assassinated, Roosevelt won his party's nomination to run for a term as president in his own right. Each of the four successor presidents who came after Roosevelt followed in his political footsteps: Calvin Coolidge in 1924, Harry S. Truman in 1948, Lyndon Johnson in 1964, and Gerald Ford in 1976. All but Ford, who lost narrowly, were then elected to their own full term as president.

Roosevelt sparked an upward spiral in the vice presidency that slowly undid the ill effects of the 19th century. Because he made the office a stepping stone to the presidency, able and ambitious politicians became more receptive to the offer of a vice presidential nomination, including Charles Dawes (1925–1929), who had served in three administrations and won a Nobel Prize, Charles Curtis, the Senate majority leader (1929–1933), and Garner, the speaker of the House (1933–1941). Their talents and experience encouraged the presidents they served to entrust them with responsibility. Adams had been the only vice president in history to meet regularly with the cabinet, for example, but in 1921 President Warren G. Harding invited Vice President Coolidge to do so, as has every president since Franklin D. Roosevelt. Garner was the first vice president to undertake a diplomatic mission for the president and to sit in on meetings between the president and congressional leaders.

During the 19th century, the pairing of a presidential and a vice presidential candidate was usually a shotgun wedding arranged by the party to heal its own divisions. The result, after the

Right: Thawing the Cold War, Soviet premier Nikita Khrushchev and Vice President Nixon toast with American wine at the US exhibit in Sokolniki Park, Moscow, in July 1959.

publicly active. To do otherwise would be regarded as irresponsible. As President Dwight D. Eisenhower said about his relationship with Vice President Richard Nixon, 'Even if Mr. Nixon and I were not good friends, I would still have him in every important conference of government, so that if the grim reaper would find it time to remove me from the scene, he is ready to step in without any interruption.' In 1949, at President Truman's request, the vice president was made a statutory member of the National Security Council.

To be sure, some modern vice presidential roles are relatively unimportant – chairing study commissions, attending state funerals, exhorting the party faithful, and so on – but others are quite substantial, including diplomatic representative, liaison to Congress, and, beginning with President Jimmy Carter's vice president, Walter F. Mondale, wideranging senior presidential adviser. During the 1960s and 1970s vice presidents began to accumulate institutional resources to help them fulfill their growing responsibilities. Modern vice presidents have a large and professional staff, an office in the west wing of the White House, a weekly private meeting with the president, access to other presidential meetings and papers, an official mansion,

Below: Vice President Mondale (right) applauds as Chief Justice Warren Burger shakes President Carter's hand following his taking of the oath of office on January 20, 1977.

and a significant voice in administration policy-making.[3] Even the vice presidential seal of office has changed. The old seal showed an eagle at rest; the new one displays a wingspread eagle with a claw full of arrows and a starburst at its head.

A second change in the post-war status of the vice presidency is that more attention has been paid to the nomination of competent and loyal vice presidential candidates. Indeed, from 1948 to 1992, nominees for vice president have had, on average, as much experience in high political office as nominees for president. Winning votes for the ticket in the presidential election is still the goal when choosing a running mate, but voters now care more about a potential vice president's ability to step into the presidency than they do about having all regions of the country or factions of the party represented in the White House. The exceptions to careful selection of a vice presidential candidate demonstrate the rule – the widely doubted competence of Spiro T. Agnew in 1968, Geraldine Ferraro in 1984, and Dan Quayle in 1988 and 1992 became an issue in each presidential campaign and cost the ticket votes. As for loyalty, presidential nominees now conduct thorough investigations of prospective running mates to find out if they will be like-minded and faithful lieutenants in office. Vice presidents, unlike cabinet and staff members, are constitutional officers who cannot be fired; their loyalty to the president must be ascertained in advance.

A concern for competence and loyalty in the vice presidency also characterized the solution that Congress invented to a recurring problem of

the executive that the challenges of the postwar era had made urgent – vice presidential vacancies. The Twenty-fifth Amendment, which became part of the Constitution in 1967, established a procedure for selecting vice presidents in unusual circumstances. Before then, the vice presidency had been vacant for parts of 16 out of 36 administrations: seven times because the vice president died, once because the vice president resigned, and eight times because the president

Below: After eight years as vice president, George Bush then became president with former Indiana senator Dan Quayle as his vice presidential running mate, a controversial choice of candidate that took many by surprise.

Above: A former director of the Central Intelligence Agency (CIA), Vice President George Bush chairs a meeting of the Crisis Management Team to discuss a proposed transfer of technology to the Soviet Union.

died and the vice president succeeded to the presidency.[4] The new amendment stated that 'whenever there is a vacancy in the office of the Vice President, the President shall nominate a Vice President who shall take office upon confirmation by a majority of both Houses of Congress,' voting separately. This procedure came in handy, albeit in circumstances its authors scarcely had imagined, in 1973, when Vice President Agnew resigned as part of a criminal plea bargain and

Above: Chief Justice Burger administers the vice presidential oath to Nelson A. Rockefeller in the Senate on December 19, 1974. The selection of this rich liberal antagonized many Republicans.

Below: Bill Clinton presenting his administration's environmental plan to protect ancient forest in the Pacific northwest. Vice President Gore (behind) had advocated such acts as a senator.

was replaced by Ford, and in 1974, when Ford became president after President Nixon resigned in disgrace and appointed Nelson A. Rockefeller to fill the vacated vice presidency.

The final enhancement of the post-war vice presidency is that the vice president has become the presumptive front-runner for a future presidential nomination by the party. Not counting Vice President Al Gore (whose chances for a future run at the White House are highly rated), 7 of the 10 most recent vice presidents – Richard Nixon in 1960, Hubert H. Humphrey in 1968, Walter F. Mondale in 1984, George Bush in 1988, and Truman, Johnson, and Ford, the three postwar successor presidents – have subsequently been nominated to run for president.

What accounts for the recent ascendancy of the vice presidency in the politics of presidential nominations? The two-term limit that was imposed on presidents by the Twenty-second Amendment in 1951 made it possible for the vice president to step forward as a presidential candidate during the president's second term without alienating the president, as Nixon did in 1960 and Bush did in 1988. In addition, the roles that Vice President Nixon developed, with Eisenhower's encouragement, as party builder (campaigning during election years and raising funds between elections) and as public advocate for the administration and its policies, uniquely situated Nixon and his successors to win friends among the party activists who influence presidential nominations.

Winning a presidential nomination is not the same as winning the election, of course. Indeed, some of the very vice presidential activities that are most appealing to the party rank-and-file may repel the broader electorate. Days and nights spent fertilizing the party's grass roots with fervent, sometimes slashing rhetoric can alienate voters who look to the president for unifying leadership. In addition, although only the president can plausibly take credit for an administration's successes, the vice president is fair game for attack by the other party's presidential candidate for its shortcomings. Such attacks allow the vice president no good response. The vice president who tried to stand apart from the administration would alienate the president and cause voters to wonder why the criticisms were not voiced earlier, when they might have made a difference. The vice president may say instead that loyalty to the president forecloses public disagreement. But that course is scarcely less perilous. Strength, independence, vision, and integrity are the qualities most voters seek in a president, not loyalty to the boss.

Still, no office provides a likelier passage to the presidency than the vice presidency – Bush won handily in 1988, Hubert H. Humphrey came close in 1968, and Nixon, having failed narrowly in 1960, was victorious eight years later. Politically, at least, the modern vice presidency is more in the Adams–Jefferson tradition than at any time since the days of Adams and Jefferson.

Notes

1. Sources for the quotations and history in this chapter may be found in Michael Nelson. *A Heartbeat Away*, Washington, D.C., 1988 . See also Irving G. Williams, *The Rise of the Vice Presidency*, Washington, D.C., 1956; and Joel K. Godstein, *The Modern American Vice Presidency*, Princeton, New Jersey, 1982.

2. Sidney M. Milkis and Michael Nelson, *The American Presidency: Origins and Development, 1776–1993*, Washington, D.C., 1994.

3. See Paul C. Light, *Vice-Presidential Power: Advice and Influence in the White House*, Baltimore, 1984; and Joseph A. Pika, 'The Vice Presidency: New Opportunities, Old Constraints,' in Nelson (ed.), *The Presidency and the Political*

System, 4th edn, Washington, D.C., 1995, pp. 496–528.

4. The vice presidents who died in office (all of natural causes) were: George Clinton in 1812, Elbridge Gerry in 1814, William R. King in 1853, Henry Wilson in 1875, Thomas A. Hendricks in 1885, Garret A. Hobart in 1899, and James S. Sherman in 1912. Vice President John C. Calhoun resigned in 1832 to accept election as US senator from South Carolina.

Harold F. Bass, Jr.

4

ELECTING THE PRESIDENT

The quadrennial presidential election process is marked by
bewildering and sometimes infuriating complexity. Yet through more
than two centuries, presidential elections have been the arena in which
many of the great dramas of American politics have been played out –
the establishment of the new government, the ending of slavery,
war and peace, the basic role of government, and more.

The first presidential inauguration:
George Washington takes the oath at Federal Hall.

Every four years, without fail, on the Tuesday after the first Monday in November, Americans troop to the polls to vote for president. Every four years, again without fail, at noon on the January 20 following the election, the person who has won swears a constitutionally-prescribed oath to 'preserve, protect, and defend the Constitution of the United States' and begins a new four-year term.

'Every' and 'without fail' are strong words that invite skeptical scrutiny. Yet from 1789 to 1996, the pattern of quadrennial elections has been unbroken, even through the Civil War of the 1860s and the Great Depression of the 1930s. This pattern has its origins in the Constitutional Convention of 1787, and its enduring strength in more than two centuries of history.

THE FRAMERS' DESIGN

The presidency emerged from the deliberations of the 55 delegates to the Constitutional Convention. Much of the time the Framers devoted to creating the executive office focused specifically on the issue of presidential selection.[1] Ultimately, the Convention decided on election by an electoral college.[2]

The electoral college, detailed in Article II, Section 1 of the Constitution, was quite complicated. It placed responsibility for presidential selection in the hands of electors, chosen in the states by methods prescribed in each state. Each state would appoint a number of electors equal to the size of its representation in Congress.

The designated electors would meet in their respective states. There, each elector would cast a presidential ballot for two persons, only one of whom could be from the elector's state. The results of the balloting in each state would be forwarded to the capital of the federal government.

The person receiving the most votes, providing that this was a majority of the electors, would become the president.

If no person received a majority, or if more than one tied with a majority, then the House of Representatives would choose the president. Each state delegation would have a single vote, and a majority of the states would be necessary for election. Under this contingency procedure, if the electoral college balloting resulted in a tie between individuals with a majority, the House would choose one of them. If no one received a majority, then the House would choose from among the top five recipients of electoral votes. Once the president was chosen, the individual with the second greatest number of electoral votes would automatically become vice president.

ELECTIONS WITHOUT POLITICAL PARTIES, 1789–1792

In 1789, shortly after the ratification of the Constitution, states selected electors to vote in the first presidential election. Initially, the states adopted diverse methods for choosing electors: legislative selection, popular election, or some combination of the two. Sixty-nine electors cast ballots. In the absence of any overt campaigning, George Washington's name appeared on every ballot, making him the electoral college's unanimous choice. John Adams, the runner-up, became vice president. In 1792, the electoral college balloting produced the same outcome. Four years later, Washington declined to be a candidate for a third term.

Below: Dated 1815, this painting by Krimmel is the earliest known representation of an American election. The scene is election day in Philadelphia with campaigners outside Independence Hall.

FEDERALISTS V. DEMOCRATIC-REPUBLICANS, 1796–1824

Following Washington's retirement announcement, the consensus that had prevailed in the electoral college disappeared. Clear partisan divisions already present within the government surfaced in the larger body politic. When the electors cast their ballots in 1796, John Adams received a narrow majority, closely followed by Thomas Jefferson. Thus, Adams became president and Jefferson vice president.

President Washington and Vice President Adams had been kindred spirits in their general perspective on politics and policy. When partisan division arose, Washington deplored it and refused to identify openly with any faction, insisting on remaining above the fray. Adams, however, with reservations, gravitated toward the Federalist Party.

The acknowledged Federalist leader, Alexander Hamilton, had been setting the political agenda within the government during the early 1790s. By 1796, Adams had become the leader of a faction within the Federalist ranks.[3] Jefferson, along with his chief lieutenant, James Madison, served as leader of the emerging opposition Democratic-Republican Party.[4]

National political parties in the United States began as governmental factions. Subsequently, they developed organizational machinery to conduct public campaigns for the presidency. In turn, elements within the electorate began developing enduring attachments to the parties.[5]

The presidential selection method developed by the Constitution's Framers had not anticipated the development of political parties. Nor could it endure their abiding presence. In 1796, the constitutional requirement that gave the presidency to the highest vote-getter in the elec-

toral college balloting and the vice presidency to the runner-up produced an awkward situation. During the next four years, Vice President Jefferson became increasingly visible as the symbol and advocate of partisan opposition to Adams' presidential leadership.

As 1800 approached, a rematch of the 1796 election loomed. Neither Adams nor Jefferson wanted an outcome in which the victor would be president while the loser promoted opposition from the vantage point of the vice presidency. The political organizations that each presided over sought in a disciplined fashion to select presidential electors committed to a party ticket: Adams and C. C. Pinckney for the Federalists, Jefferson and Aaron Burr for the Democratic-Republicans.

These efforts proved exceedingly successful. A clear majority of the electors cast their ballots for both Jefferson and Burr. But because every Democratic-Republican elector voted for both Jefferson and Burr, the balloting produced a tie between the two.

The Constitution called for the House of Representatives, voting by states, to break the deadlock. The 'lame duck' Federalist legislators still dominated the chamber, and many of them preferred Burr. Eventually, they assented to the unquestionable intention of the electoral college majority and elected Jefferson president.

The election of 1800 showed that the Framers' method of presidential selection could not accommodate the parties' practice of presenting presidential tickets. Congress responded by proposing a constitutional amendment that revised the voting procedures in the electoral college. The states quickly ratified the proposal, and the Twelfth Amendment became part of the Constitution shortly before the 1804 presidential election.

The Twelfth Amendment separated the electors' balloting for president and vice president. The failure of the electoral college to arrive at a majority in the presidential balloting would still send the election to the House, which would choose among the top three candidates in the electoral college vote. With this constitutional change, the electoral college has successfully arrived at a majority choice in every subsequent election save one, 1824.

The Twelfth Amendment clearly altered the status of presidential electors in the constitutional system. The Framers had envisioned electors as independent trustees within their respective states, demonstrating disinterested, wise judgments. With the adoption of the Twelfth Amendment, electors became deputies of their sponsoring political parties.

Even before the Twelfth Amendment transformed the electoral college, the congressional caucus had become the means by which the political parties nominated their presidential tickets.[6] As early as 1796, like-minded senators and representatives of both the Federalist and Democratic-Republican persuasion met informally to discuss presidential politics and issue recommendations. By 1804, the now dominant Democratic-Republicans had formal political links. They publicly encouraged potential presidential electors to elect President Jefferson for a second term and to substitute vice presidential nominee George Clinton for the discredited Aaron Burr.

Thus, the coming of political parties established a new expectation for presidential selection. Previously, significant informal standards, such as national identity, personal probity, and distinguished public service, had accompanied the formal qualifications of age, residency, and citizenship stipulated under the Constitution. Now came a decisive new standard – party nomination.[7]

Furthermore, the exclusive character of two-party competition that developed in the 1790s has proved remarkably stable. During the past two centuries, the party labels have changed, and the coalitions of voting groups have shifted significantly. But with only a few conspicuous exceptions, the voters' choice in presidential elections has been between the nominees of the two major political parties. To be sure, many minor parties have routinely competed for president, but they have normally operated at the extreme margins: never winning, only occasionally affecting outcomes, and fading away after one or two elections.[8]

The victory of the Democratic-Republicans over the Federalists in the election of 1800 sent Federalist electoral fortunes into steep decline. In 1804, Jefferson coasted to re-election over Federalist challenger C. C. Pinckney.

Four years later, Jefferson followed Washington into voluntary retirement after two terms. The Democratic-Republican caucus designated Secretary of State James Madison of Virginia as its presidential nominee. Federalist Party leaders met secretly in New York and again put forward Pinckney. The Democratic-Republicans won a convincing victory.

In 1812, a poorly-attended congressional caucus of Democratic-Republicans re-nominated Madison. A separate party caucus of dissident New York legislators put forward 'favorite son' DeWitt Clinton, who also received the endorsement of Federalist leaders. With the United States now at war with Great Britain, the presidential electors preferred the incumbent Madison.

The election of 1812 clearly displayed the incapacity of the Federalist Party to compete at the national level. However, the governing Democratic-Republican Party, having convincingly vanquished the opposition, now faced the specter of factional strife.

When the Democratic-Republican caucus met in 1816 to choose its presidential ticket, the Party's nomination had become tantamount to election. The top contenders were Secretary of State James Monroe of Virginia, Madison's heir apparent, and Secretary of War William Crawford of Georgia. Monroe won a narrow endorsement from the caucus, which was followed by an impressive victory in the electoral college.

Four years later, neither inter-party nor intra-party opposition emerged to Monroe's re-election. The incumbent won an overwhelming victory, approaching Washington's record of unanimous support.

The congressional caucus faced increasing opposition in the decade of the 1820s. The absence of party competition undermined its legitimacy. Further, a wave of democratization was sweeping the country. The congressional caucus came to symbolize discredited elitism, enabling a handful of partisans to select the president. In the constitutional context of separation of powers and checks and balances, the congressional party's power to designate the chief executive seemed inappropriate.[9]

Coinciding with the decline in legitimacy of the congressional caucus were two significant developments in the operation of the electoral college.[10] One concerned the selection of electors. The Constitution had left it to each state to decide how to select its electors. In keeping with the trend to democratization, and reflecting more liberal suffrage requirements, the states opted for popular selection of electors.

The second change was the move toward a unit, or 'winner-take-all', rule within each state. Under the unit rule, a state's electors would be

Left: This well known painting is called 'The Old House of Representatives' and is by Samuel F.B. Morse. The ceremonial lighting of the chandelier is depicted.

chosen as a slate, unanimously committed to a party ticket. As such, the state parties would each put forward a slate of electors for the consideration of the voters. Whichever slate received the most votes would be designated to cast all of that state's electoral votes.

These changes rooted the decision of the electoral college in the prior actions of the voters in a way that democratized presidential selection. They also raised the possibility that the winner of the popular vote could lose in the electoral college, as would occur in 1824, 1876, and 1888. The far more usual outcome, however, has been for the 'winner-take-all' rule to magnify a small popular vote margin into a more substantial electoral vote majority.

The end of inter-party competition nationally during Monroe's presidency heightened intraparty rivalries. With the 1824 election approaching, several prominent aspirants emerged within the Democratic-Republican Party: John Quincy Adams, William Crawford, John Calhoun, Henry Clay, and Andrew Jackson.

Crawford won the endorsement of a poorly-attended congressional caucus in February. Calhoun withdrew, but the other presidential aspirants and their supporters refused to accept the caucus's decision as binding and continued their presidential quests. The popular vote resulted in a plurality victory for Jackson, as did the electoral vote. But, in the multi-candidate field, Jackson fell well short of the constitutionally-prescribed electoral vote majority.

Thus, as in 1800, the election went to the House of Representatives, which, voting by states, was bound to choose among the top three electoral college vote-getters: Jackson, Adams, and Crawford. The Twelfth Amendment's revision of the contingency procedure eliminated Clay, who ran fourth. But Clay, the incumbent Speaker of the House, emerged as the power-broker in the resulting House election. Clay gave his crucial support to Adams, who won a narrow victory.

Thus, the system bypassed the plurality winner in both the popular and electoral vote, Andrew Jackson. Embittered, he immediately embarked on an energetic campaign to reverse the verdict in the next presidential election.

DEMOCRATS V. WHIGS, 1828–1856

The Democratic-Republican Party never recovered from its fragmentation in 1824. A second era of party competition soon developed as the Party's factional wings transformed themselves into autonomous political parties in their own right.[11] The more powerful Jackson faction dropped the Republican portion of the party label, styling itself as the Democrats.

The anti-Jacksonians initially called themselves the National Republicans before settling on a new party label, the Whigs. The 1828 rematch between Adams and Jackson went decisively to Jackson.

Four years later, Jackson's partisan supporters called for a national convention of the state parties to meet and formally nominate him for a second term. The new institution immediately took hold. The national party convention replaced the discredited caucus as the means by which political parties nominated their presidential tickets.[12] Reflecting the democratizing spirit of the age, the convention greatly broadened the base of popular participation in presidential nominating politics.

Above: A campaign image for the Clay-led Whig ticket in 1844. One of the Whigs' three main figures, known as the Great Triumvirate, Clay sought the presidency three times but never won.

In 1832, the Democratic convention named Jackson and Martin Van Buren as its standard-bearers. The opposition had met in their own nominating convention in December 1831, putting forward Henry Clay. In the subsequent election, the Democratic ticket easily prevailed.

Democratic superiority in this new era of two-party competition became even clearer in 1836. Following Jackson's retirement, the Democrats nominated Van Buren as his successor. The Whigs, not as well organized nationally, promoted several 'favorite son' candidacies. They hoped to prevent any candidate from attaining an electoral college majority and thus send the presidential election to the House. The strategy failed as the Democratic ticket won, making Van Buren the first vice president since Jefferson to be elected president.

Four years later, the Whigs achieved their first national success, defeating Van Buren's bid for re-election. Their nominee was William Henry Harrison. His potent public image as a heroic military leader dated from his success at the Battle of Tippecanoe in 1811. Harrison had defeated Henry Clay at the 1840 convention because the delegates preferred a popular hero who could attract support from voters who had yet to identify with the party label and cause. To heighten the ticket's bipartisan appeal, the convention selected John Tyler of Virginia, a disaffected Democrat, as his running-mate. In the general election, the Whig ticket won decisively in the electoral college.

Harrison died in April 1841, shortly after his inauguration, and Vice President Tyler succeeded to the presidency. But Tyler lacked a base of party support in Congress and the electorate. The persistent Clay garnered the Whig presidential nomination in 1844, facing 'dark horse' Democrat James K. Polk of Tennessee in the general election.

A former representative and governor, Polk had not been a leading contender for the Democratic nomination. Van Buren was initially the choice of most delegates, but the party rules required a two-thirds majority. Finally, on the ninth ballot, Polk emerged from relative obscurity as the compromise candidate. The general election went in his favor.

Polk did not seek re-election in 1848, and the Democrats nominated Lewis Cass. Meanwhile, the Whigs reverted to their successful 1840 strategy and nominated a popular and prominent military leader, General Zachary Taylor, a hero of the recently completed Mexican War. Taylor and running-mate Millard Fillmore convincingly won the November election.

In July 1849, Taylor died in office. The Whig dream of using the presidential office to transform the party into a ruling majority died with him. Fillmore, who inherited the presidency, lacked both the nonpartisan popularity of Taylor and a strong base of political support within his own party. His quest for the party nomination in 1852 met with failure.

Instead, the Whigs chose another Mexican War hero, General Winfield Scott, as their standard-bearer. Meanwhile, the increasingly salient slavery issue had been fragmenting their precarious electoral coalition along regional lines. The Democrats also faced regional division regarding slavery. They finally settled on a 'dark horse' nominee, Franklin Pierce of New Hampshire, whose bare popular majority won him a substantial electoral vote victory. With Scott's defeat, the Whigs disappeared from the presidential scene.

In 1856, Pierce experienced the unique indignity of being the first elected president to have a national party convention reject his bid for

Below: General Winfield Scott, losing Whig in 1852. He resisted the anti-immigrant, anti-Catholic prejudices within the party – evident in society with the Know Nothings – and allied with anti-slavers, choices which cost him dear.

renomination. The Democratic convention turned instead to James Buchanan of Pennsylvania.

Buchanan's chief general election opposition came from John C. Fremont, the nominee of the newly-formed Republican Party.[13] Buchanan won the presidency by sweeping the South while narrowly carrying several key Northern states. But the slavery issue transformed triumph into pyrrhic victory. The Democratic majority disintegrated during Buchanan's term as president.

THE CIVIL WAR ALIGNMENT, 1860–1892

In 1860, several candidates sought the presidency. Two represented the irreconcilable regional factions of the Democratic Party: Northerner Stephen Douglas of Illinois, and Southerner John Breckenridge of Kentucky, who was serving as vice president under Buchanan. The nascent Republican Party nominated Douglas's home state rival, Abraham Lincoln. Another new party, the Constitutional Unionists, named John Bell of Tennessee as their standard-bearer. Bell ran a strong campaign in the border states, prevailing in Virginia, Kentucky, and Tennessee. Breckenridge swept the rest of the South. Douglas finished second in the popular vote, but ran a distant fourth in the electoral vote. Lincoln won a popular vote plurality and an electoral college majority. His election hastened the secession of the Southern states and the outbreak of the Civil War.

Lincoln's victory in 1860 inaugurated a new era of Republican domination of presidential elections that included an unparalleled string of six consecutive victories.[14] In 1864, with the Civil War still raging, Lincoln was re-elected. Reflecting the name and spirit of Union, and seeking to broaden the base of party support, the Lincoln-led Republicans altered their presidential ticket. They replaced incumbent vice president Hannibal Hamlin of Maine with the military governor of Tennessee, Democrat Andrew Johnson.

The absence of the Southern states from the 1864 election severely crippled the opposition Democrats. The South had long been a bulwark of Democratic electoral support. Northern successes on the battlefield enabled the Union ticket to prevail comfortably against the Democrats.

Six weeks into his second term, in the immediate aftermath of the South's surrender, Lincoln fell victim to an assassin's bullet. As president, his successor Andrew Johnson lacked party support and quickly found himself embroiled in bitter conflicts with congressional Republicans over Reconstruction policy.

In 1868, the Republican national convention unanimously designated General Ulysses S. Grant, the victorious Union commander, to head the party ticket. The Democrats, still suffering from the absence of much of their Southern base, rejected President Johnson's overtures and nominated New Yorker Horatio Seymour. The 'Grand Old Party' (GOP), as the post-war Republicans labeled themselves, won the heated campaign. Four years later, Grant easily won a second term.

Scandals in the Grant administration revived Democratic prospects as the 1876 presidential election approached. The Democrats nominated New York governor Samuel Tilden. In the general election, he faced Republican Rutherford B. Hayes, the governor of Ohio. Although

Above: In the 1860 election the Democrats split with John C. Breckinridge (above) taking the South and Stephen Douglas polling second to Lincoln, a Northern-based Republican (right).

Tilden won a narrow majority in the popular vote, the electoral college outcome was not clear. Tilden received 184 electoral votes, one short of the required majority, while Hayes won 165. Controversy attended the remaining 20 electoral votes. One elector was found to be ineligible, and both parties claimed the votes of three Southern states.

The bicameral Congress proved unable to resolve the certification dispute because of divided party control. The congressional leadership decided to establish a bipartisan electoral commission to address the disputes and to abide by the determination of that body. Republican commissioners outnumbered Democrats by a single vote.

With the scheduled March 4 presidential inauguration looming, the Commission voted along strict party lines. It certified all 20 Hayes electors, clearing the way for his 185–184 election by the electoral college on the eve of the inauguration.[15]

Hayes did not seek re-election, and the 1880 Republican convention took 36 ballots to select his successor, 'dark horse' James A. Garfield. Garfield, a member of Congress from Ohio, was paired with Chester A. Arthur, a controversial New York politico. They defeated a Democratic ticket led by Winfield Scott Hancock.

On July 2, 1881, a disappointed federal office seeker shot President Garfield, who died on September 19. Arthur succeeded to the presidency but, like his predecessor 'accidental' presidents, he lacked sufficient party strength to win the presidential nomination in his own right in 1884. Instead, the convention turned to James G. Blaine of Maine.

In the general election, Blaine faced Democrat Grover Cleveland, the governor of New York. Cleveland won the close election, becoming the first Democrat to be elected president since the slavery issue had divided and almost destroyed the party.

NATIONAL REPUBLICAN CHART

PRESIDENTIAL CAMPAIGN, 1860

REPUBLICAN CANDIDATES FOR PRESIDENT AND VICE-PRESIDENT, Nominated by the National Republican Convention, at Chicago, May 18th, 1860.

MAP OF THE UNITED STATES, SHOWING THE RELATIVE PROPORTION OF FREE AND SLAVE TERRITORY.

Published at H. H. LLOYD & CO.'S Book and Map Agents' Depot, 25 Howard Street, New York.   Agents wanted.

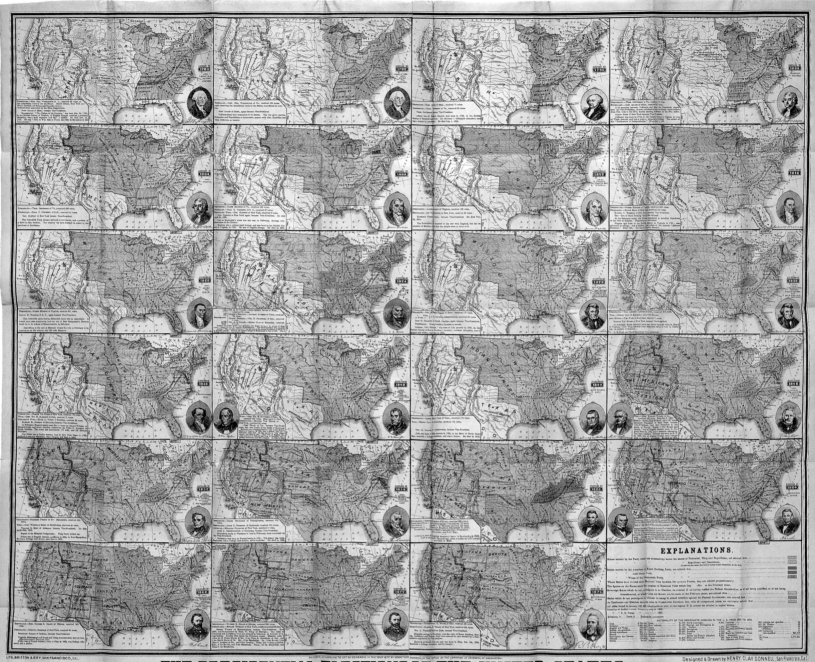

THE PRESIDENTIAL ELECTIONS OF THE UNITED STATES.

In 1888, Cleveland stood for re-election against Republican Benjamin Harrison, the grandson of the ninth president. Although the president secured the popular vote, he fell short in the electoral college balloting.

The two paired off again in 1892. This time Cleveland triumphed. To date, he is the only president to be elected to nonconsecutive terms.

A NEW ALIGNMENT, 1896–1928

In 1896, the Civil War-era party system gave way to a new pattern. Republican fortunes continued to flourish in presidential elections, but amid shifting party coalitions and alignments.[16] That year, the Democrats nominated populist William Jennings Bryan of Nebraska, an eloquent advocate of Southern and Western agricultural interests. The Republicans countered with William McKinley of Ohio, who appealed to the established industrial and financial interests of the North and East. Both parties competed for the votes of Northern urban workers. McKinley emerged victorious.

Four years later, McKinley and Bryan squared off again. Republican Vice President Garret A. Hobart had died in office, and the Republican convention nominated Theodore Roosevelt of

Above: This colored map records the presidential elections up to 1877 and is interesting not only because it shows the distribution of party and candidate votes, but also because the expansion of the nation, which affected the voting patterns, can be seen quite starkly.

Below: These items are souvenirs from President McKinley's inauguration on March 4, 1897. They include a ticket to the Senate wing of the Capitol for the event itself, as well as a ticket for the evening supper, and a dance card and menu for the Inaugural Ball that night.

New York to replace him. Again, McKinley won, with an increased margin of victory.

McKinley's assassination in 1901 made Roosevelt president. Roosevelt (or TR as he became known) identified with and promoted the causes of the Progressive reform movement. In 1904, TR shattered precedent by becoming the first vice presidential successor to capture his party's presidential nomination. In the general election, he easily defeated a conservative Democrat, Alton B. Parker.

Roosevelt declined to pursue renomination in 1908, instead passing the torch to the man he viewed as his political heir, Secretary of War William Howard Taft. The Democrats turned again to William Jennings Bryan, who lost for the third time.

Taft's policies proved to be more conservative than Roosevelt's. This alienated the former president, who re-entered the political fray with a 1912 nomination challenge. Taft's tight control of the party organization, especially in the South, enabled him to prevail at the convention. Bitter in defeat, Roosevelt declined to support his party's nominee; he bolted the convention and mounted a substantial third party effort under the banner of the 'Bull Moose' Party.

Meanwhile, the 1912 Democratic convention needed 46 ballots to agree on a nominee. The front-runner, Champ Clark of Missouri, attained a majority on the tenth ballot, but, like Martin Van Buren in 1844, he fell short of the required two-thirds. Finally, the Democrats nominated a candidate who was identified with the still-rising tide of progressive reform, New Jersey governor Woodrow Wilson.

Owing to the division within the Republican coalition, Wilson won pluralities in forty states and overwhelmed his opponents in the electoral college. Roosevelt's third-party effort surpassed the Republicans, who carried only two states.

Four years later, Wilson sought re-election. This time he faced a united Republican Party led by Charles Evans Hughes. The tight election turned on the late returns from California. The Golden State narrowly went for Wilson, who thus became the first Democratic incumbent since Andrew Jackson to secure re-election as president.

In 1920, advocating a 'return to normalcy,' the Republicans recaptured the White House. Their presidential nominee was Senator Warren Harding of Ohio. Harding and his running-mate, Governor Calvin Coolidge of Massachusetts, soundly defeated their Democratic counterparts, Governor James Cox of Ohio and New Yorker Franklin D. Roosevelt.

President Harding died in 1923, amid a rising tide of scandal that was enveloping his administration. His successor, Coolidge, unstained by corruption, followed TR's path and secured the 1924 Republican nomination without significant opposition.

In contrast, the Democrats faced severe intra-party division. It took them more than two weeks and 103 ballots to compromise on 'dark horse' John W. Davis of West Virginia. Coolidge won an easy victory. Again emulating Theodore Roosevelt, after a full term as president in his own right, Coolidge did not choose to run for re-election in 1928. The Republicans nominated Commerce Secretary Herbert Hoover to run against the Democratic candidate, New York governor Al Smith. The Republicans achieved a convincing victory.

In 1929, the first year of Hoover's term, the Great Depression hit the United States. This economic downturn, occurring on the Republicans' watch, devastated their electoral fortunes.

THE NEW DEAL ALIGNMENT, 1932–1948

In 1932, Franklin D. Roosevelt, who had succeeded Smith as governor of New York, now replaced him at the head of the national Democratic ticket. The result was a victory of historic proportions for Roosevelt. The election produced a fundamental realignment of partisan identification and loyalty. The Democrats now became the country's new majority party.[17]

Having advocated and delivered a 'New Deal' of domestic reform to the voters, FDR won overwhelming re-election in 1936. That summer, the Democratic national convention abrogated its longstanding two-thirds rule, settling thenceforth for a simple majority in choosing the presidential nominee. This was in line with what had always been the Republicans' practice.

In 1940, Roosevelt shattered the traditional two-term limit on presidential tenure. With the economy recovering and Europe at war, he secured the Democratic nomination. Then he soundly defeated Republican Wendell Willkie in the general election.

The Japanese bombing of Pearl Harbor on December 7, 1941, brought the United States into the Second World War. Roosevelt focused his attention on his weighty responsibilities as commander-in-chief. The 1944 election arrived with the war still raging in both Europe and the Pacific. Roosevelt stood for renomination, receiving it without significant opposition. The

convention, with FDR's blessing, named Harry S. Truman of Missouri as the vice presidential nominee. The Roosevelt-Truman ticket won a comfortable victory.

Roosevelt died in April 1945, less than three months into his fourth term, and was succeeded by Vice President Truman. Although Truman presided over the successful prosecution of the war, the voters handed the ruling Democrats a decisive defeat in the midterm elections of 1946. The Republicans took majority control of both houses of Congress for the first time since 1930.

In 1947, the Republican Congress proposed an amendment to the Constitution limiting presidential tenure. Ratified as the Twenty-second Amendment in 1951, it declared that no person could be elected president more than twice. Nor could a president who had served more than half of his predecessor's unexpired term be elected more than once. The amendment restored the two-term tradition, this time with the binding authority of constitutional law.

In 1948, Truman faced an uphill battle to win a presidential term in his own right. He prevailed at the Democratic national convention, but the Democrats experienced factional division on two fronts. Many conservative Southern Democrats proclaimed their allegiance to the traditional banner of states rights and rallied to the 'Dixiecrat' candidacy of South Carolina governor J. Strom Thurmond. On the left, a progressive faction backed former Vice President Henry A. Wallace.

The Republicans, confident of victory, renominated New York governor Thomas Dewey, Roosevelt's opponent in 1944. Truman waged a feverish campaign. In November, the voters defied the pollsters' predictions and gave Truman a popular plurality and a decisive electoral vote majority. The outcome showed that the Roosevelt coalition remained solid enough to survive both the passing of its namesake and significant intra-party division.

Below: Nearly rejected by his party, President Truman waged a blistering campaign in 1948, traveling 32,000 miles to speak to voters directly. Here he addresses a crowd in Iowa from his train.

THE POST-NEW DEAL ALIGNMENT, 1952–

The 1948 election thwarted the Republicans' dream of 'returning to normalcy' and forced them to come to grips with their new minority status within the electorate. They responded in 1952 by taking a page from the Whig textbook on presidential campaign strategy, nominating a Second World War military hero, General Dwight D. Eisenhower. Although Eisenhower had never participated in partisan politics, his personal popularity guaranteed a broad national following. The 1952 Democratic nomination went to Governor Adlai Stevenson of Illinois. With Eisenhower heading the ticket, the Republicans won an easy victory. In 1956, Eisenhower and Stevenson again competed for the presidency, with the same result.

In 1960, with Eisenhower constitutionally ineligible to seek re-election, the Republicans nominated his two-term vice president, Richard Nixon. Nixon was the first incumbent vice president to win a presidential nomination since Martin Van Buren in 1836. The Democrats countered with Senator John F. Kennedy of Massachusetts. Kennedy's nomination marked the culmination of a distinctive stage in the evolution of party nominations, while pointing the way to a new one.

The national nominating convention had emerged in the Jacksonian era as a democratizing device, designed to increase popular participation in presidential selection. Over the years, however, powerful state party leaders had come to exercise tight control over convention decisions.

Around the turn of the 20th century, the Progressive Movement, embraced by both Theodore Roosevelt and Woodrow Wilson, sought to reinvigorate the cause of democracy. Its leaders advocated primary elections, by which voters would directly identify the party nominee.

At the presidential level, in a few states, primaries became the means of designating delegates to attend the national convention. This development affected the strategies used by some presidential aspirants. The primaries provided candidates with an avenue for displaying their popular appeal to the state party leaders who still dominated the process.[18]

John F. Kennedy, lacking at the outset much support from the party organization, decided to contest several primaries in 1960. A string of impressive primary victories convinced the powerful party leaders that JFK would be an attractive nominee who could recapture the presidency for the Democrats. His vice presidential running-mate was Senator Lyndon B. Johnson of Texas.

Kennedy and Vice President Nixon, the Republican nominee, battled to a virtual standstill in 1960. In the tightest election in the 20th century, Kennedy finally triumphed. Kennedy's assassination in Dallas, Texas, on November 22, 1963, placed Vice President Johnson in the Oval Office. After easily winning the nomination in 1964, Johnson went on to a convincing victory.

As his term progressed, Johnson's popularity steadily declined. Controversies plagued his foreign and domestic policies. Nevertheless, most political observers expected him to seek and win another Democratic presidential nomination in 1968.

Surprisingly strong primary challenges, first by Senator Eugene McCarthy and later by Senator Robert Kennedy, showed that the president's political base had become very precarious. Johnson responded by withdrawing his name from consideration for renomination.

The nomination ultimately went to Johnson's vice president, Hubert Humphrey, but the bitter campaign left the Democrats divided and weakened. Alabama governor George Wallace bolted the party and mounted a third-party effort. Wallace echoed the 1948 'Dixiecrat' movement in seeking and finding substantial voter support below the Mason-Dixon line.

The Republicans turned again to Richard Nixon, accompanied on the ticket by Maryland governor Spiro Agnew. The popular vote narrowly favored Nixon, though neither major party candidate came close to a majority. Wallace carried five Southern states. Nixon's popular votes proved sufficient in the electoral college.

Nixon sought re-election in 1972. The Democrats, still reeling from the strife and division of 1968, nominated Senator George McGovern of South Dakota. McGovern was both the promoter and beneficiary of significant reforms of the delegate selection process for the party's national convention. These reforms expanded the opportunities for popular involvement through primaries and open caucuses. Although the national convention endured as an institution, control of nominations shifted decisively from the party organization to the voters.[19]

Significantly, since 1952, no convention of either major party has taken more than a single ballot to designate its presidential nominee. The enduring pattern of first-ballot victories is in marked contrast to the multi-ballot norm of the past. Clearly, conventions no longer choose the nominee; instead, they mostly ratify decisions made earlier in the nominating process, in presidential primaries.[20]

These developments have dramatically increased the role of the mass media in presidential selection. Unlike the general election campaign, in which voters can rely on party identification in making their decisions, presidential primaries pit fellow partisans against each other. Ordinary voters depend on the media for information regarding candidates and issues.[21]

In turn, independent political consultants and the personal organizations assembled by each presidential aspirant have supplanted the old-style party bosses in campaign management and organization. No longer do party organizations mobilize thousands of the party faithful for door-to-door campaigning. Modern technology allows presidential candidates to enter the voters' living rooms via the electronic media. Such changes have made modern presidential campaigns far more lengthy and expensive than their predecessors.[22]

The Nixon-Agnew ticket won an impressive endorsement from the electorate in 1972. The decisive victory raised Republican hopes that a new era of extended GOP control of the presidency had begun.

Yet neither Nixon nor Agnew remained in office by the time of the next presidential election. Both resigned in disgrace amid allegations of scandal. Agnew was the first to depart. He resigned the vice presidency in October 1973. Acting under the authority of the recently-ratified Twenty-fifth Amendment, Nixon nominated Gerald Ford, the leader of the Republican minority in the House of Representatives, to be vice president. Both houses of Congress confirmed the nomination, making Ford the nation's first unelected vice president.

Meanwhile, Nixon himself faced increasing political assault concerning Watergate. The Watergate affair encompassed a wide range of abuses of power by the president and his top aides. Facing certain House impeachment and likely Senate conviction and removal, Nixon resigned the presidency in August 1974.

The new president, Gerald Ford, occupied an unprecedented political position, bereft of any national party nomination or authorization from the voters. In Ford's quest for the 1976 Republican presidential nomination, he faced a strong challenge from former California governor Ronald Reagan, who led the ascendant conservative wing of the party. Nevertheless, Ford narrowly prevailed.

In the general election, Ford faced Democrat

Below: A technician makes final adjustments to one of the microphones prior to the first debate, on domestic policy, between Gerald Ford and 'outsider' Jimmy Carter on September 23, 1976.

Jimmy Carter. A former governor of Georgia, Carter, like McGovern in 1972, had risen from relative obscurity through a strong performance in the presidential primaries. With lingering vestiges of Watergate bedeviling the Republicans, Carter won a narrow victory.

The Democrats' prospects deteriorated along with Carter's popularity over the next four years. In securing renomination, Carter had to overcome a strong primary challenge from Senator Edward Kennedy of Massachusetts. Reagan captured the GOP nomination. In the November election, independent candidate John Anderson, a Republican member of Congress, attracted support from centrist voters of both parties.

Reagan won a narrow popular majority that translated into an enormous electoral vote victory. Coming in the wake of Ford's defeat in 1976, Carter's loss demonstrated the heightened vulnerability of presidential incumbents in the last quarter of the 20th century.

In 1984, Reagan overpowered Democrat Walter Mondale, who had been Carter's vice president. The key to his extraordinary electoral showing was his appeal to 'Reagan Democrats.'

Reagan's vice president, George Bush, captured the Republican presidential nomination in 1988, facing off against Massachusetts Governor Michael Dukakis. Bush's comfortable victory was noteworthy because, for the first time since Martin Van Buren in 1836, an incumbent vice president was elected president. Further, it was the first time since 1928 that the Republican Party had captured the presidency in three successive elections.

Following his election, Bush rose to extraordinary heights in public opinion polls as the voters rallied behind his leadership in the 1991 Gulf War. But his popular support evaporated as the economy became mired in recession. In his 1992 re-election effort, Bush first dismissed primary challenger Patrick Buchanan. In the general election, he faced both Democrat Bill Clinton, the governor of Arkansas, and businessman Ross Perot, an independent.

In this multi-candidate race, the Democrats prevailed. Although Clinton's popular vote total fell well short of a majority, he easily surpassed the necessary electoral vote standard. Perot's impressive popular showing carried no states and thus garnered him no electoral votes. Bush's decisive loss made him the third president of the last four to be voted out of office.

CONCLUSION

Clinton's 1992 election raised more questions than it answered about the direction of contemporary politics. Since the 1950s, the post-New Deal party system has featured significant departures from the patterns of the previous 150 years.

The traditional pattern featured sustained electoral dominance by one party, occasionally

interrupted but then quickly reinstated, until a critical realigning election transformed the electoral landscape.[23] The initial party competitors in the 1790s were the Federalists and the Democratic-Republicans. The election of 1800 catapulted the Democratic-Republicans into a generation of domination that lasted until 1824.

Democrats and Whigs battled in the second era of party competition from the late 1820s until the 1850s. The Democrats dominated this era, winning six of eight presidential elections. The divisive slavery issue that plunged the nation into the Civil War claimed both parties as victims, ending this era.

The critical election of 1860 marked the emergence of the Republicans as the party to beat in presidential elections. For more than three decades, the Republicans usually prevailed, although often by slim margins. In 1896, they significantly expanded their base of electoral support and their typical margin of victory.

The onset of the Great Depression in the late 1920s paved the way for the rise of the Democrats, beginning with Franklin D. Roosevelt's victory in 1932. The Roosevelt coalition won five consecutive presidential elections.

The eleven presidential elections since Truman's 1948 victory have featured routine

Above: Democratic candidate Bill Clinton can afford to look on during 1992's second debate as independent candidate Ross Perot interrupts President George Bush in order to make a point.

alternations in party control of the presidency. A plausible explanation for the current pattern is that party labels no longer mean much in presidential elections. Instead, the voters appear to be focusing on each election's candidates and issues in deciding their presidential votes. This shift has produced a more volatile electorate and diminished the prospect that any party will ever develop a strangle-hold on the presidency as in the past.[24]

Looking to the future, the two-party system itself may no longer contain and structure voters' choices. In previous eras of electoral competition, minor parties often emerged to address issues that the major parties were ignoring or temporizing. Eventually, the major parties would incorporate the disaffected voters who were attracted to the minor parties, restoring two-party competition. But can the weakened contemporary two-party system withstand the mounting evidence of deep voter dissatisfaction? That is the great unresolved question of presidential politics on the eve of the new century.

Notes

1. For a thorough account of the Convention deliberations dealing with the presidency, see Thach, 1969.

2. See Peirce and Longley, 1981: 10-30; also see Sayre and Parris, 1970.

3. See Dauer, 1953.

4. See Cunningham, 1957.

5. For general treatments of the origins of political parties and party competition in the United States, see Charles, 1957; Chambers, 1963; Nichols, 1967; and Hofstadter, 1969.

6. See Ostrogorski, 1899; Thompson, 1902; Morgan, 1969.

7. Remini, 1976: 30–31.

8. See Smallwood, 1983.

9. See Ceaser, 1979: 112–21; Ceaser, 1982: 15–16.

10. Peirce and Longley, 1981: 44–47.

11. See Remini, 1959; McCormick, 1966; Carroll, 1970.

12. David, Goldman, and Bain, 1960: 17–19; Chase, 1973.

13. See Gienapp, 1987; Holt, 1978.

14. See Moos, 1956; Morgan, 1969; Kleppner, 1979.

15. Haworth, 1906.

16. See Kleppner, 1972; 184–95; Burnham, 1981: 1002–23.

17. See Anderson, 1979.

18. Ceaser, 1982: 22–29.

19. See Shafer, 1983: Ceaser, 1982; Polsby, 1983.

20. See Shafer, 1988.

21. See Patterson, 1980.

22. See 'The New Style of Campaigning: The Decline of Party and the Rise of Candidate-Centered Technology' in Agranoff, 1976.

23. See Key, 1955; Key, 1959; Burnham, 1970; Sundquist, 1983; and Clubb, Flanigan, and Zingale, 1980.

24. For a discussion of this concept of dealignment, see Carmines, McIver, and Stimson, 1987.

Stephen L. Robertson

5

THE SEAT OF
PRESIDENTIAL POWER

The White House is important because of the work that
goes on there – if the presidency is the most important office
in the world, the White House is the seat of that power. The
White House is also important because of what it symbolizes
to the American people – a democratic palace
whose lease they hold.

The loneliness of power: John F. Kennedy at
his desk in the Oval Office of the White House.

In one way, the president is a very lonely man. The ultimate responsibility for decisions that affects thousands, often millions, of people, is his alone. As a sign on President Truman's desk noted, 'the buck stops here.' Thus we often think of the president, bowed under the pressure of his office, working alone at his desk, late at night.

In a broader sense, however, the president is never alone. He is surrounded by hundreds of people who are there solely to assist him. Some of them provide political advice and information; others serve his personal needs; others protect him and his family. Together, these people constitute the White House, the seat of presidential power.

THE POLITICAL WHITE HOUSE

The political component of the White House is the Executive Office of the President and, more particularly, the White House Office. The presidency is far more than a single person; indeed, the modern presidential establishment is a bureaucracy with hundreds of employees, all of whom work for the president. The Executive Office of the President (EOP) is the president's tool for coping with Congress and the far-flung executive branch.

The EOP is a collection of agencies whose only tie is their direct responsibility to the president. The components of the EOP have changed many times over the years as the needs of the presidency have changed. Today, key elements of the EOP are the National Security Council, Office of Management and Budget, Council of Economic Advisers, Office of the Special Representative for Trade Negotiations, and White House Office. Of these, the closest to the president is the White House Office.

Although the whole of the EOP does the president's business, it is the White House Office that contains the president's closest advisers. Of the entire presidential establishment, the White House Office is the most loyal to the president. It exists solely to look after his interests. It can be a tremendous asset, advancing the administration's programs and steering clear of the potential pitfalls that undermine a president's credibility. Indeed, much of a president's success depends on the ability of the White House staff to plan and promote his programs.

THE DEVELOPMENT OF THE WHITE HOUSE STAFF

The White House Office is a relatively new player in American politics. Prior to the Buchanan administration, Congress refused to provide any money to hire staff for the president. If the president wanted someone to help him with his mail, he had to pay that person out of his own pocket. (President Washington paid his nephew $300 per year to assist with his correspondence.) Even after the first appropriation for staff was made for Buchanan in 1857, the amount was small; consequently, the pay was low and the staff remained small. (For example, President Benjamin Harrison kept his entire staff on the second floor of the White House.) With certain notable exceptions, it was also of poor quality.

All this changed following the report of the Brownlow Commission. The commission had been appointed by Franklin D. Roosevelt in 1936 to study the presidency and recommend ways in which it could be improved. Echoing earlier studies, the commission noted that 'the president needs help' in running the government

Above: President Clinton and Vice President Gore under the South Portico for a symbolic cutting of red tape to mark the first anniversary in September 1994 of the National Performance Review to streamline the government.

and recommended 'salvation by staff.' The commission report went on to recommend that

> these assistants . . . would not be assistant presidents in any sense. Their function would be . . . to assist [the president] in obtaining quickly and without delay all pertinent information possessed by any of the executive departments so as to guide him in making his responsible decisions; and then, when decisions have been made, to assist him in seeing to it that every administrative department and agency affected is properly informed . . . They should be men in whom the president has personal confidence and whose attitude and character are such that they would not attempt to exercise power on their own account. They should be possessed of high competence, great vigor, and a passion of anonymity.[1]

Brownlow's report was submitted to the president in January 1937. After some delay, Congress agreed to it, and on September 8, 1939, Roosevelt signed Executive Order 8248, giving birth to the Executive Office of the President. The new EOP contained the White House Office (WHO).

From that beginning, the EOP and the WHO have grown enormously. Initially, Roosevelt hired only three administrative assistants, and the total White House staff did not exceed 65 during his years in office. When Harry S. Truman ascended to the presidency, he decided that Roosevelt's staff was too large and resolved to shrink it. He failed to do so, however, for reasons that have continued to fuel the growth of the White House Office.

The growth of the WHO has been fueled by a change in the role of government in the United States, along with a change in public expectations of the federal government. After World War II, the United States was unable to return to its traditional isolationist foreign policy. The military and political threat posed by the Soviet Union led to the Cold War and kept the United States active abroad. At home, the Great Depression of the 1930s, which had overwhelmed state and local resources and forced the federal government to a level of activism never before seen, had led people to expect more from the government. As time went on, the federal government provided benefits such as medical insurance for the elderly and wrestled with social problems such as poverty and discrimination. The increasing demands to deal with more numerous and complex problems inevitably caused the government to expand. The White House staff grew to cope with it.

Besides the increase in public expectations of government in general and the president in particular, other forces led to a growing White House. The expansion of congressional staff created a symbiotic relationship with the White House in which each branch's staff grows in response to the other's growth. Presidents also have enlarged their staff in order to establish better links to different segments of the body politic. As scholar Thomas Cronin has noted,

a partial listing of staff specializations that have been grafted on to the White House in recent years . . . [forms] a veritable index of American society: budget and management, national security, economics, congressional matters, science and technology, drug abuse prevention, telecommunications, consumers, national goals, intergovernmental relations, environment, domestic policy, international economics, military affairs, civil rights, disarmament, labor relations, District of Columbia, cultural affairs, education, foreign trade and tariffs, the aged, health and nutrition, physical fitness, volunteerism, intellectuals, Blacks, youth, women, Wall Street, governors, mayors, 'ethnics,' regulatory agencies and related industry, state party chairmen.[2]

The desire to 'put one's best foot forward' has led to the expansion of the communications and public relations arms of the WHO. As the media age has progressed, presidents have added more help to get their message across and win support from the public.

Finally, the distrust that most presidents have of the permanent bureaucracy has fueled staff growth. Most presidents have found the bureaucracy to be ponderous and unresponsive, at best; some, such as Nixon, have believed it to be actively hostile to them. Presidents want to achieve. Faced with a balky bureaucracy, presidents have tended to consolidate as much power to formulate and execute policy in the White House as possible, thereby bypassing a major obstacle to their activism. In sum,

the White House was allowed to keep growing because there was no resistance to growth. Indeed, creating another White House office was often the easiest way to solve a personnel or constituent problem, a conferring of high status with little effort. The White House was the only place in government where the president could totally control expenditures and was free to move personnel and establish units at will.[3]

Thus the White House Office grew steadily through the Nixon administration. Although Roosevelt had a peak total of 65 permanent staffers, Eisenhower had 355, Johnson nearly 500, and Nixon, who particularly distrusted the bureaucracy, more than 600. In reaction against Nixon's 'imperial presidency,' later presidents have attempted consciously to cut back on their staff. Carter and Reagan held the line at about 450 each, while Clinton reduced his staff to around 400. Despite their efforts, deeper cuts have proven infeasible. What is more, in some cases the reductions have been cosmetic, created by rearranging the organizational chart so that some staff, while still doing the president's work, no longer appear in the WHO. Because the president sometimes borrows help or has people doing his work while working in other agencies, a precise count of the staff is difficult to obtain.

The staff has diversified as well. Roosevelt employed a handful of generalists, any of whom could take any problem thrown their way. Eisenhower, a career military officer, introduced more specialization into the staff, and each subsequent administration has tended to be more specialized as the WHO has grown. Today, the staff typically includes a chief of staff, who oversees its operations; a special counsel, who is the president's lawyer; an appointments secretary; a set of speechwriters; a foreign policy adviser; an economic adviser; a press secretary; a public relations officer; congressional liaisons; contacts with specific interest groups, such as women, senior citizens, and business; a pollster; and whatever other advisers the president deems necessary.

The most important of these people, in most administrations, is the chief of staff. The chief is the president's doorkeeper and administrator. He controls the flow of people and paper into the Oval Office so that the president's workload remains manageable, and he follows up to make sure decisions are implemented. Doing so requires a firm hand. (One of the complaints about Clinton's first chief of staff, Mack McLarty, was that he was too nice. In contrast, H. R. Haldeman, Nixon's first chief, once described himself as 'Nixon's son-of-a- bitch.')[4] Finally, the chief sometimes has to be the president's fall guy, taking the blame for a presidential misstep in order to cover for the boss. John Sununu, already under fire for misusing government transportation, was ousted as Bush's chief when he failed to take the blame for one of the president's policy misstatements.

ORGANIZING THE WHITE HOUSE

No set way exists to organize and operate the White House. The Constitution says nothing about the organization of the executive branch, and although Congress could in theory dictate some order for the WHO, it has always been wary of encroaching on the president and so has avoided doing so. The WHO therefore is a highly idiosyncratic body that directly reflects the tastes and work habits of the man in the Oval Office.

Historically, there have been two basic approaches to organizing the White House staff. The first, the circular pattern, was introduced by Franklin D. Roosevelt and has tended to be the preference of Democratic presidents. In it, the president acts as the hub of a wheel; his senior advisers, at the end of spokes which radiate from this central position, all have ready access to him. There is no chief of staff. This arrangement can be either competitive or collegial: Roosevelt used it to play his advisers against one another and thereby elicit the most information possible, while Kennedy used it to encourage mutual intellectual stimulation and teamwork.

The advantages of a circular arrangement are that it encourages spontaneity and creativity. A greater exchange of ideas occurs, and more information flows to the president. This may be one

Below: The earliest known photograph of the White House taken in 1861 with the Jefferson statue in front. Abraham Lincoln lived there at the time, likening it to an 'old country tavern.' The occupant immediately prior to Lincoln was James Buchanan who selected this polished cotton fabric (right) for use during his tenancy.

reason why it has been preferred by activist Democratic presidents. Its drawback is the defect of its virtue – too many people with too much access to the president. In the absence of an effective chief of staff, the president may be swamped with paper and visitors to the point of paralysis. President Carter found himself deciding such trivial matters as the allocation of White House parking places. Because the circular arrangement tends toward disorder, the most recent Democratic presidents, Carter and Clinton, eventually discovered that the arrangement, at least in its pure form, did not suit their needs.

The other major staffing arrangement, the pyramid, was introduced by President Eisenhower, a Republican who had a military background and was repelled by the disorder he perceived in the Roosevelt and Truman staffs. He set up a chain of command, headed by a chief of staff whose responsibility was to see that the staff functioned properly so that information flowed upward to the president and decisions

moved downward to be executed. Access to the president was limited and only pertinent information was to be passed to the Oval Office. In Eisenhower's case, this meant that only one- or two-page summaries of policy options came to him for action; in the Nixon White House, bulky analyses were placed on the president's desk.

The advantage of the pyramid arrangement, very simply, is organization and efficiency. In its best days, the Nixon White House 'had a structure, had a way of doing things, had a flow and a follow-up system that was beyond belief. Things happened.'[5] The problem is the potential for isolating the president. Because he is shielded by his chain of command, a president may see and hear only those things that the staff brings to him, and so his information and decisions may be distorted by staff bias, errors, or incompetence.

Although most presidents have used one or other of these staff arrangements, a third model was used during President Reagan's first term. Often referred to as the 'triumvirate,' this organizational plan divided the staff into three divisions, each headed by a senior staff member who reported to the president and oversaw the lower staff. Policy development was headed by presidential Counsel Edwin Meese; political operations were headed by Chief of Staff James Baker; and White House operations were run by Deputy Chief of Staff Michael Deaver. Later a fourth division, for foreign policy, was added under National Security Adviser William Clark.

The White House during the first Reagan term can be visualized as a set of pillars supporting a platform that held up the president. The four senior staffers enjoyed equal access and responsibility. What is impressive about their arrangement, given the competitive atmosphere

Below: The library or living room photographed in 1890. It contains first editions given by writers and publishers and, like most of the rooms, has undergone many changes over the years.

that tends to be a part of the White House, is that it worked at all. Yet tensions were minimized and a number of political successes were achieved. This may be due to the personalities involved, and so the utility of this model for future presidents is doubtful. In fact, after President Reagan's first term, the senior staff members moved on and the structure collapsed into a more traditional Republican chain of command, under a single chief of staff.

Whatever arrangement is chosen for organizing the staff, certain realities about life in the White House remain. The first is that it is a very competitive place. Staffers are ambitious men and women, seeking to advance their careers, make their mark on policy, or both. Hidden agendas are common and internecine competition remains a constant potential or actual

Above: A good view of the conservatory taken in 1889. This area was replaced at the time of Theodore Roosevelt's presidency due to the need for administrative work areas.

headache for the president. As Franklin D. Roosevelt noted, it is rare, even among his personal staff, for the president to find someone who wants only to serve him.

The second reality of the White House is the pressure, which can be relentless. Presidents and their staff come into office knowing that they have no more than eight years, and, given electoral considerations, probably less, to achieve their goals. The chance to make a mark is fleeting and so a sense of urgency is always present. Moreover, the demands on the office are varied, numerous, and constant. As a result, the staff work long and hard, frequently at the expense of personal and family life, and under emotional strain. Work-weeks of 80 hours are not uncommon; sometimes aides sleep in their offices.

Of course, the pressures will vary under different presidencies. Some presidents are very demanding. For example, Lyndon Johnson was a tireless worker who demanded that his staff be available at all times, day or night. Once, having failed to reach an aide by telephone, Johnson ordered him to put an extension in the bathroom so that he would never be out of touch again. Johnson was famous for alternating lavish praise and verbal abuse upon his staff.

Presidents' workdays vary, and this also affects the staff. At one time, presidents worked relatively little. Benjamin Harrison only worked in the morning and Calvin Coolidge slept 11 hours a day. Today the demands are greater, and many presidents, seeing the enormous tasks before them, work very long days. Nixon, Ford, Carter, Bush, and Clinton all worked ten to 12 hours a day, usually adding more time at night and on weekends. Not all presidents subscribe to the 'workaholic' theory, however. Eisenhower and Reagan both believed that the president's job was to make the big decisions and that too much work dulled the mind; therefore, they delegated much work to their staff.

The third reality is that all power is derived from the president and can be bestowed or withdrawn at will. Titles mean nothing – an office that is extremely powerful in one administration can be insignificant in the next. Sometimes such a change can occur during the course of an administration.

Since there is no permanent grant of power, the reality is that, in the White House, proximity is power. Those close to the president, those who see and consult with him daily, have more power than those who do not. The more access one has, the more powerful one is. To know who has power in the White House, one can consult a diagram of the mansion and see who has what office – the closer an office is to the Oval Office, the more power the occupant has. Changes in offices indicate rising or fading influence, depending on whether one moves closer to or farther from the president. For the same reason, perks such as using the White House tennis court or eating in the White House mess are eagerly sought as symbols of access and power

The White House thus is a place that is both exhilarating and high pressured. The exhilaration comes in being so close to the source of power, in being able to speak in the president's name, in having the chance to devise and implement policies. But the pressures are intense. Demands are many and time is short. No job is secure and competition for the president's ear is fierce.

CRITICISM OF THE MODERN WHITE HOUSE

The White House staff has been subjected to a number of criticisms. The first concerns its size. Critics suggest that the staff is so large as to be unwieldy. It is very difficult for the president to supervise it effectively. Because many more aides run about claiming to act in the president's name than the president can keep track of, it is easy for 'rogue elephants' to appear – as happened, for example, in the Iran–Contra affair, when low-level aide Oliver North made policy without President Reagan's knowledge.

A second criticism is that the staff has too much power. The extreme case in this regard was the Nixon administration, in which department secretaries had to go to the White House to find out what their policy was. Such power wielded by people who are unelected and accountable only to one man (who may not be able to keep track of them) is disturbing to many.

The staff may also have a skewed perspective that distorts its view of issues. Its primary concern is to look after the president's needs, rather than promote the public interest. Furthermore, since there is no job security, and since the natural human inclination is to avoid being the bearer of bad news, the staff is strongly tempted to tell the president only what he wants to hear. Dissenters tend to be dismissed or disregarded – President Johnson kept George Ball in meetings on Vietnam so that his arguments against the war would be part of the record, but no one seriously considered them – and a collective mentality may emerge that distorts reality.

Finally, the president risks becoming the captive of his staff. The size of the modern staff almost demands a pyramid arrangement, but that tends to put the president at the mercy of those who serve as the filters and doorkeepers. Because visitors and information are screened by the staff, the president may not get all the relevant data and options may be dismissed before he has time to consider them. The degree to

which a president is isolated depends, of course, on his desire to be so. Clinton granted several people 'walk-in' privileges (perhaps too many) while Nixon was so isolated that one cabinet member had to greet him in a receiving line to discuss policy. Today, however, every president has to guard against a tendency toward isolation.

THE PERSONAL WHITE HOUSE

The White House is more than just a staff and an office building, of course; it is also the home of the president.

The White House is a 132-room mansion that combines living quarters and working offices. It is surrounded by an 18-acre estate, which is maintained by the National Park Service. On the grounds are the famous Rose Garden and the Jacqueline Kennedy Garden, where the White House chefs can come to gather herbs for cooking. The mansion is repainted every four years and each new president is allotted $50,000 to redecorate, an amount that usually is inadequate and often is supplemented with donations.

There is much more than offices and sleeping quarters in the White House. Within its walls are a gymnasium and other recreational facilities, such as a movie theater, a library, and a small

Above: The attractive garden pond in the grounds photographed in 1917. The modern White House has 18 acres of grounds with several gardens lovingly maintained by the National Park Service.

bowling alley. A tennis court and a swimming pool are just outside the mansion. The president's personal physician has an office and a small clinic for routine medical and dental care on the ground floor. There is a barbershop, a tailor's shop, a cafeteria, laundry rooms, a carpenter's shop, a machine shop, a painter's shop, and a bomb shelter.

The 'personal' White House comes with a staff of around 100 permanent, full-time employees. By all accounts, this staff takes great pride in serving the president. Additionally, the president can place a limited number of personal servants, such as valets and personal secretaries or chefs, on the government payroll. Such servants are paid on a par with the permanent staff and leave when the president does.

The White House workforce is varied enough to cope with almost anything. The most important member of the staff is the chief usher. The chief usher supervises every aspect of the staff and its operation; he is responsible for making sure

that the mansion operates smoothly and that the president's desires are carried out. This is no small job, particularly if the president is one such as Lyndon Johnson, who might invite hundreds of guests to dinner on the spur of the moment. Under the chief usher's supervision are butlers, maids, cooks, engineers, electricians, carpenters, plumbers, painters, floral designers, and seamstresses. The salaries for the staff amount to nearly $3 million a year.

WHITE HOUSE EXPENSES

Although the job comes with a nice salary and expense account and a number of perks, living in the White House is an expensive proposition. The president's annual salary is $200,000, supplemented by a taxable expense account of $50,000 and a travel allowance of $75,000.

For transportation, several limousines are available at the White House, including an armor-plated one. For short trips, the Marine Corps furnishes a helicopter for the president's use; on longer trips, Air Force One is used.

Air Force One is a $181.5 million, specially modified 747 that is used by the president for air transport. The latest version, acquired during the Bush administration, has a crew of 23, can carry as many as 70 passengers, and costs about $40,000 per hour to maintain. On Air Force One are offices and sleeping quarters, a conference room, computers and videocassette recorders, food service, medical facilities, telephones and a fax machine. The president may invite family and friends to fly on the aircraft, but unless they are on official business, they are required to pay their own fare – traditionally set at the commercial first class fare plus one dollar.

In addition to transportation, the government also provides operating expenses for the White House. Telephone service, electricity, and other utilities, along with the necessary supplies and equipment, are provided at no cost to the president. These are not insignificant expenses; the electric bill alone can run above $180,000 a year.

Although the president has these perks, the government does not pay for everything. All of the first family's personal expenses, such as toiletries, clothing, and food, are paid for by the president. So are costs incurred in housing personal guests and maintaining personal property brought to the White House. Also, any personal entertaining must be paid for by the president. Although the government will pick up the tab for official banquets and receptions, and the president's political party may pay for entertaining connected to partisan functions, any social event that cannot be labeled 'official business' will come out of the president's own pocket.

First ladies and presidents have been dismayed by the cost of living in the White House. In Rosalynn Carter's autobiography, she notes that the food bill for her first ten days was $600.[6] As a result, first families have often sought bargains, studied the budget for corners to cut, and in

Above: The new Air Force One overflying the carved presidential heads of Mount Rushmore, South Dakota. The uniquely modified Boeing 747 was delivered in August 1990 from Boeing Defense & Space Group, the first of two ordered to replace the 707-320Bs used since the Kennedy era. The aircraft is equipped to enable full functioning of the presidency in flight.

other ways looked to save money while in the mansion. In recent years, presidents have begun to save resources, too. President Carter lowered thermostats to save energy and President Clinton began a recycling program.

Presidents seldom, if ever, do their own shopping, even for personal needs; given the entourage that always accompanies the president and the crowds that collect when he goes out, a quick trip to Macy's or the corner grocer could easily become a logistical disaster. The few instances in recent years of first ladies or presidents doing their own shopping in public have been chaotic, as when Reagan tried to buy his wife a valentine card from a card shop. Consequently, the staff makes the purchases for the White House. Groceries, for example, are bought wholesale from a limited number of stores, with staff members and screened store employees selecting items from a prepared list. The merchandise is paid for by the president's personal check and loaded into government trucks for transport to the White House.

RELAXING IN THE WHITE HOUSE

Being able to relax is very important for a president. The pressure of the office can be enormous and the need to escape, at least momentarily, is great. To this end, the White House provides several recreational facilities, including a gym where the president can work out and a tennis court. The library often receives donated volumes from publishers that cater to the current president's tastes and studios supply the movie theater with new releases or old favorites that the president likes. The swimming pool was originally built for Franklin D. Roosevelt and was filled in by Nixon to make a press area; it was rebuilt with private donations by Ford.

Presidents have relaxed in a variety of ways while in the White House. The move theater was particularly popular with Carter, while Nixon was fond of the bowling alley. Both Nixon and Carter made extensive use of the library. Ford and Reagan used the gym often; Reagan went on an exercise regime after he was shot in 1981 and left the White House in better shape than he went in. Kennedy, Johnson, and Ford made frequent use of the pool. Other presidents have relaxed by jogging or hiking (Truman, Carter, Bush, and Clinton, for whom a jogging track was installed on the grounds); playing golf (Eisenhower, Ford, Bush, and Clinton); watching spectator sports (Nixon, a Washington Redskins fan, and Clinton, who rooted for the University of Arkansas Razorbacks); and playing horseshoes

Above: The White House ablaze with lights as President Franklin D. Roosevelt confers into the night with cabinet officials and Congressional leaders following Japan's unprovoked attack on Pearl Harbor on December 7, 1941.

Below: The chaotic scene in the White House Press Office on August 10, 1945 as rumors spread of Japan's surrender and reporters sought confirmation. President Truman made a formal announcement from his office on August 14.

and softball (Bush became so enamored of horseshoes that he had a pit installed at the White House).

Presidents also have felt the need to escape from the White House and leave its worries behind – symbolically, at least. Most presidents have had some sort of retreat, a place they could go to be away from the pressures of Washington. Bush had a vacation home in Kennebunkport, Maine, where he could relax by boating and fishing. Kennedy would retreat to Cape Cod, Massachusetts. Johnson went to the LBJ Ranch, not far from Austin, Texas. Nixon had homes in San Clemente, California, and Key Biscayne, Florida; Carter had his family home in Plains, Georgia; and Reagan had a ranch in the Santa Yaez Mountains of California, where he rode horseback and worked the range. Clinton took vacations in places like Martha's Vineyard and Jackson Hole.

One alternative to the White House is available to every president. In the mountains of Maryland, the government maintains a presidential retreat. Built for Franklin D. Roosevelt, who went there often, the retreat was originally named 'Shangri-La,' after the Tibetan utopia in James Hilton's novel *Lost Horizon*. Eisenhower renamed it after his grandson, and the name Camp David has continued to the present.

Above: This building was added by Charles McKim to the West Wing to free more space in the house proper during Teddy Roosevelt's tenure – it was only then that 'White House' became official use.

Below: President John F. Kennedy with his cabinet and the First Lady on January 21, 1961. Mamie Eisenhower had begun putting antiques in the state rooms and Jacqueline Kennedy continued.

Originally a rustic retreat, Camp David today is a modern complex, maintained at an estimated cost of more than $1 million a year, that includes an air-conditioned, four-bedroom lodge, several guest cabins, and numerous recreational facilities. Among these are walking trails, a riding stable, an archery range, a tennis court, a swimming pool, a trout stream, a skeet-shooting range, and a par-three golf hole. The grounds are fenced off and guarded by Marines, and no one is admitted except at the president's invitation. Camp David is perhaps the only place where the president can

Below: President Reagan has Secretary of State George Shultz in attendance as he telephones Israel's Menachem Begin in August 1982, a time when US troops were serving in Lebanon.

Above: A lone Lyndon Johnson watching three television sets simultaneously in the Oval Office as he follows news coverage of the Six Day War in the Middle East between Israel and the Arabs.

just go for a stroll.

Every president since Roosevelt has used Camp David. It is secluded and protected, yet it is close enough to Washington (30 minutes by air) and has sufficient communications equipment to keep the president posted on events as needed. Besides relaxation, the solitude at Camp David provides an ideal setting to concentrate. Numerous policies have been devised, strategies mapped out, and speeches written at the resort. Camp David has also been the site of international diplomacy, most notably the 1978 summit hosted by President Carter that led to the Egyptian–Israeli peace accord.

ENSURING THE PRESIDENT'S SECURITY

One of the less enjoyable facts of life in the White House is the presence of the Secret Service. Charged with the mission of protecting the life of the president and his family, agents of the Service are beside the president from the time he leaves the living quarters in the morning until he returns at night. Agents precede him and secure every place he goes. Presidents have often found their security detail to be a nuisance.

The Secret Service was created in July 1865 as an agency to combat the counterfeiting of US currency, which had occurred on a massive scale during the Civil War. Congress first gave the Service authority to protect the president in 1906, but continued to require annual re-authorization of that role until 1951. Over the years, the Service has added to its list of protectees the vice president, the first lady, the president's immediate family, ex-presidents, widows of ex-presidents, foreign heads of state visiting the United States, and presidential candidates. Former presidents and their widows are entitled to protection as long as they live. Although they may refuse this protection, few do.

As a protective agency, the Service's primary job is to keep the president alive and well. To this end, security is tight at the White House. The Service naturally is not inclined to reveal details about the measures available to protect the president, but a fair amount is known. For example, anyone entering the White House is checked and monitored, and all employees must wear photo badges. Incoming packages and mail are screened, by bomb-sniffing dogs if necessary. Reinforced fences with guardhouses surround the White House grounds to keep intruders out, and should someone scale the fence, television monitors and electronic sensors will detect him or her, leading to a quick response by armed guards of the Service's Uniformed Division. Plainclothes agents, who may be armed, are also on the grounds, and may be posted on the roof, alongside radar and anti-aircraft weapons. Since 1995, the street in front of the White House has been closed to vehicular traffic. If all else fails, there is a 'panic button' under the desk in the Oval Office so that the president can summon agents.

Elaborate as they are, these security measures still break down on occasion. President Hoover was eating dinner one evening when a stranger walked in off the street to join him. More recently, a visitor walked up to a window of the Oval Office and spoke to President Carter; during the Reagan administration, a man wandered the White House grounds for ten minutes before he was stopped. In 1994, a man crashed a low-flying small plane into the mansion; the radar system, which was primarily aimed upward, had failed to detect the plane and no one saw it until it was already over the White House lawn.

Security problems multiply when the president travels. The Service maintains files on individuals who might be a risk to the president, and these are checked whenever he leaves the White House. Unfortunately, no foolproof way exists to predict who is likely to be an assassin, and so one could easily remain completely unknown. In fact, none of the people who have attacked pres-

Below: President Kennedy appearing as the family man in March 1963 with his two children, John F. Jr. and Caroline Bouvier. The young, attractive 'first family' captured the nation's imagination.

Above: A pack of press photographers from a quieter era on the White House lawn in 1918. Today a news conference or photo opportunity will attract hundreds of accredited journalists.

idents since Kennedy have been in the Secret Service's files.

The itinerary for every presidential trip is planned and the route of travel mapped out; then, working with local authorities, the Service secures the airport, the roads the motorcade will travel, and the buildings the president will visit. Uniformed and plainclothes agents guard the designated areas. Overlooks are secured with sharpshooters. The exact route that the president takes, once highly publicized in order to attract cheering crowds, is now kept secret. Finally, the president travels surrounded by a protective wall of agents who try to maintain a cleared 'safe zone' around him, in order to better spot possible assailants.

This cordon of agents is the last line of defense for the president, and it is with him anytime he leaves the living quarters of the White House. Agents surround the president in public and stand guard inside and out of every room that he is in. The job is stressful; the Service must watch everyone in a crowd for suspicious actions. Since the assignment is to prevent an attack on the president, agents have to anticipate possible hostile actions. The job is also dangerous; agents are trained to become human shields, placing their bodies between the president and any assailant, taking the shots that are meant for him.

The Service's job is complicated by the fact that many presidents or other protectees co-operate only reluctantly with their guardians. The Service would prefer to keep the president away from the public, but presidents are politicians who love to plunge into a crowd to 'press the flesh.' Obviously, this destroys the 'safe zone' and makes the agent's job much more difficult. Also, being constantly surrounded by people can get tedious, and sometimes presidents try to slip away from their guardians. President Johnson used to race around the LBJ Ranch in his car, trying to lose his protective detail, and President Bush would go powerboating off Kennebunkport and try to leave his agents behind.

CONCLUSION

The president spends his term in glamor and splendor. His home is large and magnificently furnished, his transportation is luxurious and always available, and servants who take great pride in serving him are available night and day. If he wants something, it will be provided. People surround him to protect him and his loved ones. When he goes to work, hundreds of experts gather information and analysis to help him make decisions and then carry out the decisions he has made. He occupies a position of power and importance – perhaps the most important single job in the world.

But the costs are many. The demands of the office are enormous, far more than he can satisfy. The frustrations are great; the arrangement of power in the American political system makes it very difficult for any president to achieve what he wants. Much of what he does is unappreciated by supporters and condemned by foes. He has few, if any, true friends, for he is surrounded by men and women who seek to further their own ambitions. And the burden of decision, the pressure of

Above: Bathed in warm floodlighting, the White House as seen at dusk from Lafayette Square. The square was originally called President's Square but was renamed after the French hero in 1825.

responsibility, rests with him alone and cannot be shifted to another. After being president for a few months, James Garfield wondered what there was 'about the place that a man should want to get into it.' The question has been asked by many presidents. The seat of power is a very lonely place.

Notes

1. President's Committee on Administrative Management, 1937: 5.

2. Cronin, 1987: 346–47.

3. Hess, 1976: 88.

4. Rather and Gates, 1974: 240.

5. Jerry Jones, Nixon's staff secretary quoted in Wayne, 1978: 47.

6. Carter, 1984: 144.

John R. Vile

6

THE EARLY PRESIDENTS

George Washington   1789-1797
John Adams   1797-1801
Thomas Jefferson   1801-1809
James Madison   1809-1817
James Monroe   1817-1825
John Quincy Adams   1825-1829

The Constitution was little more than a piece of parchment –
a well-conceived plan of government, but still only a plan. The
challenge of the early presidents was to transform parchment
into practice. All six of them hailed from Virginia or Massachusetts,
the seedbeds of American independence. Despite George Washington's
warnings to the contrary, political parties arose and divided the early
presidents. Yet together they accomplished their main objective.
By the end of their era, the government and the presidency
were firmly established.

George Washington presides over the
signing of the Constitution of the United States.

America's first six presidents all came from two states: Virginia and Massachusetts. They were all considered to be honest and capable men. All but the last of them, John Quincy Adams, are regarded as 'founding fathers,' and he was the son of the second president, John Adams. Of the men who served as president from 1789 to 1829, only George Washington and James Monroe fought in the American Revolution. But the other four participated in the revolution in government and laws that this conflict precipitated, and, as a child, John Quincy Adams witnessed the Battle of Bunker Hill in Boston.

Four of the first six presidents were among the most intellectually gifted ever to occupy the office, and the other two, Washington and Monroe, demonstrated considerable practical judgment and leadership skills. All six presidents were landowners, all had substantial political experience prior to assuming the presidency, and all but Washington had studied law. The early presidents served at a time when it was possible for Thomas Jefferson to spend each afternoon on a solitary horse ride and for John Quincy Adams to swim in the Potomac River nude. Most of them were fairly reserved men, and probably would not have excelled at the kind of glad-handing and public speaking demanded by the modern presidency. Yet most of the early presidents won considerable trust and affection from the American people during their lives, and today all are respected as statesmen who were deeply devoted to their country and to the public offices they held.

GEORGE WASHINGTON

Born in Westmoreland County in Virginia in 1732, Washington was a national hero long before the Constitution was written. Although he received little formal education, Washington gained early experience surveying the vast lands of his native state and managing Mount Vernon, the large plantation on the Potomac River that he inherited from his half-brother Lawrence. In the 1750s, Washington served the British as a military leader in the French and Indian wars,

Below: This china plate was part of a load imported aboard the *Pallas* and divided between generals George Washington and Henry Lee in about 1785. The arms decorating it are of the Order of the Cincinnati, an organization of officers who had served in the American Revolution.

Above: This French porcelain soup tureen with gilt decoration was part of a large service purchased by George Washington from the Comte de Moustier, the French minister, in 1790.

redeeming early mistakes with courage and increased experience. Washington subsequently married a wealthy widow, Martha Custis, greatly expanded his landholdings, and was elected to the Virginia Assembly, where his service earned him a place at the Continental Congresses of 1774 and 1775. Washington was a handsome man who, at six feet, two inches, was unusually tall for his day. Because of his striking appearance, his military experience, and the rebels' need to rally the South to the Revolutionary cause, the Continental Congress approved John Adams's nomination of Washington to lead the continental army.

Washington was not a military genius, but he showed a tenacity of purpose in the face of obstacles and an ability to inspire loyalty that served the American cause well. Moreover, after successfully prosecuting the war, Washington rebuffed efforts to make him a king or dictator. In one revealing incident, he declined to lead a march on Congress by soldiers who were owed back pay. Instead, the soldiers were persuaded to disperse,[1] and, like the Roman Cincinnatus, with whom he was often compared, he retired to private life.

The war taught Washington several important lessons. As he observed the weakness of Congress under the Articles of Confederation and the constant bickering among the states, he recognized the need for a stronger plan of union.

Washington's decision to attend the Constitutional Convention in 1787 and his subsequent election as president of that body helped legitimize its proceedings. Washington spoke only once during the long summer of debates, but his sober presence enhanced the dignity of the deliberations. Because they expected him to serve as the republic's first president, the delegates invested more powers in the executive branch than they otherwise would have.

Once the Constitution was adopted, electors unanimously chose Washington as the first president, the only individual ever so honored. By contrast, John Adams became vice president with only 34 of the 69 votes cast. Following his election, Washington refused the yearly salary of $25,000 that went with his office. Always a pub-

Right: Made of walnut in about 1750 in Philadelphia, Pennsylvania, this beautiful side chair was part of the furniture of the presidential household when it was based in the city.

lic man conscious that he was on a national stage, Washington was especially careful about the precedents he set. He lent the presidency both a democratic and an aristocratic air. Accessible to the people at his residence, Washington nonetheless rode in a magnificent carriage through the streets of the nation's first capital, New York, and insisted on the prerogatives of his office. Once, while visiting Massachusetts, he pointedly waited for Governor John Hancock to call on him rather than calling on the governor. Similarly, in a dispute over General Arthur St. Clair's expedition to quell an Indian uprising, Washington asserted the president's right to withhold sensitive information from Congress.

Washington was granted broad leeway in appointing members of his cabinet, and in dismissing members without the Senate's approval – a matter the Constitution had not directly addressed. Washington chose Alexander Hamilton as secretary of the treasury and Thomas Jefferson as secretary of state, with Edmund Randolph serving as attorney general and Henry Knox as secretary of war.

Almost from the beginning, Hamilton and Jefferson were at loggerheads on public questions, and Jefferson eventually resigned. The controversy over the wisdom and constitutionality of the national bank that Hamilton proposed early in Washington's first term was only the most visible flash-point in a series of important clashes. These were soon reflected in the emerging Federalist and Democratic–Republican parties, embodying different political philosophies. Jefferson, the Democratic–Republican leader, cherished state and local institutions while Hamilton, the leader of the Federalists, was a strong nationalist. Jefferson envisioned an America that was agrarian; Hamilton looked to the development of banking, commerce, and

industry. Jefferson expressed implicit faith in the common man, but Hamilton looked to monied elites. Jefferson admired the French Revolution, but Hamilton favored the English system of government.

On the issue of the bank, Washington sided with Hamilton. Still, Washington remained a unifying figure, and political leaders of all persuasions supported him for a second term. His second inauguration took place in Philadelphia, New York's successor as the interim site of the nation's capital.

During Washington's second term, party wrangling intensified. Representative James Madison of Virginia, an ally of Jefferson's, authored a number of essays under the pen-name 'Helvidius' that questioned the president's right to declare a policy of neutrality between England and France. Hamilton sharply responded under the name of 'Pacificus'. The French Minister to America, Citizen Genet, openly criticized the president, and Washington ordered him recalled to France when his attempts to outfit a privateering ship in America embarrassed even his Democratic–Republican supporters.

In 1794, faced with a revolt among Pennsylvania farmers who opposed a federal tax on whiskey, Washington mobilized the militia and prepared personally to face down the revolt. The 'Whiskey Rebellion' fizzled out in the face of such resolve. The next year, Washington agreed to the unpopular Jay Treaty. It subjected American ships on the high seas to searches for contraband by the British navy in exchange for British withdrawal from the American northwest territory. More positively, in Pinckey's Treaty of 1795, the United States settled the boundaries of Florida with Spain, won the right to conduct commerce on the Mississippi River, and gained access to New Orleans.

By the end of his second term, Washington was exhausted and frustrated. His decision to retire unintentionally set a two-term precedent, later reaffirmed by Thomas Jefferson, that would not be broken until Franklin D. Roosevelt sought and won a third term in 1940.

Washington's retirement was interrupted when his successor, John Adams, commissioned him to take the field in case of a French invasion. Fortunately, neither war nor invasion materialized, and Washington lived out his life at Mount Vernon. When Washington died in 1799, even his political foes recognized his greatness. With more attention to book sales than to historical

Below: This blue and white Canton porcelain cup and saucer belonged to the first president, George Washington. Both the cup and saucer are decorated with Chinese pagodas.

fact, Parson Weems would soon spread legends about Washington, including the story that as a boy he had confessed to his father about chopping down a cherry tree rather than tell a lie. In contrast, Henry Lee's encomium of Washington is a flattering but still accurate assessment: Washington will ever be 'first in war, first in peace, and first in the hearts of his countrymen.'[2]

JOHN ADAMS

Few presidents were as intellectually gifted as John Adams. He was born in Quincy (now Braintree), Massachusetts, three years after Washington's birth. Educated at Harvard College, Adams subsequently taught school, studied law, and established a legal practice in Boston. In 1765, the young lawyer was stirred by the rhetoric of James Otis against the British-imposed Stamp Act and wholeheartedly embraced the patriot cause. He and Josiah Quincy nonetheless successfully defended the British soldiers haplessly involved in the so-called 'Boston Massacre' of 1770.

Adams's neighbors elected him to the Massachusetts Legislature and later to the

Above: This portrait of Washington in oils was produced in 1833 by Thomas Sully, after a more famous, unfinished work by Gilbert Stuart that was painted from life; it can therefore be assumed to offer a good likeness of the man.

Continental Congress, where he served on the five-member committee appointed to write the Declaration of Independence. Leaving the job largely to Jefferson, Adams devoted most of his time to the task of establishing foreign alliances for the revolutionary cause. From 1778 to 1788, Adams served his country abroad. He went first to France where, with his Puritanical inclinations, he was never quite at ease with either the French people or America's better-known ambassador, Benjamin Franklin. After serving at the Massachusetts Constitutional Convention (where he largely wrote the state's ground-breaking constitution), Adams represented the United States in Holland and later in England. While in England, he helped draft the 1783 Treaty of Paris, which ended the Revolutionary War. He served there until 1788, thus missing the Constitutional Convention.

A short, rotund man, five feet six inches tall, Adams was quite sensitive to criticism and con-

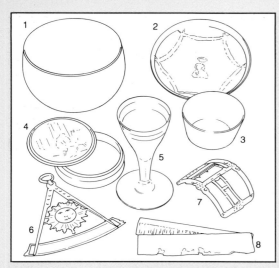

PRESIDENT GEORGE WASHINGTON

1. Cobalt blue finger bowl of blown glass made in Bristol, England.

2. Hard paste porcelain saucer, beautifully decorated with polychrome enamel and gilt. It was made in Nidervilier, France, and was given to George Washington by the Comte de Custine in 1782.

3. Tea bowl belonging to the same French set as the saucer and also made of hard paste porcelain with polychrome enamel.

4. Snuff box of papier mâché, tortoiseshell, and printed paper, made in either England or France.

5. Engraved wine glass, made of blown glass, probably in England.

6. Silver masonic jewel of silver paste, probably made in the United States. This Postmaster's jewel is thought to have been worn by George Washington at the Fredericksburg Masonic Lodge No. 4. Many American presidents have been members of the Masonic order.

7. Ornate shoe buckle made of pewter and steel, probably in England.

8. Comb with case, both made of horn in England.

cerned about his place in American revolutionary history. As the nation's first vice president, he took seriously his constitutional responsibility to preside over the Senate and broke numerous tie votes. Adams nonetheless described the job to his beloved and outspoken wife Abigail (who had admonished her husband to 'Remember the Ladies' in his work for independence)[3] as 'the most insignificant office that ever the invention of man contrived or his imagination conceived.'[4] Moreover, other members parodied Adams's vanity by nicknaming him 'His Rotundity' and 'His Superfluous Excellency.' Serving Washington faithfully, Adams subsequently earned Washington's endorsement for the presidency, although he served only a single term.

Adams's presidency was hindered from the start by party infighting. Hamilton (whom Adams would call 'a bastard brat of a Scotch peddlar')[5] had sought to deny Adams the presidency by secretly supporting South Carolina's Thomas Pinckney. Although Adams was elected in 1796, his Democratic–Republican rival for president, Thomas Jefferson, finished second and secured the vice presidency. Once in office, Jefferson refused Adams's offer to take an active part in the new administration. Moreover, Adams unwisely retained a number of Washington's cabinet members, notably Secretary of State Thomas Pickering and Secretary of the Treasury Oliver Wolcott, who conspired with Hamilton against the president and hindered his policies.

As in Washington's administration, both the French and British harassed American shipping in warring with one another. Again, Federalists generally sympathized with the British and Democratic–Republicans with the French. Adams realized that the nation was unprepared for war. Thus, even after the notorious 1798 XYZ Affair, in which France's Talleyrand refused

Below: A presentation printed copy of
An Oration, Pronounced July 5, 1819 **given to James Monroe, the fifth president, by the former president John Adams. The marble patterned boards and inscribed frontispiece are original.**

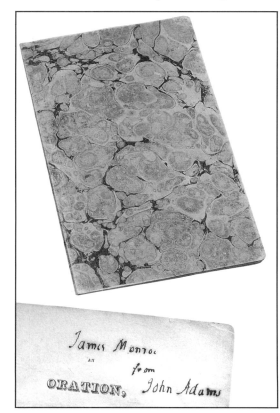

Above: An engraving of John Adams. It was during his presidency that the government moved from Philadelphia to Washington, D.C., and the president to the White House – that then, curiously, consisted of unpainted grey Virginia freestone.

to meet with American ambassadors without a bribe, Adams kept a quasi-war on the seas with France from developing into a full-blown conflict. Such statesmanship earned him the enmity of many of the Anglophile members of his party.

Less commendable was Adams's support of the Alien and Sedition Act of 1798. The Sedition Act punished those who criticized the government or the president. The laws prompted James Madison and Thomas Jefferson to write the Virginia and Kentucky Resolutions, which attempted to defend First Amendment freedoms of expression by asserting the states' rights to disregard unconstitutional federal laws.

In 1799, Adams, like Washington before him, faced a rebellion of disgruntled Pennsylvania taxpayers. Again, the revolt fizzled out, and Adams sensibly pardoned the ringleader to avoid further recriminations.

Although Jefferson was the first president inaugurated in the newly constructed capital of Washington, D.C., in 1800 Adams became the first president to live in the White House. In a letter to his wife, Adams expressed the hope that 'none but honest and wise men [may] ever rule under this roof.'[6]

Adams's most enduring legacy to the nation was his appointment of Virginia's John Marshall to serve as Chief Justice of the Supreme Court. Long after the Federalist Party disappeared from public view, Marshall expounded Federalist principles from the bench, upholding a strong national government. Marshall also elevated the Court from an insignificant bailiwick to a coequal branch of the federal government. With considerable justification, Adams later proclaimed that his 'gift' of John Marshall was the 'proudest act' of his entire life.[7]

Adams's defeat in the 1800 election resulted as much from his inability to resolve intra-party strife as from the growing strength of the Democratic–Republicans. The transition to Jefferson was peaceful but ungraceful: as his son, John Quincy, would later do, Adams left the capital before his successor's inauguration. During his twenty-five year retirement at Peacefield, his small farm in Quincy, the bitterness of the near-toothless Adams (whose condi-

Above: A daguerreotype from 1849 showing the Old Mansion, the family residence of John Adams and John Quincy Adams, at Quincy, Massachusetts, and today a National Historic Site.

tion so affected his speech as to make him too self-conscious to resume the practice of law) somewhat mellowed, and he and Jefferson began an extensive and friendly correspondence. It ended only when both died on July 4, 1826, fifty years to the day after the Declaration of Independence was adopted.

THOMAS JEFFERSON

When entertaining a group of Nobel Prize winners at the White House, President John F. Kennedy famously remarked that no more distinguished collection of talents and human knowledge had ever gathered there 'with the possible exception of when Thomas Jefferson dined alone.'[8] Jefferson may indeed be the American exemplar of the Renaissance Man. He was a farmer, diplomat, philosopher, man of letters, architect, educator, scientist, inventor, linguist, and musician.

Born in 1743 in what is now Albermarle County, Virginia, Jefferson was privately tutored before attending the College of William and Mary. He entered the practice of law after reading in George Wythe's office in Williamsburg. Serving as a member of the Virginia House of Burgesses from 1769 to 1774, Jefferson authored the 'Summary View of the Rights of British America,' which earned him a national reputation for clear and forceful writing and made him the obvious choice to draft the Declaration of Independence at the Continental Congress in 1776. Although Jefferson did not aim for novelty, his immortal defense of 'life, liberty, and the pursuit of happiness' was as elegant a statement of human rights as has ever been penned.

Before becoming president in 1801, Jefferson served as a wartime governor of Virginia (when he barely escaped from British troops) and as a member of Congress where he drafted a report in 1784 that eventually led to the Northwest Ordinance of 1787, which organized the Northwest Territory. He also was minister to France, secretary of state in Washington's first administration, and vice president under John Adams. Because he was then serving in France, Jefferson did not attend the Constitutional Convention of 1787, but his post-Convention letters influenced James Madison's subsequent

Left: This blue and white Chinese export berry bowl, with decoration, is from a dinner service owned by Thomas Jefferson.

Below: Like a number of the founding fathers and prominent early leaders, Jefferson was both anti-slavery and a slave owner. This handwritten list is an inventory, by year, of the slaves he owned. The key is from one of the doors at Monticello.

decision to press for a Bill of Rights to be added by amendment.

In the 1800 presidential election, the electoral college almost stymied what contemporaries called 'the Revolution of 1800' when all the Democratic–Republican electors (each of whom had to cast two ballots for president) who voted for Jefferson also voted for his intended vice presidential running mate, New York's Aaron Burr. Burr's refusal to step aside threw the election into the House of Representatives. 'Lame duck' Federalists bided their time through 35 ballots. Jefferson won only after Alexander Hamilton, who was even more suspicious of Burr than of Jefferson, convinced enough Federalists to withhold their votes to give Jefferson a majority. Jefferson was then saddled with Burr as his vice president.

Unlike Adams, Jefferson knew how to clean house. He appointed all the members of his cabinet from the ranks of the Democratic–Republican Party. Madison became secretary of state, Albert Gallatin, secretary of the treasury, Levi Lincoln, attorney general, and Henry Dearborn, secretary of war. Blessed with firm congressional majorities, Jefferson used his power as the Party's founder and leader to move legislation through Congress.

Jefferson inaugurated an informal style of government in Washington, D.C., receiving diplomats in informal attire and transmitting his annual 'State of the Union' messages to Congress in written form rather than delivering them in person. At the White House, the handshake replaced the bow as the standard form of greeting.

Jefferson's first term was successful by any measure. He engaged the Barbary pirates in a war over their demands for tribute. In 1803, he took an action that, although conflicting with his own narrow construction of the federal government's powers under the Constitution, remains the single greatest accomplishment of his presidency. Jefferson had sent William Livingston and James Monroe to France to purchase New Orleans and West Florida. Napoleon instead offered to sell the entire Louisiana Territory for $15 million, and the American negotiators accepted. This single purchase doubled America's land area, removed a potential enemy from its western border, and extended Jefferson's dream of an agrarian republic into the foreseeable future. He

Below: This French, open face, calendar pocket watch with key is made of yellow gold and was owned by Jefferson. The reverse is engraved 'Voucher à Paris.'

Above: Gilbert Stuart's portrait of Jefferson. Arguably his greatest presidential act was the Louisiana Purchase which doubled the United States' size and created a new power in the world.

subsequently sent Meriwether Lewis and William Clark on an exploration of the land.

Jefferson's second term was less successful. In 1805, two years after John Marshall asserted the Court's power to annul congressional legislation in the case of *Marbury* v. *Madison*, Jefferson's congressional lieutenants impeached and unsuccessfully attempted to convict Supreme Court Justice Samuel Chase for alleged intemperate remarks and behavior. Similarly, the Jefferson administration unsuccessfully prosecuted Aaron Burr for conspiring to form a separate Southwestern republic.

Like the two administrations before his, Jefferson's was bedeviled by problems arising from ongoing war between Britain and France.

Right: Martha Jefferson's deathbed adieu, a portion of Laurence Sterne's poem *Tristram Shandy*, that was completed in Jefferson's hand in 1782. He was griefstricken at her death following her failure to recover from their sixth child's birth.

Jefferson hoped to bring the two sides to terms by stopping trade with them. His embargo was a failure: it was predictably unpopular, especially in New England, and it fell much harder on American than on European business.

Jefferson lifted the embargo just before he left what he described as 'the splendid misery' of the

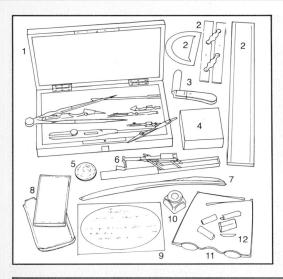

PRESIDENT THOMAS JEFFERSON

1. Drawing instruments with a wooden case. Among other things Thomas Jefferson was a highly gifted architect – he designed many buildings, including his own home, Monticello, and even the obelisk under which he is buried – and had every need of such a set of portable items.
2. Measuring instruments, including a protractor, parallelogram, and conversion rule. His collection of mathematical apparatus, acquired from the best London makers, was one of the finest in the country.
3. Folding pocket knife.
4. Paperweight.
5. Silver half-dollar dated 1809, the last year of Jefferson's presidency.
6. Pocket scales manufactured in Kirkby, near Liverpool, England.
7. Quill pen.
8. Leather-bound pocket notebook with its slipcase.
9. Blank invitation to dinner.
10. An ink well.
11. Folding spectacles.
12. A set of bifocal lenses wrapped in papers and marked as matching pairs.

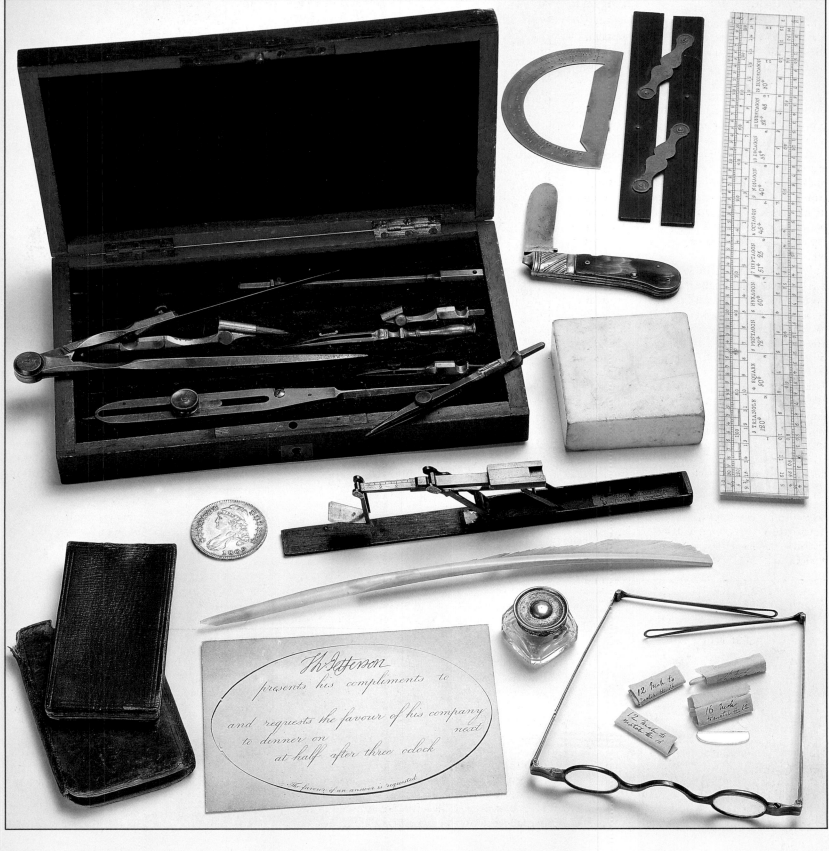

Left: An engraved portrait of Jefferson. Not an orator, the pen was Jefferson's natural means of expression, but while he was charming and even tempered he also remained very private.

In 1776, Madison was elected to Orange County's Committee of Safety, where he drilled with other troops until it became clear that his physical constitution (he weighed only about one hundred pounds and was subject to seizures) unfitted him to military life. He subsequently served as a delegate to the Virginia Convention of 1776; a member of the Virginia House of Delegates, where he worked with Jefferson to secure religious freedom; a member of Virginia's Council of State; a delegate to the Continental Congress; and a delegate to the Annapolis Convention of 1786 that served as a prelude to the Constitutional Convention.[10]

Madison carried out his most important work in his roles as a delegate to the Constitutional Convention of 1787 and as a member of the first Congress. In the former position, Madison drafted the Virginia Plan, which set the Convention's subsequent agenda. He took the leading role in its debates and is often referred to as the Father of the Constitution.

Although Madison did not fully achieve the strong central government that he advocated at the Convention, he worked vigorously for the Constitution's adoption. With Alexander

Below: James Madison was a towering intellect whose energy at the Convention was central to its success. He was, however, always insistent that the Constitution was the work of many.

presidency for his beloved Monticello. During his retirement, he founded the University of Virginia. Dying, like Adams, on the 50th anniversary of the Declaration of Independence, Jefferson requested that three achievements be noted on his gravestone. Omitting the presidency, he cited his authorship of the Declaration of Independence, his drafting of the Virginia Statute for Religious Freedom, and his role as founder of the university. At his death, Jefferson was heavily in debt, and his home was auctioned.

JAMES MADISON

Measuring six feet, two inches, Jefferson was one of the nation's tallest presidents. He was succeeded by the shortest, five foot four inch James Madison, whom the writer Washington Irving once described as 'but a withered little Apple-John.'[9] Increasingly recognized in modern times as an intellectual giant, Madison's historical reputation rests less on his presidency, a time during which Congress was ascendant and he sometimes appeared indecisive, than on his prior accomplishments.

Born at Port Conway, Virginia, in 1751, Madison grew up on Montpelier, his family's large plantation in Orange County. After studying with tutors, Madison attended the College of New Jersey – today's Princeton University – before studying, albeit never practicing, law.

Left: The Jefferson Memorial's colonnaded and domed structure has echoes of Monticello. The walls bear excerpts of two of his best known documents, the Declaration of Independence and the Virginia Statute for Religious Freedom.

Hamilton and John Jay, he authored a multi-part defense of the document, *The Federalist Papers*. Madison's contributions included the two best-known essays – *Federalist* No. 10, dealing with factions, and No. 51, elucidating the separation of powers. Madison led the defense of the new Constitution at his state's ratifying convention where he narrowly prevailed against powerful Anti-Federalist forces led by the more oratorically gifted Patrick Henry. Although Henry then blocked Madison's election to the US Senate, Madison defeated James Monroe for a seat in the House of Representatives. There Madison proposed the outline of what became the first ten amendments to the Constitution – the Bill of Rights.

After eight years of service in the House and a year in the Virginia House of Delegates, Madison became Jefferson's secretary of state and later secured his endorsement for the presidency. Despite the unpopularity of Jefferson's embargo, with which Madison was associated, he and running mate George Clinton defeated South Carolina's C.C. Pinckney in the election of 1808.

Madison's administration was dominated by foreign policy concerns. The Non-Intercourse Act, designed to cut off American trade with Britain and France, proved about as unsuccessful as the earlier embargo, and France manipulated Madison's promise to lift the new embargo against any power that respected American neutrality. Meanwhile a group of newly-elected 'war hawk' congressmen, eager to acquire Canada, pressed for war with Great Britain. Scholars still debate whether a stronger president might have successfully resisted them, but Madison did not, and America entered the War of 1812 politically divided and militarily unprepared.

Below: This walnut side chair was one of a set of 12 made in Fredericksburg or Falmouth, Virginia, in 1773 for James Madison's father and later inherited by him after his father's death.

Although 'Mr. Madison's War,' as it was often called, was not popular, Madison was re-elected in 1812 against New York's DeWitt Clinton, with Elbridge Gerry replacing the deceased Clinton on the ticket. The war petered out inconclusively and did not end the abuses on the high seas that had precipitated it. During the war, America's efforts to capture Canada were thwarted, and the nation's capital was sacked. The sacking, a humiliating event, nonetheless spotlighted Madison's popular wife, Dolley, a buxom and vivacious hostess for both Jefferson, whose wife Martha Skelton had died long before he became president, and her own less convivial husband. Dolley Madison refused to leave the White House until she had rescued what she could of the silver and Gilbert Stuart's full-length picture of President Washington, which had to be cut from its frame.

Fortunately for Madison, the army's reverses were offset by several important naval victories, and by Andrew Jackson's rout of the British in the Battle of New Orleans, unknowingly fought

Above: James Madison, 'Father of the Constitution,' whose last note read, 'The advice nearest to my heart and deepest in my convictions is that the Union of the States be cherished and perpetuated.'

after diplomats had signed the Treaty of Ghent which officially ended the war.

The War of 1812 effectively destroyed the Federalist Party. Federalist delegates from New England, who had never supported the war and had even considered secession from the Union, arrived in Washington from the anti-war Hartford Convention with their peace demands just as Americans were celebrating the victory of New Orleans and the end of the war. To his great credit, Madison used the war neither as an excuse to suppress domestic opposition nor to assume extraordinary powers.

During his long and close association with Thomas Jefferson, Madison had espoused states' rights and strict constitutional construction. His reluctance to voice support had contributed to the demise of the first, Hamilton-sponsored

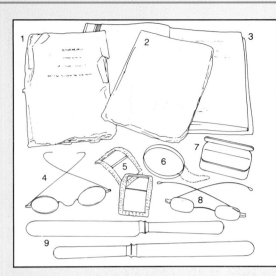

PRESIDENT JAMES MADISON

1. Printed copy of 'An Address Delivered Before the Rockingham Agricultural Society' on October 18, 1821 that was presented to James Madison by the author, William Plumer, Jr., and so inscribed. Madison himself was president of the Albemarle Agricultural Society.
2. Printed copy of 'A Dialogue Between an Assembly-man and a Convention-man on the Subject of the State Constitution of Pennsylvania.'
3. A copy of *The New Olive Branch* inscribed to James Madison.

4. James Madison's spectacles.
5. Shoe buckles with paste jewels.
6. Mrs Dolley Madison's gold bracelet. Dolley was renowned as a formidable lady of an optimistic and sociable nature. She spent a great deal of time, effort, and money in the first furbishment of the presidential house in Washington only to see it gutted by the British in 1814.
7. Mrs Dolley Madison's imitation tortoiseshell snuff box.
8. Mrs Dolley Madison's spectacles.
9. Table knives belonging to the family.

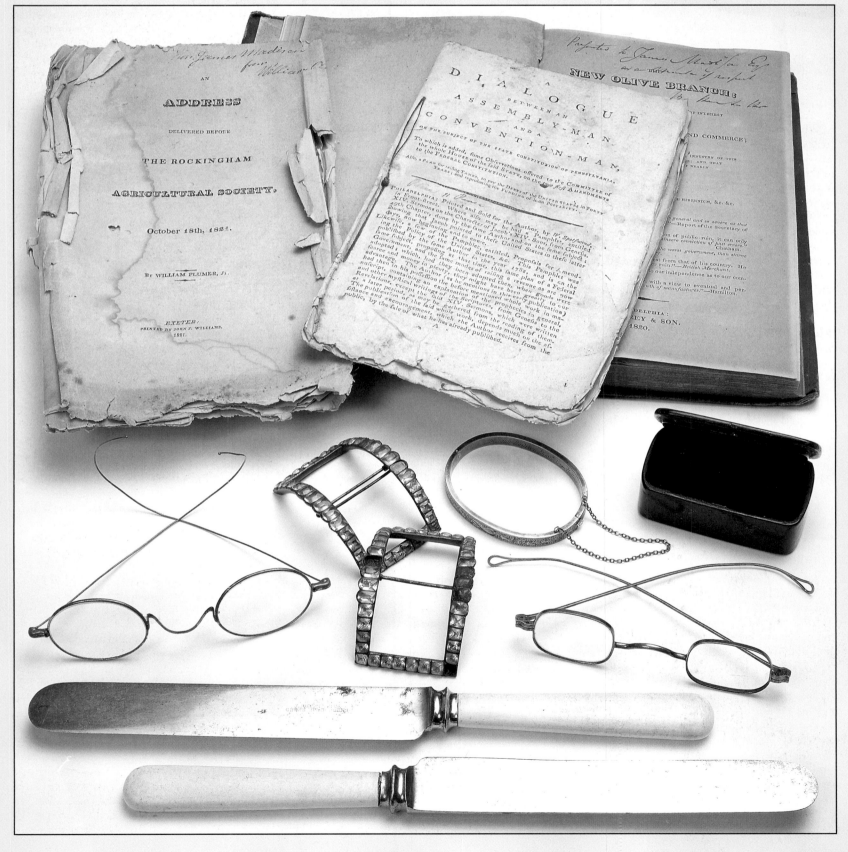

Above: This campeachy mahogany chair with an embossed black leather back was ordered by Thomas Jefferson – possibly from the joinery at Monticello – and given to his friend, and successor to the presidency, James Madison. Given that it looks exceedingly comfortable, it should come as no surprise to learn that it was one of Madison's favorite chairs.

Above: This bronze peace medal is decorated with a portrait of President Monroe. He was president during a nationalist period when, among other things, relations with the Indians were being defined. Indian leaders often wore these medals.

JAMES MONROE

It is fitting that James Monroe was the last president to wear knee breeches – he was the last of the so-called Virginia Dynasty and the last founding father who would serve as president. A large man who impressed with his directness, Jefferson once described him as a man 'whose soul might be turned wrong side outwards without discovering a blemish to the world.'[11]

Born in Westmoreland County in 1758, Monroe briefly attended the College of William and Mary before enlisting as a soldier in the American Revolution. During the war, he survived a fierce winter at Valley Forge, Pennsylvania, crossed the Delaware River with Washington in the victorious Christmas raid on Trenton, and developed a close friendship with

Below: This rectangular, brass-bound mahogany box with key has an escutcheon engraved with the words 'James Monroe, Esq.'. It was used by him to store documents.

Bank of the United States, but Madison bowed to precedent and approved the establishment of a second bank in 1816. Although he personally favored national action to construct internal improvements, Madison, like James Monroe after him, vetoed such appropriations because the Constitution did not specifically authorize them.

Madison spent nearly twenty years in retirement at Montpelier. During this time he served at a convention (which Monroe also attended) to rewrite the Virginia Constitution; like Monroe, too, he was a trustee of the University of Virginia. Madison spent his final years guarding Jefferson's reputation and opposing sectional division. When Madison died in 1836 at age 86, he was the last surviving member of the Constitutional Convention.

Above: President Monroe meeting with advisers to formulate the policy of US opposition to European recolonization of, or interference in the affairs of, the continent. This came to be called the Monroe Doctrine, although only after his death.

Washington's French aide, the Marquis de Lafayette. After studying law under Jefferson, Monroe served in a variety of positions: as a member of the Continental Congress; as a US Senator; as minister to France in the Washington administration; as governor of Virginia; as one of the two envoys who helped negotiate the Louisiana Purchase; as minister to Great Britain; and as secretary of state and secretary of war to President Madison.

Monroe's diplomacy was not always successful. To be sure, when he served as minister to France for President Washington, Monroe's elegant wife, Elizabeth – later criticized, along with her daughter Eliza, during Monroe's White House years as being too aristocratic – made a visit to see Lafayette's wife in prison that saved her life from the revolutionary government. But Monroe's work in freeing Thomas Paine, the author of *Common Sense*, backfired politically when Paine subsequently criticized Washington. Moreover, Monroe treated the French revolutionary government far more positively than Washington, who favored neutrality, intended. So, too, Jefferson later repudiated a commercial treaty that Monroe and Pinckney negotiated with the British.

Right: An engraving of President Monroe, the last of the Revolutionary leaders to attain the highest office. Curiously, he died on July 4, making a total of three of the five Revolutionary presidents who died on the same notable day.

Above: This eye-catching, red-colored French gilt armchair has a rich presidential history. It was originally purchased by President James Monroe; it was then used by President Andrew Jackson to pose for a portrait; and it was subsequently bought at a White House excess property sale by President Woodrow Wilson.

Above: This cartoon from *Judge* in 1889 shows the impact of the Monroe Doctrine on United States policy more than 50 years after its declaration. The Uncle Sam figure, in human-lion form, is barring the path to European government involvement in the Panama Canal project, the construction difficulties of which had caused the French company's liquidation. It began a period of aggressive nationalist foreign policy.

Monroe shined, however, in Madison's administration. He gained wide respect, as well as Madison's support for the presidency, when he successfully reorganized the Department of War while simultaneously serving as secretary of state. The resolution of the War of 1812 also contributed to Monroe's prestige.

In running for president as the Democratic–Republican candidate in 1816, Monroe faced a mere remnant of Federalist opposition. By 1820 the Federalist Party had died, and only an elector's desire to reserve the honor of electoral una-nimity for Washington kept Monroe from being so selected. (He won by 231 votes to 1.) After New England extended the new president a hearty welcome during a visit in 1817, observers commented on the new 'Era of Good Feeling,' and, even during the economic 'Panic of 1819,' the new label stuck.

Monroe's administration is best remembered for its foreign policy successes. The Rush–Bagot Agreement of 1818 ended conflict in the Great Lakes between the United States and Great Britain. In 1819, the Adams–Onis Treaty redeemed an unauthorized incursion by General Jackson into Florida by securing this territory from Spain.

Monroe's best-known policy was the Monroe Doctrine. Here, as in other successful areas of his foreign policy, Secretary of State John Quincy Adams played an important role. After most of the Latin American nations had achieved their independence from Spain, Monroe announced that the United States would not permit recolonization or other interference by the European powers in the Western Hemisphere. Although the policy largely depended on British naval forbearance, Monroe chose to announce his doctrine unilaterally.

One harbinger of trouble for the republic that emerged during the Monroe administration was the controversy that led to the Missouri Compromise of 1820. Missouri, a US territory, ignited the dispute when it applied for statehood.

Left: A pair of silk silhouette portraits of Mr and Mrs James Monroe, in gilt wood frames made by Charles Wilson Peale.

PRESIDENT JAMES MONROE

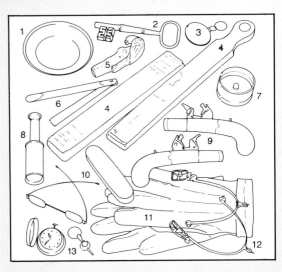

1. Piece of porcelain that was used in Monroe's White House.
2. White House door key.
3. Silver-framed, folding magnifying glass.
4. Red leather-bound razor strop presented to President Monroe on July 4, 1823.
5. Ivory cane handle carved in the form of an eagle.
6. Silver-mounted, folding razor with a handle of tortoiseshell, made in England.
7. Brass pocket compass. It was made in England as were many instruments of a scientific nature at the time.
8. Brass pocket telescope reputedly used by Monroe while scouting the British advance on Washington during the War of 1812.
9. Pair of English flintlock pocket pistols, made by Hewson in Exeter. No gentleman would be without such pistols.
10. Silver-framed spectacles with sliding, adjustable stems, together with their original case.
11. Gentleman's doe skin gloves.
12. Silver riding spurs, probably English-made.
13. Gold-cased pocket watch and key; the works are marked 'Gabriel, London'.

Right: An exquisite French-made, brass-mounted mahogany Secretaire belonging to Monroe. In 1906, some 75 years after his death, about 200 letters were found in three secret drawers when a leg was being repaired. The letters were from Washington, Jefferson, Madison, Hamilton, Burr, Franklin, Calhoun, Lafayette, and Napoleon.

As a slave state, Missouri's admission threatened to disrupt the even balance between slave and free states in the Senate. Like the other Virginian presidents, Monroe owned slaves. Like them, too, he appeared to hope for the day the institution would be eliminated. (Interestingly, because he served for a time as president of the American Colonization Society, Liberia named its capital Monrovia.) Madison believed, however, that the Constitution protected slavery, and he only reluctantly signed the 1820 compromise that, in simultaneously admitting Missouri as a slave state and Maine as a free state, also banned slavery north of latitude 36° 30′ in the old Louisiana Territory.

Although he considered Ash Lawn, a 'cabin castle' near Jefferson's Monticello, to be his home, like Jefferson, Monroe found that political service had left him in debt. He thus had to retire to Oak Hill, another house designed by Jefferson in Loudon County, Virginia. After his wife died, Monroe spent his last years with his daughter and son-in-law in New York. He died on July 4, 1831, five years to the day after Adams and Jefferson.

JOHN QUINCY ADAMS

Few men have appeared better prepared for the presidency than John Quincy Adams. Adams was a member of a distinguished family whose accomplishments continued well into the 20th century, and he was the only son of a president ever to be elected to that office. Adams was born in 1767 in Quincy, Massachusetts, in a house next door to the one in which his father was born. As a youth, he accompanied John Adams on diplomatic trips to Europe and learned several foreign languages. After attending Harvard College, he studied and practiced law.

Before becoming president, Adams served as minister to the Netherlands in Washington's administration; minister to Prussia for his father; and minister to Russia and later to Great Britain for Madison. In the latter capacity, he helped draft the Treaty of Ghent, ending the War of 1812. Adams followed this activity, as well as an uncompleted term in the US Senate (where his willingness to cross party lines and vote for Democratic–Republican proposals like the Louisiana Purchase angered his state's legislature), by serving as Monroe's secretary of state. Along the way, he married the gracious Louisa Johnson, who had been born in England of an American father and English mother.

Although the Federalist Party had withered, the election of 1824 was hotly contested by four candidates, all of them Democratic–Republicans. Congressional caucuses selected four presidential candidates. Adams was opposed by Tennessee's Andrew Jackson, Georgia's William Crawford, and Kentucky's Henry Clay. The popular General Jackson secured the greatest number of both popular and electoral votes, but because no candidate won a majority, the contest went to the House of Representatives.

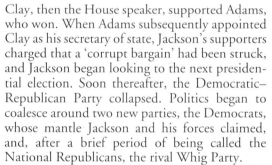

Clay, then the House speaker, supported Adams, who won. When Adams subsequently appointed Clay as his secretary of state, Jackson's supporters charged that a 'corrupt bargain' had been struck, and Jackson began looking to the next presidential election. Soon thereafter, the Democratic–Republican Party collapsed. Politics began to coalesce around two new parties, the Democrats, whose mantle Jackson and his forces claimed, and, after a brief period of being called the National Republicans, the rival Whig Party.

Party politics eclipsed other features of the Adams administration. Adams did propose a massive program of internal improvements, but Congress had constitutional qualms about such projects, and, apart from some funding for the Chesapeake and Ohio Canal, his plans went largely unimplemented. Moreover, Adams's reluctant support for the protective tariff of 1828, the so-called 'Tariff of Abominations', fueled the ongoing tension between the free and industrializing North and the agricultural, slave-based South.

Adams's somewhat gloomy and stubborn disposition, which he himself described as 'cold, austere and forbidding,'[12] did not aid his policies. His view of the statesman's role was closer to that of his predecessors than to those who would follow in the wake of President Jackson's brand of democratic populism. Retiring briefly to Massachusetts, after Jackson's election in 1828 dashed his hopes for a second term, in 1830

Below: As part of the funeral observances for Adams, following his dramatic end, this pamphlet was published: 'Proceedings of the Corporation and Citizens of Washington on the occasion of the Death of John Quincy Adams who died in the Capitol on Wednesday Evening February 23, 1848.'

Above: An oil portrait by George Peter Alexander Healy of John Quincy Adams, so far the only son of a president also to have become president. He was buried alongside his parents and wife at First Parish Church in Quincy, Massachusetts.

Adams was subsequently elected to the House of Representatives, where he served as a Whig member. He died in 1848 from a stroke that he suffered at his post in the House. Opposing slavery and the 'gag rule' that Southern represen-

tatives had imposed on anti-slavery petitions, Adams earned the title of 'Old Man Eloquent.' Far from universally loved, many Americans nevertheless respected him for a life of devoted and principled service.

Notes

1. This incident is dramatically recorded in James Flexner, 1974: 174–75.

2. Degregorio, 1993: 59–60.

3. Letter to John Adams dated March 31, 1776 in Mason and Baker, 1985: 119.

4. Bowman, 1986: 20.

5. Peabody (ed.), 1973: 373.

6. Friedel, 1987: 11.

7. Urofsky, 1988: 177.

8. Frank and Melick, 1984: 49.

9. Leish (ed.), 1968: 155.

10. Here as in other listings of offices in this essay, the author has relied on Degregorio, 1993: 59–60.

11. Leish (ed.), 1968: 155.

12. Bowman, 1986: 38.

Mark Byrnes

7

THE JACKSONIAN ERA

Andrew Jackson   1829-1837
Martin Van Buren   1837-1841
William Henry Harrison   1841
John Tyler   1841-1845
James K. Polk   1845-1849
Zachary Taylor   1849-1850
Millard Fillmore   1850-1853
Franklin Pierce   1853-1857

The United States was a roiling, rapidly expanding democracy during the Jacksonian Era. The era's namesake, known affectionately as 'Old Hickory,' both led and embodied these populist changes. But the seven presidents who served in the two decades after Jackson faced a new challenge: the increasingly bitter rift between North and South over slavery.

Daguerreotype of The White House
as it looked in or around 1846.

The presidents of this era oversaw tremendous changes; some of which, especially the growing North–South tensions, occurred despite presidential actions, and others that were sparked by the presidents, such as the spread of democracy under Jackson and the expansion of territory led by Polk.

ANDREW JACKSON

Andrew Jackson's presidency marked the beginning of the 'Jacksonian era' – a time when ordinary Americans began to improve their standing in politics and society. Jackson championed the common person and, in his own life, vividly demonstrated what someone with humble origins could accomplish.

Jackson was born in a log cabin on March 15, 1767, in the Waxhaw settlement that straddled the border between North and South Carolina.[1] His father died a few days before Andrew's birth. Never a great student, Jackson grew into a fun-loving but quick-tempered boy.[2]

At age 13, Andrew joined the American army in the Revolutionary War. In his teens Jackson studied law in North Carolina,[3] before moving to Nashville, Tennessee in 1788. There the main developments of his adult life took place: he practiced law, speculated in land, entered politics, and met his wife Rachel. The couple inadvertently married before Rachel's divorce from her first husband was final, and the ensuing gossip tormented Rachel and infuriated Andrew.[4] Over the years Jackson fought in several brawls and duels, even killing one opponent to defend his wife's honor.[5]

Jackson was elected as Tennessee's first US representative in 1796; he became a US senator the next year, and a justice of the Tennessee Supreme Court the year after that. He later served as a general during the War of 1812, earning the nickname 'Old Hickory' for his toughness. Jackson became a national hero after his

Above: Andrew Jackson by Thomas Sully. Jackson was a thoroughly populist leader, a self-made man and a national war hero.

Left: General Jackson with a submitting Creek chief following his defeat of the Indians at the Battle of Horseshoe Bend in 1814.

defeat of the British at the Battle of New Orleans in 1815. Ironically, the battle was fought after a peace treaty had been signed.

Jackson ran for president in 1824 but lost to John Quincy Adams. Jackson won more electoral votes than any other candidate, but not the majority needed to be elected. The election then went to the House of Representatives, which chose Adams. Jackson charged that a 'corrupt bargain' between Adams and one of the other candidates, Speaker of the House Henry Clay, swung the vote. After the election, Adams appointed Clay as secretary of state.

Four year later, however, Jackson defeated the incumbent Adams in the election that spawned the modern Democratic Party. He entered office determined to make the federal government more democratic and was unafraid to wield exec-

utive power to that end. Jackson vetoed 12 bills and so vigorously asserted presidential power that critics dubbed him 'King Andrew the First.'

Unhappy that many federal jobs had seemingly become lifetime positions, Jackson replaced some government employees. The jobs went to his political supporters in a practice that became known as the 'spoils system.'[6] Even though he had appointed his cabinet, Jackson instead relied on an informal group of advisers that opponents labeled the 'Kitchen Cabinet.'

Jackson split with Vice President John C. Calhoun over the issue of 'nullification.' Calhoun argued that a state should have the right to reject, or nullify, any law passed by Congress that the state considered unconstitutional. Others countered that allowing nullification might eventually destroy the Union. At an 1830

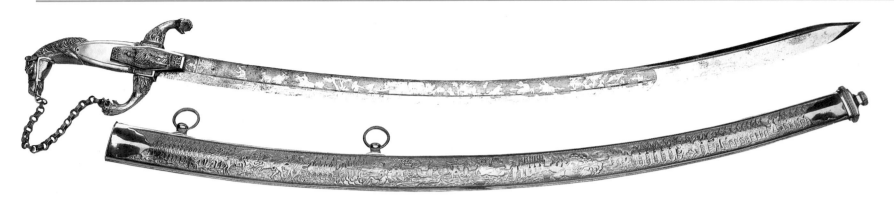

banquet Jackson glared at Calhoun and declared his opposition to nullification with this toast: 'Our federal Union – it must be preserved.'[7]

Jackson fought his biggest political battle against the second Bank of the United States. Chartered by Congress in 1816, the Bank oversaw the US currency system and regulated state banks. Jackson regarded the Bank as an elitist institution that favored business over working people. He also contended that Congress lacked the constitutional authority to establish such a Bank. Jackson therefore vetoed a bill passed by Congress in 1832 to extend the Bank's charter. Although the veto drew strong criticism, most ordinary Americans supported it, and the issue helped Jackson win re-election in 1832.

Jackson left the presidency a much stronger institution than he entered it. He saw the president as the 'tribune' and was the first president to seek political support directly from the people. This tactic of 'going over the heads' of Congress to rouse public opinion later became a hallmark

Below: Titled 'General Jackson Slaying the Many Headed Monster,' this cartoon refers to Jackson's waging of The Bank War. He used his veto in 1832 to prevent Congress extending the charter of the Bank of the United States. He called the bank a 'hydra of corruption' catering to the wealthy at the expense of the masses. It signified a major difference of opinion on the government's relationship with the nation's financial system.

Above: This presentation saber was made by Frederick W. Widmann of Philadelphia for President Andrew Jackson at the request of some 60-70 gentlemen on the twentieth anniversary of the Battle of New Orleans in January 1835. It has a pearl plaque grip and is gilt overall. The scabbard decoration depicts the battle and the blade is etched with battlescenes.

of the presidency. After his second term as president Jackson retired to his plantation, the Hermitage, near Nashville. Despite ill health, he supervised his fields and maintained his interest in politics, campaigning for Martin Van Buren in 1840 and James K. Polk in 1844. Jackson died on June 8, 1845.

PRESIDENT ANDREW JACKSON

1. The presidential seal used by Andrew Jackson. It is a copper-clad, lead seal attached to a brass base within a rosewood handle. The tag attached to it was written by President Rutherford B. Hayes.
2. Top hat with a wide mourning band, made by S.W. Handy of Washington. Excessive grief was signified by the width of the black band.
3. Needlepoint-covered hymnal that belonged to Rachel, the president's wife.
4. Miniature oil on ivory portrait of Rachel Donelson Jackson, often carried by President Jackson. Jealous of his honor, he did once kill a man in a duel after the man had cast a slur on Rachel.
5. Single-shot percussion pistol made by Philip Creamer of St Clair Co., Illinois, and given by President Jackson to General John H. Eaton. The silver thumb escutcheon is engraved 'Andrew Jackson.'
6. Gentleman's pocket watch made by Hunter of Liverpool, England.
7. A stick pin made of a pearl surrounded by rubies.
8. Gold spectacles with case, made by John McAllister & Co., Philadelphia.

MARTIN VAN BUREN

Martin Van Buren swept into the White House in the election of 1836 as Jackson's handpicked successor. Many Americans blamed Van Buren for the severe economic depression that hit the country soon afterward, however, and they threw him out of office in the next election.

Van Buren was born in Kinderhook, New York, on December 5, 1782[8]. His father owned a tavern and a farm. At age 14, Van Buren began to study law and he demonstrated such promise that his mentor allowed him to sum up a case before a jury at age 15. In 1801 Van Buren moved to New York City to continue his studies. He gained admission to the bar two years later.

An enthusiastic believer in Jeffersonian democracy, Van Buren entered New York politics as a Democratic-Republican. While serving in the New York legislature from 1812 to 1820, Van Buren helped organize an effective political party organization, or 'machine,' called the 'Albany Regency.' The machine helped him get appointed as attorney general of New York, a post he held from 1815 to 1819, and as a US senator in 1821. In 1828 he was elected governor of New York, but he resigned two months into his term to become secretary of state in the administration of his close political ally, Andrew Jackson. Van Buren became Jackson's most trusted adviser.

In 1831 Jackson nominated Van Buren to be ambassador to Great Britain, but the Senate, which was controlled by the newly formed opposition Whig party, rejected him for partisan reasons. Jackson chose Van Buren as his vice presidential running mate in the 1832 election and made clear that he wanted Van Buren to succeed him as president. After his term as vice president, and with Jackson's continuing support, Van Buren easily won the Democratic nomination for president in 1836. He went on to defeat several Whig candidates.

Less than three months after Van Buren took office, a major economic depression, the so-called 'Panic of 1837, struck the nation. Ironically, some of the financial measures taken by Van Buren's predecessor and mentor, Andrew Jackson, helped cause the crash. During the depression, hundreds of banks and businesses around the country collapsed and many Americans suffered. True to his belief in a limited government, Van Buren did not seek legislative solutions to the crisis. Even though the depression was not Van Buren's fault, he received much of the blame for it.

Van Buren made an easy target for the Whigs in 1840, led by presidential candidate William Henry Harrison.[9] The Whigs portrayed Van Buren, a natty dresser who had refurbished the White House, as an uncaring, aristocratic dandy. After his defeat, Van Buren retired to his mansion near Kinderhook.[10] In 1848 he ran unsuccessfully for president on the antislavery Free Soil ticket. Van Buren died on July 24, 1862.

Below: The signature of Martin Van Buren. As one of the leaders of the 'Albany Regency' he became America's first political boss.

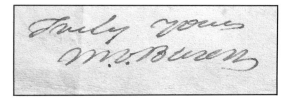

WILLIAM HENRY HARRISON

William Henry Harrison served as president for only one month – the shortest presidential tenure in American history.

Harrison was born in Charles City County, Virginia, on February 8, 1773 – the last president born a British subject. From a prominent and well-to-do family (his father, Benjamin Harrison V, signed the Declaration of Independence), Harrison attended Hampden-Sydney College and briefly studied medicine. In 1791 he quit medicine, joined the army, and went to the Northwest (modern-day Ohio).

After seven successful years in the army, Harrison was named secretary of the Northwest Territory and later governor of the Indiana Territory. As governor, Harrison oversaw the settling of frontier areas previously controlled by American Indians. When Indians led by the charismatic chief Tecumseh threatened the

Above: An engraving of Van Buren after a painting by Alonzo Chappel. His adroitness in organizing satisfactory outcomes to political problems earned him the nickname of the 'Little Magician.'

settlers, Harrison spearheaded the defense. His subsequent victory at the 1811 Battle of Tippecanoe brought him national prominence.

Harrison commanded the American army in the Northwest during the War of 1812 and won a major victory against combined British and Indian forces at the Battle of the Thames in 1813. After the war he served stints in the Ohio state senate, Congress, and as US minister to Colombia. He also devoted much attention to his Ohio farm.

Despite his return to private life in 1829, Harrison's past military exploits ensured his continuing status as a national hero. Looking for such a hero, the Whig Party nominated Harrison to run for president in 1840. His campaign con-

Left: This campaign ribbon for 1840 was made in Baltimore. The slogan is 'Our Country's Hope – Harrison & Reform.' His campaign was notable for its sloganeering and lack of platform, concentrating on his supposed personal qualities.

sisted of slogans and gimmicks rather than issues. When political opponents charged that Harrison would be happy living in a log cabin and drinking hard cider, the Whigs cleverly seized the theme and portrayed Harrison as a simple but honorable frontiersman. Even though Harrison had been born in a Virginia mansion and currently lived in a grand Ohio house, the 'log cabin' theme struck a chord with the public. 'Old Tippecanoe' defeated the Democratic incumbent, Martin Van Buren.

On March 4, 1841, the 68-year-old Harrison delivered a one hour and forty minute inaugural address – the longest in presidential history – wearing no coat or hat despite the inclement weather. He caught a cold, later developed pneumonia, and died on April 4. Harrison thus became the first president to die in office.

Below: A mezzotint by John Sartain of President William Henry Harrison. Ironically, he is depicted wearing a jacket and cape but he died of pneumonia contracted from a cold caught at his inauguration due to his refusal to wear a coat in chilly weather.

Above: Another former Indian fighter, Harrison ran for president under the slogan 'Tippecanoe and Tyler too.' This silk ribbon is from the Virginia Convention in 1840 that approved the balanced ticket with former Democrat Tyler.

JOHN TYLER

John Tyler was the first vice president to become president due to the death of his predecessor. Subbed 'His Accidendcy' by critics, Tyler experienced a rocky time during his three years and eleven months in the White House.

Tyler was born to a prominent family in Charles City County, Virginia (like Harrison), on March 29, 1790. He attended the College of William and Mary and later studied law under his father. Interested in politics from an early age, Tyler served variously in the Virginia legislature, as governor of Virginia, and in both the US House and Senate between 1811 and 1840.

Tyler, like his father's friend Thomas Jefferson, advocated strict interpretation of the Constitution and a limited national government. A states' rights Democrat, he drifted toward the Whig Party in the 1830s because he disagreed with many of President Jackson's politics. In 1840, hoping to capture Southern votes, the Whigs picked Tyler to run for vice president with presidential nominee Harrison. The Whig ticket marched to victory with the slogan 'Tippecanoe and Tyler too.'

Tyler was sworn in as president on April 6, 1841, two days after Harrison's death. His Whig colleagues were initially confident that the new president would uphold party principles, but they soon learned otherwise. Consistent with his belief in a limited national government, Tyler rejected much of the Whig agenda (which favored an activist national government) and twice vetoed Whig-backed bills to re-establish a

Above: This beautiful, inlaid music box was made in Geneva by Ducommun Girod. It belonged to John Tyler and his wife. He married twice – his first wife died soon after he became president.

Above: This betrothal ring (left) of jet black stones belonged to Tyler's wife. It contains a lock of his hair. Hair is also in the gold memorial brooch (right) that is engraved on the reverse 'Veto President and Friend of Ireland.'

Left: An engraving of President John Tyler after a painting by Alonzo Chappel. As the first vice president to assume the presidency because of death, his was a difficult tenure to see through.

national bank. After the second veto, all but one of his Cabinet members resigned and furious Whigs vilified Tyler.[11] In January 1843 Whigs in the House tried unsuccessfully to pass an impeachment resolution against Tyler. This was the first attempt in history to impeach a president.

Despite his political troubles, Tyler accomplished a great deal as president. He approved the Pre-Emption Act, which sped settlement of the Western frontier; oversaw the Webster-Ashburton Treaty, which ended a long-running dispute with Canada over Maine's boundary; and led the push to annex Texas.

Perhaps Tyler's greatest achievement was the confident way he assumed the presidency after Harrison's death. The Constitution was vague on the matter of succession, and some argued that Tyler should merely act as caretaker until a special presidential election could be held. Tyler rejected that notion, however, and insisted on wielding all the powers of the office until the end of the four-year term. To underscore his position, Tyler quickly moved into the White House, gave an inaugural address, and went so far as to return unopened any mail addressed to 'Acting President' Tyler. His succession set a vital precedent that has been followed ever since.

A man without a political party, Tyler chose not to run in the election of 1844. He retired to a quiet life in Virginia with his second wife, Julia.[12] In 1861 Tyler headed an unsuccessful peace mission seeking compromises on the issues dividing the North and South. He later supported Virginia's secession from the Union and was elected to the Confederate House of Representatives. He died on January 18, 1862, before taking his seat.

JAMES K. POLK

Although not among the most fabled presidents, James K. Polk enjoyed remarkable success in fulfilling his presidential agenda. He presided over a period of dramatic territorial growth for the United States.

Born in Mecklenburg County, North Carolina, on November 2, 1795, Polk moved with his family to Tennessee in 1806. Polk's

PRESIDENT JAMES K. POLK

1. Set of French porcelain manufactured by Edward Honore in 1846 and purchased by William W. Corcoran, the official purchasing agent, from Alexander Stewart and Co. in New York. Polk was the first president to employ such an agent to acquire furnishings for the White House, for it was only in March 1845 that Congress allocated a fund to be used for the purpose. The service carries the official presidential seal (with 27 stars for the then states) and cost $979.40.

2. Smoking jacket of black satin damask tailored in a Turkish style. The jacket was given by the president to his brother, Marshall, and was subsequently passed down through the family.

3. Bible on which James K. Polk took the presidential oath on March 4, 1845. Alexander Hunter, marshal of the District of Columbia, presented it to Sarah. (President Cleveland began the custom of presidents supplying their own family Bibles for the ceremony.)

4. Ivory, gold-mounted cameo of James K. Polk that belonged to Sarah.

5. Ivory-handled presidential seal.

Left: An engraving of President Polk. He enlarged the nation massively by settling the issues of Texas, California, and Oregon Territory, but it did not ease North-South tensions.

Above: Polk's appeal to the people in 1844 was for territorial expansion and the creation of a continental nation. His support for Texas' annexation won him the Democratic nomination.

Below: This ivory fan is believed to have been given by Polk to his wife for the inauguration. Adorned with the first eleven presidents, it is inlaid with silver and gilt paper.

father prospered there and sent him to college at the University of North Carolina. After graduating in 1818, Polk returned to Tennessee where he studied law, entered politics, and became friends with Andrew Jackson. That friendship bolstered Polk's political career.

Polk served briefly in the Tennessee legislature before winning election to the US House of Representatives in 1825. He served in the House 14 years and was Speaker during his last four years there (Polk is the only Speaker to become president). As speaker, Polk worked closely with President Jackson. Polk supported Jackson so long and so consistently that he earned the nickname 'Young Hickory.' At Jackson's urging, Polk retired from the House to run for governor of Tennessee in 1839. He won that election but lost his 1841 re-election attempt and another race for governor in 1843.

Considered a likely vice presidential nominee for the Democrats in 1844, Polk surprisingly emerged at the convention as the compromise candidate for president – becoming the nation's

Above: This mahogany veneered table with a marble mosaic top in the form of the national symbol of the United States was presented to Polk after he had retired. The thirty stars represent the number of states in the Union at the time.

first 'dark horse,' or unexpected, presidential candidate.[13] His Whig opponent was Henry Clay. Polk was not as well known as Clay, so Whigs taunted: 'Who is James K. Polk?' Democrats responded with a slogan of their own, '54-40 or Fight!,' meaning that the US should fight with Britain if necessary to obtain disputed Oregon territory all the way North to the latitude of 54° 40′. Polk firmly believed in 'Manifest Destiny' – the notion that the United States was destined to control the continent from sea to sea.

Right: A daguerreotype of, left to right: (sitting) Attorney General Mason, Secretary of War Marcy, President Polk, and Secretary of the Treasury Walker; and (standing) Postmaster General Johnson, and Secretary of the Navy Bancroft.

Above: An engraving of Zachary Taylor in uniform as a major general in the Mexican War. Although yet another war hero, he was actually the first career military man to be elected president.

Left: A colored lithograph promoting Taylor as the people's choice for president to join the previous holders of the office, all arranged around him for added impetus. Part of his appeal lay in his unpretentious demeanor which had earned him the nickname 'Old Rough and Ready' – an epithet that struck a chord in the frontier nation that the United States was at the time.

Polk won the 1844 election and set out to fulfill his promise to expand American territory. He compromised with Britain by agreeing to split Oregon at the 49th parallel and tried unsuccessfully to buy California from Mexico. The United States and Mexico were already squabbling over Mexico's refusal to accept the recent American annexation of Texas, a former Mexican possession. In 1846, after Polk ordered American troops to occupy a disputed border area, war erupted between the two nations.

As he did in all executive matters, Polk closely supervised the war effort. In doing so, he set the important precedent that the president, even without personal military experience, has final control over American military operations. After winning the war in 1848, the US forced Mexico to cede the California territory (which comprises all or part of modern-day Arizona, California, Colorado, Nevada, New Mexico, Utah, and Wyoming). Polk also achieved his two other main goals as president, lowering the tariff and re-establishing an independent treasury.

Polk pledged when he accepted the nomination in 1844 that he would not run for re-election. He kept that promise, becoming the first president not to seek a second term. Exhausted by the long hours he kept as president, Polk retired to Tennessee after his term ended in March 1849.[14] He died of cholera just a few months later, on June 15.[15]

Left: A Brooks Brothers clothing advertisement depicting the home of Zachary Taylor near Baton Rouge as part of their series about historic American mansions.

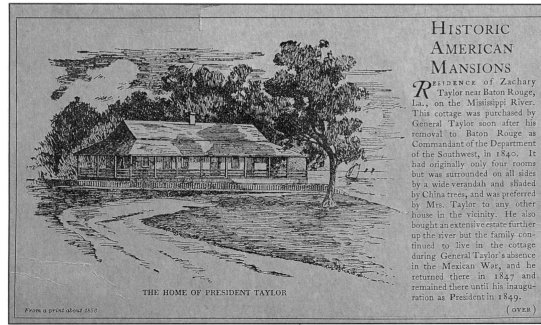

HISTORIC AMERICAN MANSIONS

RESIDENCE of Zachary Taylor near Baton Rouge, La., on the Mississippi River. This cottage was purchased by General Taylor soon after his removal to Baton Rouge as Commandant of the Department of the Southwest, in 1840. It had originally only four rooms but was surrounded on all sides by a wide verandah and shaded by China trees, and was preferred by Mrs. Taylor to any other house in the vicinity. He also bought an extensive estate further up the river but the family continued to live in the cottage during General Taylor's absence in the Mexican War, and he returned there in 1847 and remained there until his inauguration as President in 1849.

THE HOME OF PRESIDENT TAYLOR

From a print about 1856

(OVER)

ZACHARY TAYLOR

Zachary Taylor gained national fame as a general during the Mexican War. Nicknamed 'Old Rough and Ready' by his troops because of his unpretentious demeanor, Taylor parlayed his popular standing into a winning campaign for president.

Taylor was born in Orange County, Virginia, on November 24, 1784, but his family moved to the Kentucky frontier when he was an infant.[16] The little schooling he received there came from tutors. Taylor began a military career in 1808 and spent the next several decades fighting American Indians during the War of 1812, the Black Hawk War, and in Florida. In 1838 he reached the rank of general.

As war with Mexico loomed in 1846, Taylor was ordered to the Rio Grande with about 4,000 troops. The Mexicans attacked, war was declared, and Taylor led his men in a series of victorious battles. Taylor seemed poised to lead the invasion of Mexico City, but President Polk – apparently hoping to deny glory to the Whig general – gave the job to a fellow Democrat, General Winfield Scott, instead.[17] Taylor still achieved glory, however, in the stunning defeat of a much larger Mexican force led by General Santa Anna at the Battle of Buena Vista in 1847.

Taylor's military heroics made him an irresistible presidential nominee for the Whig Party in 1848. The Democrats nominated Senator Lewis Cass of Michigan. Fierce public debate focused on the issue of slavery, especially whether slavery should be permitted in territories acquired as a result of the Mexican War. Taylor was noncommittal, but his background as a Southerner and a slave-owner won him many Southern votes while his military experience made him attractive in all regions of the country. Martin Van Buren's entry into the race as the candidate of the Free Soil Party, which wanted to ban slavery in newly acquired territories, drew votes away from Cass, and Taylor won the election.[18]

As president, Taylor opposed the extension of slavery and fought a measure in Congress (which later became the Compromise of 1850) that sought a middle ground on the issue. He also rejected the idea that states could secede from the Union and threatened to use force if necessary to preserve it. The slavery debate was still raging when Taylor died suddenly on July 9, 1850, after only 16 months in office.[19]

MILLARD FILLMORE

Elected vice president as Zachary Taylor's running mate, Millard Fillmore assumed the presidency upon Taylor's death. As president, Fillmore reversed Taylor's policy and worked for passage of the Compromise of 1850, a series of laws that helped postpone civil war for a decade.

Fillmore was born in a log cabin in Cayuga County, New York, on January 7, 1800. Helping his father work the family's rented farm, he received little formal education as a boy. Apprenticed to a clothmaker at age 14, Fillmore attended a one-room school when he could. With the help of his teacher, whom he later married, Fillmore continued his education and became a lawyer at age 23. Good-natured and outgoing, he entered politics and served three one-year terms in the New York legislature.

In 1830 Fillmore opened a law practice in Buffalo, New York. There he helped organize the local Whig Party and got elected to the US House of Representatives, serving from 1833 to 1835 and 1837 to 1843. He retired from Congress and ran, unsuccessfully, for governor of New York. In 1847 Fillmore was elected Comptroller of New York, and served in that position until chosen as the Whigs' vice presidential nominee in 1848. Interestingly, Fillmore and Taylor did not meet each other until after the election.

The Compromise of 1850 was the leading issue of Fillmore's presidency. One controversial provision of the Compromise required the federal government to return runaway slaves to their masters. Fillmore's acceptance of this provision infuriated many Northern Whigs, who worked to deny him the party's presidential nomination in 1852. The Whig Party never recovered from its internal split over the Compromise of 1850; it

Above: **This metal campaign token, made in New York – his home base – depicts a bust view of Fillmore. He was the last Whig Party nominee to serve as president.**

soon began to disintegrate. Fillmore was the last president from the party.

Fillmore returned to Buffalo after his term.[20] He refused to join the emerging Republican Party, and in 1856 he ran unsuccessfully for president under the American Party (also called the Know Nothing Party) banner.[21] He died of a stroke on March 8, 1874.

Below: **President Fillmore in about 1850. During his term of office the issue of slavery really came to the fore, but the famous Compromise of 1850 only held the Union together temporarily.**

PIERCE

FRANKLIN PIERCE

Almost unknown outside his home state of New Hampshire before his presidential bid in 1852, Franklin Pierce served in the White House during a time of increasing tension between the North and South. Pierce tried to ease the sectional divisions, but he wound up exacerbating them.

Left: This image of Franklin Pierce was created by the Bureau of Engraving and Printing. Civil war moved a step closer during his term as a result of the Kansas-Nebraska Act. Interestingly, he always pronounced his name 'Purse.'

Pierce was born on November 23, 1804, in Hillsboro, New Hampshire. His father was a Revolutionary War veteran who had later served two terms as governor of New Hampshire. In 1824 Pierce graduated from Bowdoin College. There he had become close friends with classmate Nathaniel Hawthorne, who later wrote a flattering biography of Pierce to boost his presidential campaign. Pierce studied law and entered politics as a Democrat.

The good-looking and affable Pierce enjoyed a rapid political rise. Entering the New Hampshire legislature in 1829, he became its speaker only two years later. Pierce then went to Congress, serving in the House from 1833 to 1837 and in the Senate from 1837 to 1842. Pierce resigned from the Senate in 1842, hoping to earn more money and satisfy his wife's desire to return to New Hampshire. He opened a law practice in Concord, New Hampshire, but remained active in party affairs.

Soon after the start of the Mexican War, President Polk commissioned Pierce as a colonel in the army. Quickly promoted to general, Pierce served under General Winfield Scott on the march to Mexico City.[22] He resumed both his law practice and his prominent place in New Hampshire Democratic politics after the war.

Four strong candidates vied for the 1852 Democratic presidential nomination, including two who would be nominated in future elections: James Buchanan (1856) and Stephen Douglas (1860). Lewis Cass and William L. Marcy also competed for the 1852 nomination. None had enough support to win the nomination, however, so the convention chose Pierce as a compromise candidate. Pierce was undoubtedly a dark horse nominee, as James K. Polk had been eight years earlier, but Democrats embraced him with this slogan: 'We Polked you in 1844; we shall Pierce you in 1852!'[23]

Both Pierce and his Whig opponent, Mexican War hero General Winfield Scott endorsed the Compromise of 1850. Pierce, a Northerner who sympathized with the South, had more appeal nationally and won the election. Two months before taking office, Pierce's only surviving child, 11 year-old Benjamin, died in a train wreck before his parents' eyes. Pierce and his wife thus entered the White House exhausted and grief-stricken.[24]

As president, Pierce's most fateful move was to support the Kansas-Nebraska Act of 1854, which allowed settlers in the newly organized territories of Kansas and Nebraska to decide for themselves whether to allow slavery.[25] The measure's sponsor, Senator Stephen Douglas of Illinois, believed it would encourage settlement of the West and thereby facilitate the construction of a transcontinental railway. Instead, the law destroyed the uneasy truce between the North and South and

Below: Pierce's birthplace at Hillsborough, New Hampshire, depicted in 1854, 50 years after his birth. His was a well known New England family with his father serving twice as state governor.

Above: An attractive, hand-tinted broadside of President Franklin Pierce and his predecessors, printed by Charles Magnus of New York. As such it is a typical, patriotic symbol of the mid-19th century period.

prompted a violent struggle between pro-slavery and anti-slavery settlers for control of Kansas.[26]

The disastrous consequences of the Kansas-Nebraska Act ruined Pierce's political career. The Democratic Party refused to renominate him in 1856. He remained a controversial figure in retirement, and during the Civil War he harshly criticized the politics of Abraham Lincoln. Pierce died in Concord, New Hampshire, on October 8, 1869.

Notes

1. The exact site of his birth is still disputed, although Jackson believed that he was born on the South Carolina side of the border.

2. Jackson proudly recalled how he had been selected, at age nine, to read the newly-arrived Declaration of Independence to a group of illiterate frontiersmen.

3. One long-time resident of Salisbury described Jackson as 'the most roaring, rollicking, game-cocking, horse-racing, card-playing, mischievous fellow that ever lived in Salisbury (Boller, 1981: 73).

4. They married after Rachel's divorce became final, but she was still wounded by talk of her adultery.

5. Jackson exchanged gunfire with John Sevier, then governor of Tennessee, in 1803, and killed Nashville lawyer Charles Dickinson three years later in a duel in which Jackson was also seriously wounded.

6. The term comes from the Roman adage, 'To the victor go the spoils of the enemy.' Jackson believed that rotating government workers made a more democratic system. But he actually replaced less than 20 percent of federal workers during his two terms in office.

7. Freidel, 1977:62.

8. Van Buren was the first president born as an American citizen.

9. The Democrats could not agree on a vice presidential nominee, so Van Buren ran without one – the only

presidential candidate in history to do so.

10. Democrats in 1840 used the phrase 'O.K.' to express support for Van Buren, whose nickname was 'Old Kinderhook,' and thereby helped popularize the slang expression.

11. Secretary of State Daniel Webster did not resign.

12. Tyler's first wife, Letitia, was incapacitated by a stroke in 1839. She lived as an invalid in the White House until her death in 1842. From his two marriages, Tyler had 14 children live to maturity – more than any other president.

13. Benjamin Disraeli used the phrase 'dark horse' in his 1831 novel to refer to an actual horse. The term probably first took on a political connotation after Polk's election. (Safire, 1993:166-67).

14. Polk reportedly once boasted that he was the 'hardest-working man in this country.' (Voss, 1991:30).

15. Polk's retirement, barely three months, was the shortest of any president's.

16. Among Taylor's numerous cousins were James Madison and Robert E. Lee.

17. Taylor and Scott had quite different personalities. Taylor was informal and unconcerned with his appearance or military protocol; Scott was such the opposite that he was nicknamed 'Old Fuss and Feathers.'

18. The presidential election of 1848 was the first in which voting took place in all the states on the same day.

19. In 1991 experts exhumed Taylor's body to test a theory

that he had been assassinated by poisoning. They judged that he died of natural causes.

20. During a 1855 visit to Britain, Fillmore declined an honorary degree from Oxford University, modestly saying that he did not deserve the honor. He remarked: 'I have not the advantage of a classical education, and no man should, in my judgment, accept a degree he cannot read.' (Boller, 1981:112).

21. The party, called 'know nothing' because members refused to discuss its activities with outsiders, opposed immigration and proposed anti-Catholic measures.

22. En route to Mexico City, Pierce injured his knee in a fall from his horse. When he later aggravated the injury just prior to a battle, he fainted from the pain and lay on the ground until the battle was over. Political foes later claimed that the incident revealed Pierce's cowardice.

23. DeGregorio, 1993: 202.

24. Pierce's wife, Jane, did not attend the inauguration and remained in seclusion upstairs in the White House for almost two years.

25. The notion that the people of a territory should decide whether to allow slavery there was known as 'popular sovereignty.' Senator Stephen Douglas and other advocates thought the approach might ease the national crisis over slavery by devolving the decisions on its expansion to the territories

26. It was clear from the beginning that Nebraska would choose not to allow slavery.

Mark Byrnes

8

THE CIVIL WAR PRESIDENTS

James Buchanan	1857-1861
Abraham Lincoln	1861-1865
Andrew Johnson	1865-1869

The Civil War tore the new republic asunder.
The first president of this era, Buchanan, failed by
refusing to lead. The era's last president, Johnson,
failed by pushing too hard. But in between
was Lincoln, heretofore undistinguished, but once
in office, history's greatest president
and the savior of the Union.

President Andrew Johnson and other dignitaries watch as the main
Union forces review for the last time along Pennsylvania Avenue in May 1865.

Sectional conflict engulfed the nation, and its presidents, from 1857 to 1869. James Buchanan tried ineffectually to avert the war. Abraham Lincoln presided over the Union war effort and, in the process, greatly stretched the powers of his office. Andrew Johnson battled political enemies in Congress over how to reconstruct the nation after the war. Although the powers and naitonal role of the presidency swelled during the Civil War, after it the institution declined in influence and remained diminished for several decades.

JAMES BUCHANAN

James Buchanan served as president during the tumultuous years just before the Civil War. Despite his considerable political experience, he failed to avert the coming disaster.

Buchanan was born in a log cabin at Cove Gap, Pennsylvania, on April 23, 1791. As a boy he worked in his father's store and also received a good education. He graduated from Dickinson College in 1809 and then studied law in Lancaster, Pennsylvania. Buchanan entered politics as a supporter of the Federalist Party.

Initially opposed to the War of 1812, Buchanan volunteered for duty after the British burned Washington, D.C., in 1814. After brief military service, he served in the Pennsylvania legislature from 1814 to 1816. He retired from politics in 1816, but, after an unhappy romance,[1] returned in 1821 and was elected to the US House of Representatives. While there, Buchanan gravitated to the Democratic Party and became a supporter of Andrew Jackson.

Jackson rewarded Buchanan by making him minister to Russia in 1832. After two successful years, he returned to America and became a US senator for Pennsylvania. He served in the Senate until 1845, when James K. Polk appointed him as secretary of state. Buchanan held that position during a time of great territorial expansion for the United States.[2] He left public office in 1849 when the Whig Party took over the presidency.

Buchanan sought the 1852 Democratic presidential nomination but lost it to Franklin Pierce, who later appointed him minister to Great Britain. Working in London, Buchanan missed the controversy over the Kansas–Nebraska Act that politically wounded many Democrats, including Pierce.

Buchanan returned home and won the 1856 Democratic nomination for president. Promising to work for conciliation between the North and South, Buchanan defeated Republican John C. Fremont and 'Know Nothing' Party candidate Millard Fillmore in the presidential election.

As president, Buchanan walked a tightrope in trying to appease both the North and the South. Many people thought, however, that he actually favored the South. Buchanan personally opposed slavery but did not think it could be legally abolished under the Constitution. He also endorsed the Supreme Court's *Dred Scott* decision of 1857, which ruled that Congress lacked the authority to outlaw slavery in the territories, and supported admitting Kansas to the union as a slave sate. Sectional tensions continued to rise.

Despite the stormy politics of the time, White House social life glittered during the Buchanan administration. Buchanan's niece, Harriet Lane, presided as hostess – Buchanan being the only president never to marry.

By 1860 the Democratic Party had divided

Above: A steel engraving of James Buchanan, the only bachelor president in the history of the United States (to date) and one of the oldest ever elected. He was slow to grasp the realities of sectionalism and the growing signs of confrontation.

Right: This signature of Buchanan's on an envelope is prefaced by the word 'Free.' The president and other political officers had the privilege of a free mail service by the use of such a signature, or 'free frank.'

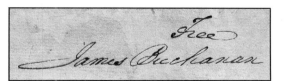

into Northern and Southern wings over the slavery issue; neither wing wanted to nominate Buchanan for president.

The Democratic cleavage sealed the election of Republican Abraham Lincoln, whose views on slavery made him anathema to the South. In response to Lincoln's victory, South Carolina seceded from the Union in December 1860 and was quickly followed by six other states.

Buchanan, still president when secession began, denied that states had the right to secede but believed that the federal government had no legal power to stop them. His proposed compromises went nowhere, and matters were at a stalemate when he turned over the presidency to his

successor. Obviously relieved, Buchanan told Lincoln, 'If you are as happy on entering . . . this house as I am in leaving it, you are the happiest man in the country.'[3]

Buchanan retired to his Pennsylvania mansion, where he strongly supported the Union and President Lincoln. He also wrote a book defending the policies of his own administration. Buchanan died on June 1, 1868.

ABRAHAM LINCOLN

Abraham Lincoln became president at the moment of his country's worst crisis. As he left Illinois to travel to his inauguration, Lincoln described the task facing him as 'greater than that which rested upon [George] Washington.'[4] At the time, many Americans wondered whether Lincoln was up to the job. Today most scholars rank him as America's greatest president.

Lincoln was born on February 12, 1809, in a log cabin near Hodgenville, Kentucky. His father, Thomas Lincoln, was a farmer and carpenter. His mother was Nancy Hanks Lincoln. At age seven, Abraham moved with his family to Spencer County, Indiana, where he helped his father build the family's log cabin. Abraham did farm chores and received only a sporadic education,[5] yet he read voraciously when given the opportunity.

In 1818, when Abraham was nine years old, his mother died. A year later his father remarried. Abraham took an immediate liking to his stepmother, Sarah Bush Johnston Lincoln. He grew to be a tall young man who loved to tell stories and jokes. Throughout his youth, Lincoln worked on his father's farm and occasionally was hired out to neighbors. He could skillfully wield an ax to split logs for fence posts – an attribute later highlighted in his campaign for president.

When Lincoln was 21, his family moved to Illinois. A year later, he moved on his own to New Salem, Illinois, where he worked as a clerk in a general store. He served briefly in the army during the 1832 Black Hawk War, but he saw no fighting.[6] Upon his return home he was

Right: The inauguration of Abraham Lincoln on March 4, 1861. He spelt out in no uncertain terms in his address the dangers to the South of their seceding and where blame for war would lie.

Above: A collection of objects all connected with President Abraham Lincoln. This beautiful dessert plate (left) is part of Lincoln's White House china. It was made by Hariland in Limoges, France. The tin poncet box (top right) was used on Lincoln's desk, as was the brass call bell (right, center) to summon people into his office. The Swiss-made gold watch was presented by him to a friend, US Marshal Ward H. Lamon. The gold chain is made from nuggets mined in California in 1849.

appointed New Salem's postmaster and also became a partner in a general store. The store soon failed, but Lincoln's perseverance in paying off his debts from that enterprise helped earn him the nickname 'Honest Abe.'

In 1834 Lincoln won election as a Whig to the Illinois state legislature, where he served eight years. He quickly demonstrated skill in debate and public speaking. Lincoln also studied law during this period. He received his law license in 1836 and moved to Springfield, the capital of Illinois, the next year. He practiced in two different partnerships before joining with William H. Herndon in 1844. That partnership was never formally dissolved. Lincoln became a highly successful lawyer and handled cases throughout much of Illinois.

In Springfield, Lincoln met and courted Mary Todd, a southern belle from a well-to-do family in Lexington, Kentucky, who was living with her sister in Springfield. After a stormy courtship, Lincoln and Mary married on November 4, 1842. The Lincolns had four sons, only one of whom (Robert) lived to adulthood. The couple apparently had a loving relationship, but Mary increasingly suffered from mental instability. The pressures of the White House exacerbated

Above: The nickname 'Honest Abe' was not just a campaign innovation but something attached to Lincoln earlier in life. This political banner was intended to be suspended from a building.

Below: Physically, Lincoln has always been described in far from generous terms, but his unattractiveness – tall, long-necked, and with a gaunt, bony face – was more than outweighed by his inner qualities. Significantly, the words he uttered, which still ring so powerfully today, were carefully crafted in his own hand.

her problems, adding to Lincoln's woes.[7]

Lincoln was elected to the US House in 1846. He found serving in the House unsatisfying, however, and did not seek re-election. Lincoln returned to Illinois in 1849 and resumed his legal career. He prospered and became one of the best known lawyers in the state.

The growing national controversy over slavery in the 1850s propelled Lincoln back into politics. Although he did not advocate abolishing slavery where it already existed, Lincoln regarded it as a moral evil and strongly opposed its extension into new territories. He therefore denounced the theory of popular sovereignty, which held that the people of a territory should decide whether slavery would be permitted there. In 1856 Lincoln joined the new Republican Party, which opposed slavery.

In 1858 the Illinois Republican Party nominated Lincoln to run for the Senate against incumbent Senator Stephen A. Douglas, the leading advocate of popular sovereignty. Lincoln accepted the nomination with a prophetic speech: 'A house divided against itself cannot stand. I believe this government cannot endure, permanently half slave and half free.'[8]

Lincoln and Douglas argued the slavery issue in a series of seven debates across Illinois. Douglas defended popular sovereignty while Lincoln opposed the extension of slavery under any circumstances and condemned slavery as 'a moral, social and political evil.'[9] Lincoln lost the close election[10] but emerged as a national figure because of the highly publicized debates. In early 1860 he delivered a speech at Cooper Union in New York City that further impressed Republicans. The audience cheered Lincoln's

Left: This parade torch was used during Lincoln's 1860 campaign at Chattanooga, Tennessee. The tin canister can hold combustible material and is mounted with a wick.

Above: This 2nd Model Burnside Carbine, serial number 593, was presented by Lincoln to the Governor of Kentucky for his efforts to preserve the Union. A plaque (right) on the obverse butt bears an engraving to this effect.

conclusion: 'Let us have faith that right makes might, and in that faith, let us, to the end, dare to do our duty as we understand it.'[11]

The Republican Party nominated Lincoln for president in 1860. The Democratic Party split into two factions; Northern Democrats nominated Stephen A. Douglas while Southern Democrats nominated John C. Breckinridge of Kentucky, the sitting vice president. A fourth party, the Constitutional Union Party, nominated former senator John Bell of Tennessee.

Lincoln won just 40 percent of the popular vote but easily carried the electoral college.

Between Lincoln's election and his inauguration, seven Southern states seceded from the Union (four more followed later) and formed the Confederate States of America. In his inaugural speech, Lincoln declared that although he would use force if necessary to 'hold, occupy, and possess' federal property in the South, he hoped war would be avoided. He told Southerners, 'In your hands, my dissatisfied fellow countrymen, and

not in mine, is the momentous issue of civil war. The government will not assail you. You can have no conflict, without being yourselves the aggressors.'[12]

Tragically, the war came. On April 12, 1861, Confederate forces fired on the federal Fort

Below: President Lincoln discussing a draft of the Emancipation Proclamation with his cabinet. This war measure affected slaves only in areas under Confederate control.

Sumter in South Carolina's Charleston harbor. Congress was not in session, but Lincoln immediately increased the size of the military, ordered a blockade of Southern ports, and suspended the writ of habeas corpus.[13] With these and other decisions, Lincoln stretched to the utmost his powers as commander-in-chief. Critics charged that some of Lincoln's actions exceeded the president's constitutional authority – a charge that Lincoln admitted. He argued that the extraordinary circumstances demanded extraordinary action from the president.

At the outset, both the North and the South expected to win the war quickly. Instead it dragged on for four bloody years, costing more American lives than any other conflict. The North was shocked to lose the war's first major clash, the Battle of Bull Run, in July 1861.[14] After the defeat, Lincoln placed General George B. McClellan in command to reorganize the Union army. McClellan proved to be an excellent organizer but a reluctant fighter. Union forces in the West led by General Ulysses S. Grant were more active and more successful.

Although he detested slavery, Lincoln's overriding goal in the war was always the preservation of the Union. 'What I do about slavery, and the colored race, I do because I believe it helps to save the Union,' he wrote.[15] Lincoln feared any attempt to abolish slavery completely would cost him the crucial support of the border states.[16] By the summer of 1862, however, Lincoln decided to issue the Emancipation Proclamation to boost Northern morale and win support from abroad. The decree stipulated that slaves living in areas still in rebellion on January 1, 1863, would be free.[17]

On July 4, 1863 the Union won two major military victories at Vicksburg, Mississippi, and

Above: Lincoln at Antietam (or Sharpsburg) in September 1862. The Union victory saved the federal capital and a relieved Lincoln issued a preliminary Emancipation Proclamation.

Below: This double-wicked parade torch is made of pressed tin and was used in Lincoln's campaign in 1860. The term 'wide awake' torch came from the campaign slogan used by the Republicans.

Below: These mourning badges are made of black fabric backing affixed to various images of the assassinated president. They were usually worn on the lapel of the coat.

Above: The procession entering the grounds for the dedication of the Gettysburg National Cemetery on November 19, 1863. The distinctive batons, scarves, and tall silk hats identify the marshals in the crowd scene.

Gettysburg, Pennsylvania. Later that year, in ceremonies dedicating a cemetery on the Gettysburg battlefield, Lincoln gave one of the greatest speeches in American history.[18] Only about two minutes long, the Gettysburg Address simply and eloquently honored the men who had died and linked their sacrifice to the cause of human freedom.[19] Lincoln ended by expressing his faith that 'this nation, under God, shall have a new birth of freedom – and that government of the people, by the people, for the people, shall not perish from the earth.'[20]

Despite the major Union victories in 1863, the war dragged on. In 1864 Lincoln placed Grant, a general known for his willingness to fight, in charge of all Union armies. Grant and his troops began to move on the Confederate capital of Richmond, Virginia, and, in a series of battles, encountered Confederate forces led by General Robert E. Lee. Meanwhile, Union General William Tecumseh Sherman captured the city of Atlanta and proceeded to Savannah, Georgia, on his destructive 'march to the sea.'

Lincoln was determined that the presidential election of 1864 should not be postponed.

Left: This ebony cane, with a silver cap engraved 'A. Lincoln,' was found in the box at Ford's Theatre where the president was assassinated. The silk rosette with tassel is from Lincoln's coffin cover and was given to Miss Harriet Sterling of Cleveland, Ohio, on April 28, 1865.

America thus became the first nation in history to hold a national election during a civil war. The Republicans nominated Lincoln for president and Andrew Johnson of Tennessee, a leading pro-Union Democrat, for vice president.[21] The Democrats nominated former Union general George B. McClellan, whom Lincoln had removed from command, for president.

Lincoln's prospects for re-election appeared slim throughout much of 1864. He wrote that 'it seems exceedingly probably that this administration will not be reelected.'[22] Many Northerners complained that the war was taking too long and condemned General Grant, whose forces had suffered heavy casualties, as a butcher. The outlook for Lincoln brightened, however, after a string of Union military victories, including Sherman's capture of Atlanta. Lincoln won the election with 55 percent of the popular vote.

Below: This marble-topped, two-tiered mahogany table was used by President Lincoln to serve iced water in the cabinet room of the White House. He refused to serve hard liquor.

Above: Lincoln delivering the Gettysburg Address, one of the most famous of all political speeches, but not so readily appreciated at the time. It is notable for its brevity – just ten sentences long and taking two minutes to deliver, its short and direct nature must have been a relief to a crowd that had listened to Edward Everett for two hours.

The Union army began to grind down the Confederates, and by the time of Lincoln's second inauguration on March 4, 1865, the end of the war was in sight. Lincoln began to consider how best to reconstruct the Union. Although many in Congress opposed him, he envisioned a process that would be fairly lenient toward the

Below: This gem-sized tint mounted on card and surrounded by a mourning wreath is typical of the popular observances sold commercially at the time of the president's death for family albums.

Above: The Petersen House opposite Ford's Theatre. Lincoln, shot in the head behind the ear, lay dying here on the night of April 14, 1865, and died the next morning, surrounded by his family and members of the cabinet. His assassin, John Wilkes Booth, was a well known actor who saw Lincoln as the source of the South's problems and had planned with other conspirators since 1864 to kidnap him – the plan escalating to murder after a kidnap attempt failed. At left are Booth's carte de visite and a ticket from that night's theater performance – *Our American Cousin*, a comedy.

South. Lincoln expressed his hopes in his second inaugural address:

> With malice toward none, with charity for all, with firmness in the right as God gives us to see the right, let us strive on to finish the work we are in, to bind up the nation's wounds, to care for him who shall have borne the battle and for his widow and his orphan, to do all which may achieve and cherish a just and lasting peace among ourselves and with all nations.[23]

Managing the Union war effort exhausted Lincoln. His staff was small and he worked endless hours. He wrote letters and speeches, made numerous political and military appointments, toured army hospitals, and, during certain times each week, saw anyone who wanted to see him. The immense pressure of the war made it difficult for Lincoln to sleep or relax, and he suffered frequent bouts of depression. Through it all, however, Lincoln managed to retain his compassion and his sense of humor.

On April 9, 1865, Lee surrendered to Grant at Appomattox Court House, Virginia, bringing the Civil War to an end. Five nights later, while Lincoln was watching a play at Ford's Theater in Washington, the well-known actor and Confederate sympathizer John Wilkes Booth shot and killed him.[24] The nation mourned deeply as a train carried Lincoln's body home to Springfield for burial. Although frequently criticized in life, in death Abraham Lincoln underwent a near apotheosis.

Below: The burden of having to replace the nation's assassinated political leader was greatly increased in the aftermath of the Civil War, and the onerous task fell to Andrew Johnson.

Above: Lincoln lying in state on a bier, his coffin flanked by a uniformed guard of honor, prior to his body being transported to the place of burial in Springfield, Illinois.

ANDREW JOHNSON

Thrust into the presidency by the assassination of Abraham Lincoln, Andrew Johnson faced the politically volatile question of how to reconstruct the Union after the Civil War. He fought bitterly with Congress and was the only president ever to be impeached.

Johnson was born in Raleigh, North Carolina, on December 29, 1808. His father's death in 1812 left the already impoverished family even poorer.[25] Johnson received no formal education and became an apprentice to a tailor at age 13. After two years of his scheduled six-year apprenticeship, Johnson ran away from his master. He earned money by tailoring in the Carolinas before moving in 1826 to Greenville, Tennessee, where he opened his own tailor's shop.

The next year Johnson married Eliza McCardle, who taught him to write and do basic math and encouraged him to improve his reading. Johnson worked hard and prospered as a tailor. He soon entered local Democratic politics and became a rousing stump speaker. Taking Andrew Jackson as his model, Johnson championed the common man and attacked the wealthy planters who dominated Tennessee politics.

Beginning in 1828, Johnson won election to a series of offices: alderman and then mayor of Greenville, state representative and senator, and US representative. He served as governor of Tennessee from 1853 to 1857 and as US senator from 1857 to 1862. In Congress Johnson vigorously advocated the Homestead Act, finally passed in 1862, which granted free frontier land to poor settlers.

Although Johnson believed that the Constitution protected the institution of slavery, he also fiercely opposed secession – even after

Above: Andrew Johnson has the dubious distinction of being the only president ever to be impeached. This contemporary sketch depicts the vote being taken in the Senate chamber on May 16, 1868. Senator Ross of Kansas is voting 'not guilty,' thereby helping Johnson to acquittal by 35 to 19, one vote short of the two-thirds required.

PRESIDENT ANDREW JOHNSON

Above: The carte de visite of Andrew Johnson plus three gallery tickets to the Senate impeachment trial. Despite the ordeal he later served, albeit briefly, as a senator, the only former president, to date, to do so.

Tennessee left the Union in 1861.[26] The only Southern senator to reject the Confederacy and remain in the Senate after his state seceded, Johnson was glorified in the North but reviled as a traitor in the South. Many Tennesseans hung him in effigy. In March 1862 President Lincoln appointed Johnson military governor of Tennessee, part of which the Union army had captured by that time.

As military governor, Johnson sought to restore federal authority in Tennessee and to maintain order until civil government resumed. He required officeholders and voters to pledge loyalty to the Union and took other measures to expunge Confederate influence from the state.

At Lincoln's urging, the Republicans chose Johnson to balance the 1864 ticket as Lincoln's vice presidential running mate. The two swept to victory, and Johnson was inaugurated as vice president on March 4, 1865.[27] On April 14 Lincoln was assassinated; Johnson took the presidential oath the next day at the hotel where he had been staying.

The Civil War had ended just days before Lincoln's death, but Johnson still faced the daunting prospect of reconstructing the Union. Lincoln had planned to bring the Southern states back into the Union quickly and with few restrictions. Johnson sought to implement such a

Left: Reconstruction was a difficult policy to see through and assessing it is still a topic of debate. Johnson was accused of being too lenient to those who had started the war and unsympathetic to the aspirations of black Americans. He vetoed many measures and it took a Radical Republican Congress to override his veto in order to enact a more far-reaching Reconstruction rather than merely a restoration of the South to the union.

plan, but encountered stiff resistance from some Republican members of Congress, called 'Radical Republicans,' who demanded more severe terms of reconstruction. This disagreement set the stage for a rancorous political battle between Johnson and Congress.

Led by the Radical Republicans, Congress tried to replace many of Johnson's reconstruction policies with harsher ones of its own. Johnson vetoed many of those bills, further infuriating his opponents. Congress overrode some of the vetoes and also passed some laws to restrict the power of the president. Johnson challenged one such law, the Tenure of Office Act,[28] when he fired Secretary of War Edwin Stanton. Congress then initiated impeachment proceedings against Johnson.

On February 24, 1868, the House of Representatives voted to impeach Johnson. The politically motivated charges did not stand up in the subsequent Senate trial, and Johnson was acquitted – although by only a one-vote margin.[29] The outcome established the precedent that the impeachment process should be used only when a president abuses the powers of the office – not merely when he is unpopular in Congress.

Johnson held on to the presidency, but lost most of his political strength. After unsuccessfully seeking the Democratic nomination for president in 1868, he returned to Tennessee. There he failed in races for the US House in 1871 and the Senate in 1872. He finally won election to the Senate in 1875, but served only a few months before his death on July 31, 1875.[30] Johnson was the only former president to serve in the Senate.

Notes

1 In 1819 Buchanan became engaged to Ann Coleman. The couple had a disagreement, however, and Ann went to stay with relatives in Philadelphia. She died suddenly there; rumor said she committed suicide.

2 Buchanan's role was somewhat limited since Polk oversaw most details himself.

3 Voss, 1991: 39.

4 Anderson, 1970: 207

5 Lincoln later estimated that altogether he received about one year of formal education. As a result, Lincoln said, 'When I came of age I did not know much.' Freidel, 1977: 100.

6 The men of Lincoln's company elected him captain – an early indication of his leadership ability.

7 Some people incorrectly suspected Mrs Lincoln of secretly supporting the Confederacy because she came from the South and had several relatives who served in the Confederate Army.

8 Anderson, 1970: 135.

9 Freidel, 1977: 103.

10 At that time a state's US senators were chosen by the state legislature.

11 Anderson, 1970: 196.

12 Anderson, 1970: 216.

13 This step enabled Union officials to imprison suspected Southern sympathizers without bringing formal charges against them.

14 Especially surprised were the civilians – many carrying

picnic baskets – from Washington, D.C. who had gone to observe the battle expecting an easy Union victory.

15 Anderson, 1970: 227.

16 The border states – Missouri, Kentucky, Maryland, and Delaware – allowed slavery but had stayed loyal to the Union.

17 In reality, the proclamation freed no slaves immediately since it could not be enforced in areas still controlled by the Confederacy.

18 Lincoln initially thought the speech was a flop. He told a friend, 'That speech won't scour. It's a flat failure.' Ward, 1991: 262.

19 The commonly told story that Lincoln scratched out the speech on the train to Gettysburg is untrue; he carefully prepared it.

20 Anderson, 1970: 249.

21 In 1864 the Republican Party called itself the National Union Party because it included some Democrats who supported Lincoln.

22 Anderson, 1970: 255.

23 Anderson, 1970: 269.

24 Booth and other Southern sympathizers had conspired to kill Lincoln, Vice President Johnson and Secretary of State William H. Seward. Seward was stabbed but recovered from his wounds; the attack on Johnson did not materialize. After the shooting, Booth fled to a barn in Virginia where federal troops shot him to death. Eight others were convicted of taking part in the conspiracy, and four of them were hanged.

25 Johnson's mother supported the family by sewing and taking in laundry.

26 Johnson's Greenville home was in mountainous east Tennessee, where pro-Union sentiment was strong.

27 Johnson embarrassed himself badly on inauguration day. Recovering from an attack of typhoid fever, Johnson took a few swigs of whiskey to fortify himself before his swearing-in ceremony. The whiskey, combined with his weakened condition and a stuffy Senate chamber, made Johnson tipsy, and his ensuing speech was incoherent. The incident left Johnson with a reputation as a drunkard.

28 This law required the president to get Senate permission before firing any official, including cabinet members, whose appointment required Senate confirmation. The law reversed the precedent established in George Washington's administration that the president could remove appointees on his own authority.

The Supreme Court declared the Tenure of Office Act unconstitutional in 1926.

29 A two-thirds majority was needed to convict Johnson and remove him from office. Seven courageous Republican senators bucked considerable political pressure and joined their Democratic colleagues in voting against President Johnson's conviction.

30 On his instructions, Johnson was buried with his body wrapped in an American flag and his head resting on a copy of the Constitution.

Stephen H. Wirls

9

THE 'GILDED' AGE

Ulysses S. Grant   1869-1877
Rutherford B. Hayes   1877-1881
James A. Garfield   1881
Chester A. Arthur   1881-1885
Grover Cleveland   1885-1889
Benjamin Harrison   1889-1893
Grover Cleveland   1893-1897
William McKinley   1897-1901

The typical president of a century ago offered better leadership
than the times and a recalcitrant Congress allowed. Nonetheless,
the leadership of these presidents, Democrats and Republicans alike,
set the stage for expanded presidential power in the 20th century.

The wreck of the USS *Maine* in Havana Harbor on February 16, 1898,
the day after the explosion. Two months later the Spanish-American War began.

The 'Gilded Age' is an era of forgotten presidents. Yet obscurity is not a fate that most of them deserve. Their task, to rescue the presidency from a domineering Congress, was not glamorous, but their victories and their virtues merit high praise. These presidents found the will and the weapons to recover the executive's equal constitutional status and leave the presidency on the doorstep of its modern era.

The battles between the Gilded Age presidents and Congress were fought in an atmosphere of social and political turmoil. The era was inaugurated by the first assassination of a president and concluded by the third. Despite being a 'golden age' of political parties, it was accompanied by astounding political corruption. Economically and politically, the life of the nation was transformed by the process of industrialization and the laying of 140,000 new miles of railroad. Emerging from the Civil War, the nation wondered if it could ever again be made whole; yet by 1901 it was ruling a country, the Philippines, on the other side of the world. The moral rent between North and South over slavery was replaced by social and economic conflicts between the industrial East and the agrarian West. Reconstruction's noble mission to aid emancipated blacks was replaced by the brutal and demeaning tyranny of racial segregation.

ULYSSES S. GRANT

The abject state of the presidency can be traced back to the battles between President Andrew Johnson and congressional Radicals, who declared war on the president and his office. However, the significance of Johnson's narrow escape from being removed by impeachment is often exaggerated. A conviction probably would have had only a minor effect on the future of the

presidency. With the inevitable emergence of less fervent policy disputes, sounder politicians, and favorable public opinion, the office would have recovered as it did, albeit in fits and starts.

That recovery was to have begun with the next president. The Republican Party's inevitable choice was General Ulysses S. Grant, the most revered man of the day: 'To doubt Grant is to doubt Christ.'[1] Born Hiram Ulysses, Grant claimed later in life that he was 'more of a farmer than a soldier.'[2] Yet he displayed virtues as a soldier that were little evident in his other efforts as farmer, peddler, rent collector, shop clerk, and president of the United States.

Below: President Ulysses S. Grant photographed by Mathew Brady or an assistant in about 1870. The photographic plate was found by accident in a barn in New York state.

Below: This armchair, made of maple and with turned legs and a rush seat, was used by President Grant at the inaugural of his successor, Rutherford B. Hayes, in 1877.

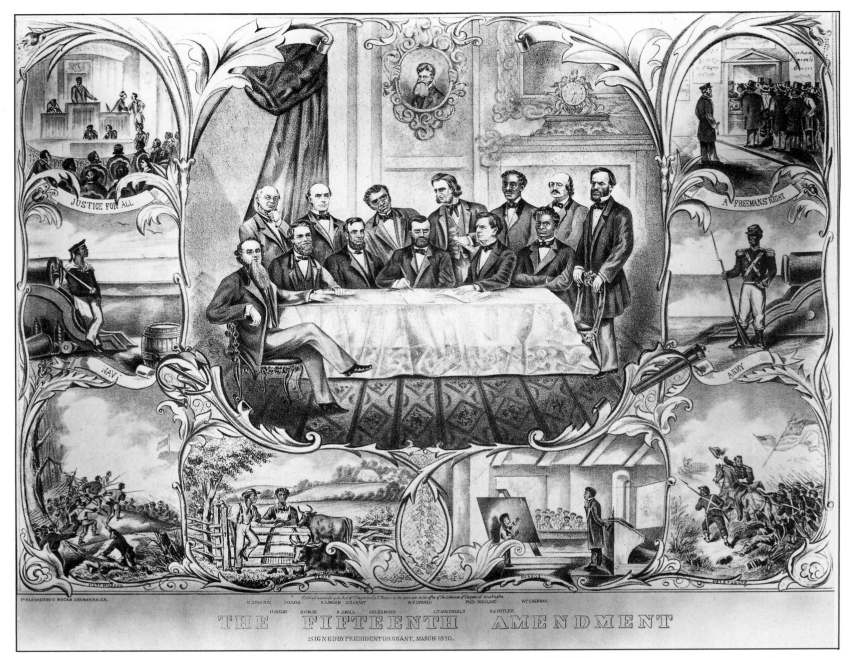

Above: A contemporary engraving, published in Savannah, Georgia, of the signing of the Fifteenth Amendment by President Grant in March 1870 that extended suffrage to male ex-slaves. He is flanked, symbolically, by Lincoln and Seward.

Many hoped and expected that this dogged warrior would be another Andrew Jackson, and Grant's presidency began forcefully. He refused to make any appointments until Congress repealed the Tenure of Office Act. This obnoxious statute had, in effect, give the Senate control of the executive branch. In the end, the Senate balked, and Grant wilted, accepting a bill that removed only some of the Act's intrusiveness. Moreover, there was no change in the arrogant pretensions of the Senate, and Grant considered it his duty to follow the advice of senators when making executive branch appointments.[3]

Treating his office as more honorific than political, Grant did not lead the nation. His mediocre cabinet was assembled without any particular course of action in mind. Grant was instead dominated by a 'kitchen' cabinet of

Right: A salad plate from 'The Flower Set,' a 587-piece service purchased from J.W. Boteler & Brother, Washington, D.C., for use by President Grant. The set was designed by the painter Lissac for a French company, Hariland & Co., in 1868.

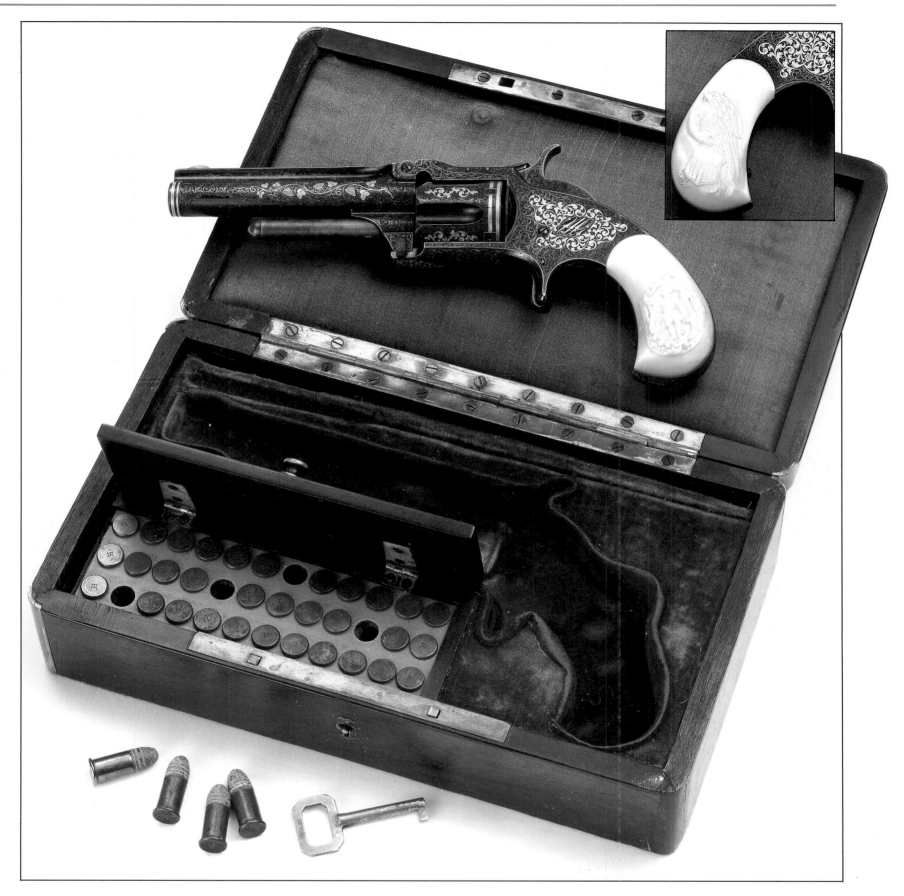

Above: This spectacular Smith and Wesson Model 1½ Second Issue Revolver was presented to President Grant by the manufacturer on August 1, 1870. The beautifully-cased pistol is factory engraved on both sides with gold inlay and has a carved pearl grip. The grip has different designs on either side (see inset American eagle). The case carries the initials 'USG' inlaid in gold on the left side of the frame.

powerful Republican senators, each with his own factional and personal concerns.[4]

Grant did propose reforms to improve the quality of federal administration, and he refused to spend funds appropriated for 'works of purely private and local interests, in no sense national.'[5] Yet these were mere skirmishes in this era of unconstrained profiteering and epidemic corruption. For example, railroad companies, using their control of routes and rates, regularly extorted favorable measures out of city councils and state legislatures. If this method failed, the needed votes could be purchased.[6] One of the more egregious scandals was the wholesale theft of federal distillery tax revenues by the 'Whiskey Ring.' Among its ranks were a number of federal officers, as well as Grant's own private secretary. Grant, loyal to the end, defended his secretary and pushed his Treasury Secretary, who was investigating the scandal, out of office.

Henry Adams neatly captured the sorry politics of this period.

While the Executive . . . resigns himself with the significant consolation that this is the people's government, and the people may accept the responsibility, the members of the lower house are equally ready with the excuse that they are not responsible for the action of Senators and the Senators, being responsible to no power under Heaven except their party organs, which they control, are able to obtain precisely what legislation answers their personal objects or their individual conception of the public good.[7]

RUTHERFORD B. HAYES

The corruption in and around the two Grant administrations had split the Republican Party, and the 1876 convention hoped that Rutherford B. Hayes would reunite it. Once in office, however, Hayes would earn the enmity of many Republican leaders for putting the presidency and the public good ahead of the interests of his party. But first he had to win one of the most bizarre presidential contests in the nation's history.

With a depressed economy and the national shame of corruption hanging around its shoulders, the Republican Party's prospects for victory in 1876 were bleak. Having nominated a proven reformer, Governor Samuel J. Tilden of New York, the Democrats waged a promising campaign, augmented by widespread and murderous intimidation of Southern Republican voters, both black and white.[8] For their part, the Republicans poured money into key states and once again 'waved the bloody shirt,' reminding the nation that the Democratic Party was the party of armed rebellion.[9] On election night, though, the Republican cause seemed to be lost.

Then General Dan Sickles, famous for shooting his wife's lover and having an affair with the deposed Queen of Spain, found a glimmer of hope in the returns. The Republicans rallied and sent their troops into three critical Southern states to make sure that the votes were counted in the right way. Particularly in Louisiana, a fair sum of money was spent persuading election boards and fending off Democratic attempts to buy them back.[10]

Below: A Republican campaign ribbon for the Hayes-Wheeler ticket during the controversial election of 1876. Made of silk, the ribbon was mass produced in Paterson, New Jersey.

After the dust settled, each of the three states submitted two sets of electoral votes. The ensuing constitutional and political crisis dragged on for months, and Congress eventually appointed an independent commission to resolve the ballot question. The Republicans, by chance, ended up with a one-vote edge on the commission, and the commissioners, voting along strict party lines, awarded Hayes a one-vote electoral college majority.[11] Hayes was, with some justification, dubbed 'His Fraudulency,' but the evidence suggests that, but for the Democratic intimidation of Southern Republicans, Hayes would have won outright.[12]

Even more controversial than Hayes's election was the change in the federal government's reconstruction policy offered by the Republicans in exchange for Democratic acquiescence to the commission's decisions. Southern Democrats sought, among other things, 'home rule': that is, withdrawal of the Federal troops supporting Reconstruction governments and enforcing the

Above: A portrait of Rutherford B. Hayes from an original negative made by Brady just prior to Hayes's inauguration as president. He announced in advance that he would serve only one term.

Fourteenth and Fifteenth Amendments to the Constitution. Republican leaders promised that Hayes would comply, and Hayes did withdraw the troops.[13]

Against the charge that Hayes callously traded the well-being of millions for the White House stands a life of earnestly moral concern for the welfare of Southern blacks. As an attorney before the Civil War, Hayes offered his legal services to defend fugitive slaves. He later joined the Republican Party and the Union army in order to combat slavery. After the war, Representative Hayes supported radical reconstruction in Congress, and Governor Hayes considered Ohio's ratification of the Fifteenth Amendment to be one of his two great achievements.[14] As president, however, Hayes had reasonable doubts

PRESIDENT RUTHERFORD B. HAYES

1. A top hat, typical of the president's attire, that was bought from W.B. Davis Co., Cleveland, Ohio.
2. Grand Army of the Republic cane with a cast head. Hayes was very active with veteran's groups after the civil war.
3. A silver-headed presentation cane. The head is engraved 'Presented to Gov. R.B. Hayes by W.H. Turner, USN, January 1, 1871.
4. Large porcelain serving platter depicting a vivid American turkey, made by Hariland & Co., Limoges, France.
5. Plate depicting a wolf howling at night, from a series by painter Theo R. Davis known as 'On the Plains at Night.'
6. Cup and saucer decorated with bamboo shoots, created by Theo R. Davis.
7. Oyster plate made by Hariland & Co., Limoges, France, and also painted by Theo R. Davis.
8. Flowered deep dish made by Hariland & Co., Limoges, France, and also painted by Theo R. Davis.
9. Cuff links belonging to President Hayes. Still in their original velvet case, the links were a gift from his wife, Lucy, and carry her image.

about the effectiveness of federal troops in securing social and political equality for Southern blacks. As an alternative, he worked for a revival of the Southern Republican Party and for an honorable Southern policy toward the voting rights of blacks.[15]

These efforts were futile. Southern whites united as Democrats and labored to disenfranchise blacks. Hayes's later calls for appropriations to protect black voting rights were ignored by a Democratic Congress. The experiment was, Hayes admitted in 1878, 'a failure' and a stain on an otherwise admirable administration.[16]

Hayes was far better prepared for the presidency than Grant. After one term in the House, he served as governor of Ohio from 1868 to 1872 and from 1875 until his inauguration as the nation's chief executive. At Harvard, where he studied law, Hayes had been a student of

Below: Reconstruction remained a central issue and the withdrawal of federal troops from the South appeared to indicate that Hayes's government no longer wished to enforce the constitutional amendments which were providing a measure of social and political equality for black citizens; in fact, he wished to create a strong Southern Republican bloc but failed.

Justice Joseph Story, the leading interpreter of the Constitution. Hayes now brought Story's lessons, fortified by self-confidence and integrity, to the beleaguered national office.[17]

Unlike Grant, Hayes was determined to run the executive branch. To do so required an assault on the custom of 'Senatorial courtesy': that is, if one senator objected to a particular nominee, the rest of the Senate would vote against confirmation. Presidents were left with a choice between bowing to senators' wishes or working without a cabinet.[18]

Hayes, however, would 'make no appointment to take care of anybody' and submitted nominees of his own choosing.[19] He salted that wound by nominating Carl Schurz, a noted proponent of civil service reform. Outraged, Republican Senate leaders stalled. But Hayes's choices were impeccable, and the delay only exposed the Senate's arrogance. Public opinion and newspaper editors supported Hayes, and the senators backed down. Hayes had taught future presidents a lesson about the strength of their office when executive determination is coupled with favorable public opinion.

Hayes's investigation of the huge New York City Customs House triggered another battle with the Senate. The Customs House was the patronage breadbasket of Senator Roscoe Conkling's New York Republican machine, and the powerful senator fought back.[20] The president was again unshakable in the face of defeats and criticism: 'I am right and I shall not give up the contest.'[21] Hayes won the day and then worked to institute merit and tenure systems in other field offices of the federal government.[22]

Hayes repelled other assaults on the integrity of his office. To evade Hayes's veto of vicious legislation eliminating all federal protection for black voting rights in the South, House Democrats resorted to political extortion. They attached these measures as 'riders' onto vital appropriations bills that the president would feel compelled to sign. Responding to the challenge, Hayes vetoed five bills in three months: 'No precedent shall be established with my consent to a measure which is tantamount to coercion of the Executive.'[23]

Hayes's administration is notable not for any lasting initiative in policy, but rather for paving the way, by courageous example, for institutional revival. A few years after the Hayes administration, Mark Twain predicted that 'its quiet & unostentatious, but real & substantial greatness, would steadily rise into higher & higher prominence.'[24]

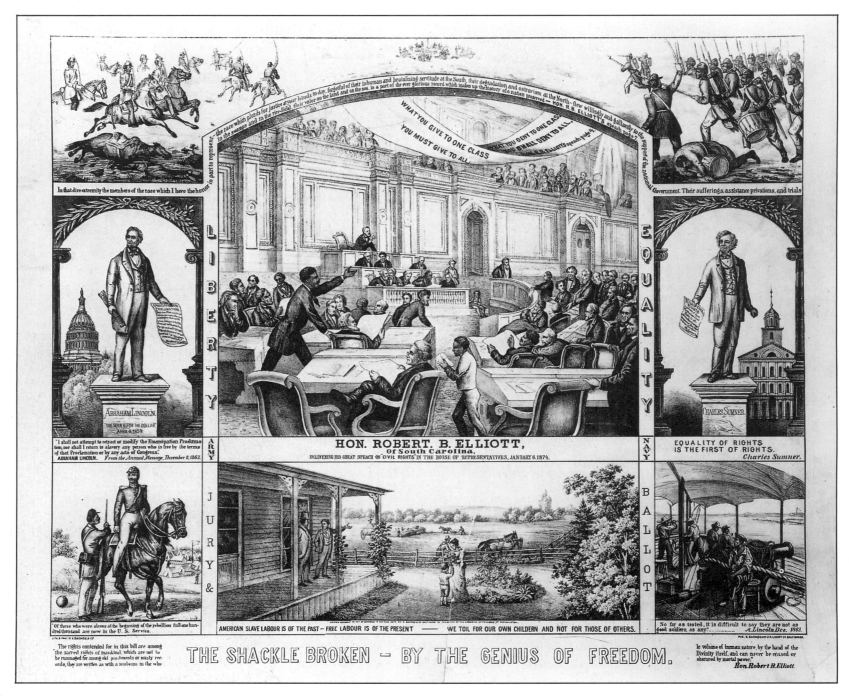

THE FIFTEENTH AMENDMENT.

CELEBRATED MAY 19ᵗ 1870.

Above: A lithograph depicting the celebrations that accompanied the passing of the Fifteenth Amendment. Hayes was proud of the fact that the state of Ohio ratified the amendment when he was governor.

JAMES A. GARFIELD

Hayes was the first sitting president since Polk to decide against running for a second term. The Republican Party was again riven with faction, and no candidate, including Grant, entered the 1880 convention with a majority of delegates. On the 36th ballot a dark horse, James A. Garfield, was chosen to lead the ticket. As a gesture toward the Grant wing, the convention nominated for vice president Chester A. Arthur, a Conkling crony whom Hayes had dismissed from office. The goodwill gesture was costly for Garfield. On July 2, 1881, after shooting the president in the back, Garfield's lunatic assassin explained: 'I am a Stalwart! Arthur is now President!'[25]

Garfield's death may have been a great public loss, for he had considerable talent and promise. He had risen far from a poor and fatherless boyhood. His first career, as an academic, began with assiduous and loving study of classical languages and literature. In 1859, after rising to the presidency of Hiram College, Garfield traded bickering professors for factious politicians and won a seat in the Ohio legislature.[26] During the war against the 'giant Evil' of slavery, Garfield was promoted to major general. He then sat in the House of Representatives for 17 years, serving as chairman of the powerful Appropriations Committee and as minority leader of his party. In 1881, he brought this experience and his incisive understanding of constitutional government to the White House.[27]

Like Hayes, yet against his intentions, Garfield made his mark battling the Senate. In making appointments, the new president tried, at first, to unite his party by accommodating the wishes of key senators. Yet when Conkling tried to defeat one of his nominees, Garfield struck back: 'I'm going to find out whether I am merely a recording clerk for the Senate or chief executive of the United States.'[28] To avoid the appearance of thwarting the president, the Senate planned to confirm all but this one nominee. Garfield immediately withdrew the other names, and the embarrassed Senate approved the president's choice.

Garfield, a compromiser by disposition, seemed to have been annealed by these experiences. But for nought. After less than a year in office, Garfield was dead, and the sorrowful nation was disturbed by another shock: Arthur was now president!

Below: President James A. Garfield promised to win back some respect for the presidency but his term was cut short by an embittered man, Charles J. Guiteau, who had failed to get a job in the new administration's bureaucracy.

PUBLISHED BY CURRIER & IVES   COPYRIGHT 1880, BY CURRIER & IVES, N.Y.   115 NASSAU ST. NEW YORK

FARMER GARFIELD
Cutting a Swath to the White House.

Above: This hexagonal desk calendar was set by President Garfield on the morning of July 2 prior to his going to the railroad station that day where he was mortally wounded by his assailant.

CHESTER A. ARTHUR

Chester Alan Arthur was a gentleman: distinguished in appearance, versed in literature, an expert fisherman, and an abolitionist. He was also a skilled administrator. During the Civil War, Arthur was efficient and scrupulously honest as Quartermaster General of New York State, a position of unbounded opportunities for graft: 'If I had misappropriated five cents, and on walking down town saw two men talking on the street together, I would imagine they were talking of my dishonesty, and the very thought would drive me mad.' He left this position poorer than he entered it.[29]

Although honest, Arthur was also a major gear in Conkling's New York party machine. Appointed by Grant to the New York Customs House, he used this patronage empire to become party 'boss' of New York City.[30] President Hayes removed Arthur from that post not because Arthur was personally corrupt but because he was dedicated to using federal service as a tool of party organization.[31]

The vice presidency had not changed that side of 'Chet,' and Arthur worked openly against

Above: Son of a farmer, Garfield was the last of the 'frontier, log cabin-background' presidents. His attack on corruption is depicted here in a Currier & Ives lithograph as he cuts a swathe through fraud and calumny.

Garfield in the battles with Conkling. The presidency was, it seems, another matter. As one disappointed crony noted: 'He isn't Chet Arthur any more, he's the President.'[32]

President Arthur became a relatively enthusiastic reformer. He pursued Garfield's investigation of postal route fraud, vetoed appropriations that did not serve 'the general welfare,' and otherwise promoted responsible management of the government's budget surplus.[33] Most important and surprising was Arthur's support for the nation's first major civil service reform legislation.

The system of federal service at this time was corrupt and inefficient. Offices were awarded as

Right: This mourning ribbon of black silk with green fringe was produced to commemorate the assassination of President Garfield. Shot in the back on July 2, he suffered all summer until he finally died on September 19.

Cleveland wanted to run an efficient, but purely Democratic administration and, therefore, was not enthusiastic about civil service reform. Indeed, he began his term by dismissing hundreds of federal officials to make way for office-hungry Democrats.[38] To secure these removals, however, the president had to go head-to-head with the Republican Senate, which demanded, and was refused, related papers and documents. This confrontation led to the repeal of the Tenure of Office Act in 1887 and marked the end of the Senate's pretention to control executive appointments.[39]

'His Obstinacy' dominated the executive branch and wielded the constitutional powers of the presidency like a sledgehammer. He used the veto with a record-setting zeal to attack wasteful practices, especially the profligate and fraudulent awarding of Civil War pensions. Congress eventually responded to his calls for pension reform. But Cleveland did not involve himself in shaping

Above: Chester A. Arthur (his signature, right), previously a spoilsman of Conkling, distanced himself on becoming president and supported a civil service based on a non-political merit system.

payment for party loyalty, and officers were generally more adept at milking opportunities than at doing their public duty. This perversion of public service was encouraged by the parties, which required their vassals to devote working hours to party business and to fill the party coffers with 'assessments' from their public salaries.[34]

Presidents tended to favor civil service reform, at the very least, to relieve them from the hordes of patronage seekers that streamed through the White House from sun-up to long after dark.[35] The Republican Party saw the light only after a disgusted public crushed it in the 1882 congressional elections. In 1883, President Arthur signed the Pendleton Act into law. This Act established a merit system of hiring and outlawed kickbacks to the party. Although the hiring provisions of the Act covered only about 10 percent of federal employees, it was the beginning of the end for the federal spoils system.[36]

Arthur's honorable service as president was not rewarded with a party nomination in 1884.

GROVER CLEVELAND

The Republicans' newfound religion of reform could not save them from the voters in 1884. The economy was depressed, labor strife was rampant, and the nomination of James G. Blaine, who was tainted with corruption, split the party. The 'Mugwump' faction promised to support any honest Democrat, and the Democratic Party obliged by nominating the hard-nosed governor of New York, Grover Cleveland.[37] Not even Cleveland's typically forthright admission of having fathered, years before, an illegitimate child could prevent his election.

Right: A campaign ribbon from President Grover Cleveland's 1888 re-election bid. Undaunted by his failure he defeated his successor, Benjamin Harrison, four years later and served a second term – the only president to do so in this way.

BENJAMIN HARRISON

The new president, Benjamin Harrison, rivaled Grant in lack of political experience. The one-term senator was, however, inoffensive to the various party factions and hailed from a crucial swing state, Indiana.

Harrison's distinctive contributions were in foreign affairs. He revived and pursued with considerable success Arthur's policy of increasing trade and lowering tariffs through reciprocal trade agreements with individual countries. To complement the policy of expanding foreign trade, Harrison's Navy Secretary persuaded Congress to fund a much-needed modernization of the navy.[43]

Leadership in domestic policy, however, would not be forthcoming from this White House. Harrison believed that the President 'should have no policy distinct from that of his party and that is better represented in Congress than in the executive.'[44]

Surprisingly, Congress actually took the policymaking lead. Through most of the Gilded Age, the houses of Congress had been organized for little more than distributing the government's largess to various particular interests.[45] Otherwise, the public's business was held hostage by faction and filibuster. After the Republican victory in 1888, Speaker of the House Thomas Reed decided to convert the House into a vehicle for implementing the majority party mandate. Reed ran the House without much regard to Harrison, between whom 'the dislike was cordial and undisguised.'[46]

The Congress of 1889–91 enacted almost the

the legislation to his liking, and he rewarded Congress's efforts with a veto. This was typical.

Cleveland's two administrations are notable both for bold legislative initiatives and for failures to lead Congress to acceptable results. The tenaciously independent chief executive never

Below: This bronze Peace Medal dates from 1889 and bears the high relief image of President Benjamin Harrison on one side (seen here) and an Indian and soldier on the reverse. During his Senate career he had championed the Indians.

Above: This paper Chinese lantern, replete with patriotic symbols, was a piece of campaign paraphernalia used during Harrison's bid for the Republican nomination at the 1888 convention. He was successful on the eighth ballot.

adjusted to the requirements of a policy leader and 'confused the necessity for tact with the sin of weakness.' His approach to legislative politics was exquisitely tactless. He eschewed appeals to popular opinion, hated the increasingly intrusive press, and insulted legislators of both parties regularly.[40]

Moreover, Cleveland could not, for the political life of him, embrace a middling position that would unite his party. With good reason, Cleveland believed that the high tariff was reducing foreign trade and creating a budget surplus that kept needed capital out of circulation. Against the advice of party leaders, he called for lowering the tariff: 'Perhaps I made a mistake from the party standpoint; but damn it, it was right.'[41] To what effect? Cleveland and his party were defeated in 1888, and the Republicans proceeded to enact the extremely protectionist McKinley Tariff.[42]

Right: A silk campaign ribbon for the Harrison-Morton ticket approved at the 1888 Republican convention. One of the administration's greatest actions was the passing of anti-trust legislation.

Right: A paper Chinese lantern from the Cleveland presidential campaign camp. It was made by the same Ohio company, Sprague and French, that made the Harrison lantern.

Right: A paper Chinese lantern from the Cleveland presidential campaign camp. It was made by the same Ohio company, Sprague and French, that made the Harrison lantern.

entire Republican platform, including the Sherman Anti-trust Act – the first major step toward federal regulation of business.[47] But another major achievement, the McKinley Tariff, contributed to high prices and the defeat of the Republicans in the following elections. In 1892, Cleveland became the only defeated president to be returned to office.

GROVER CLEVELAND

In 1893, the high hopes of the victorious Democrats were rudely greeted by a financial panic and severe depression. As agricultural prices plummeted in the drought-plagued West, bankrupted farmers sought a cure for their woes in an inflationary monetary policy and, specifically, the free coinage of silver.[48] Cleveland, however, was convinced that a weak currency was ruining the economy, and he pursued a return to a strict gold standard with unprecedented determination. He called a special session of Congress in summer of 1893, fought off all compromises and strong-armed members of Congress by withholding patronage appointments.[49]

Cleveland's success angered Congress, divided his party, and effectively estranged the western 'populists.'[50] Cleveland lopped off another bloc of voters, industrial labor, with his ill-conceived use of federal troops in the Pullman Strike of 1894.[51] The man who had won the Democratic Party's only presidential victories between James Buchanan (1856) and Woodrow Wilson (1912) left office highly unpopular and thoroughly

Below: The crowd assembled in front of the Capitol in 1893 for Grover Cleveland's second inauguration as president. In office he faced an economy in acute depression.

Left: Two inaugural ball souvenir programs; on the left is one from McKinley's of March 4, 1897, and on the right is one from Cleveland's first ball held on March 4, 1885 – note the small broom attached for the promised 'clean up.'

McKinley entered the House of Representatives in 1877 on the day of Hayes's inauguration, and through a close relationship with his old Civil War commander, he became familiar with White House politics. After only four years in the House, McKinley was made chairman of the powerful Ways and Means Committee, an excellent apprenticeship in the art of reconciling diverse interests.[56] In 1891, after 12 years in the House, he captured the governorship of Ohio and served for four years before being nominated on the first ballot of the 1896 Republican convention.

McKinley's election ended a long period of regularly divided government. In 1894, the Democrats lost an astounding 113 seats in the House, giving the Republicans a 139-seat majority. In 1896, McKinley won the presidency with the widest margin of victory (4 percent) since Grant's re-election. For the next 36 years, until Franklin D. Roosevelt's victory in 1932, the Republicans dominated the national government.

With the confidence of both business and labor, McKinley charted a boldly moderate course. 'Mr. McKinley,' according to Herbert Croly, 'represented, on the whole, a group of ideas and interests as nearly national as could any political leader of his generation.[57]

Ideas alone do not win the day, and McKinley assiduously acquired other means of influencing Congress. One was patronage: he used an executive order to roll back Cleveland's extension of the merit system to make way for thousands of Republicans.[58] Another was popularity. His numerous speaking tours made him as personally known to the country as was possible in an age without electronic media, and he wooed the press by receiving correspondents socially and giving them regular access to his aides. In these ways, he made himself daily news.[59]

repudiated by a party convention that swooned before the silver-tongued populist, William Jennings Bryan of Nebraska.

The enduring effects of the second Cleveland administration were the consolidation of the Populist movement and the emergence of a new Republican majority. But it took an upward swing in the economic cycle and the political genius of William McKinley to transform this into a lasting majority.

WILLIAM McKINLEY

In historians' ratings of presidents, William McKinley is consistently ranked below Grover Cleveland.[52] Yet the accomplishments of the McKinley administration are the greater in both number and importance. Evidently, the raters put a high value on Cleveland's principled assertiveness, even though its effects were regularly disastrous.[53] Moreover, they must assume that McKinley himself had little to do with the significant accomplishments of his administration.

Elihu Root, probably the most intelligent and accomplished member of McKinley's administration, explained the enigma:

> He had a way of handling men so that they thought his ideas were their own. He was a man of great power because he was absolutely indifferent to credit. His great desire was 'to get it done' . . . [and] McKinley *always had his way.*[54]

Personable and shrewd, McKinley was a master of persuasion.[55]

He was also far better prepared for the White House than any other president of the era.

Left: McKinley's campaign ribbon – with an actual photograph of the candidate – with his slogan 'Patriotism, Protection and Prosperity.' Once president he delivered the highest tariff yet seen.

Below: McKinley had stated that no wars of conquest were wanted, but during his administration a lot of overseas territory was annexed. These American troops are advancing on Manila in 1898.

Right: This Eagle No. 3 inkpen and glass inkwell were used by President McKinley on April 25, 1898, when he signed the resolution of Congress declaring war with Spain – a war owing much to newspaper-incited populist imperialism.

McKinley used popularity, patronage, the press, and tact to breech, if quietly, the wall between the White House and Capitol Hill. As a contemporary noted, 'We have never had a President who had more influence with Congress than McKinley.'[60]

McKinley's first term was rich with irony. His first inaugural address asserted forcefully that: 'We want no wars of conquest, we must avoid the temptation of territorial aggression.' Yet his administration is most noted for the war with Spain, and many of McKinley's foreign and trade policies were shaped by the nation's new colonial possessions.

For 13 months, and in the face of political and personal attacks, McKinley resisted the cries for war and pursued negotiations.[61] When it was clear that Spain would not grant Cuba autonomy, McKinley bought time to prepare for war in 1898.

The Spanish–American War came, McKinley ran it, and in ten weeks it was won.[62] The ground war in Cuba was a fiasco, but the naval war in the Philippines was an efficient triumph. Admiral George Dewey destroyed the Spanish fleet in Manila Bay without losing a man. Driven, in part, by his general policy of expanding foreign trade, McKinley then used his considerable resources to outmaneuver the anti-imperialist forces in the Senate and secure a peace treaty with Spain that ceded the Philippines to US control.[63]

These policies and events led to McKinley's most ambitious diplomatic initiative, the 'Open Door' policy. He and Secretary of State John Hay labored long for agreements with the major trading powers to maintain China's political integrity and to keep its ports open to US trade.[64] In a related measure, McKinley stretched the president's commander-in-chief power by ordering US forces into China, a nation at peace with the United States. He sought both to protect American lives and property during the Boxer Rebellion and to keep a US hand in any event involving foreign powers in China.

McKinley's domestic and foreign policies intertwined in other ways. After failing to secure a general tariff reduction in 1897, the president vigorously pursued the alternative route of reciprocal trade agreements. A battle for Senate ratification of two reciprocity treaties inspired another speaking tour. The key speech was delivered at the Pan-American Exposition in Buffalo. Following the speech, McKinley was shot by an anarchist on September 6, 1901. He died eight days later.[65]

In 1900, aided by an economic upturn, McKinley had been re-elected in a landslide and had declared: 'I can no longer be called the President of a party. I am the President of the whole people.'[66] This was not exactly accurate. In the 1890s, Populism in the southern states had evolved into a viciously racist movement that disenfranchised blacks and subjected them to a thorough and degrading social segregation.[67]

Two eras met in 1901 as the last Union soldier to sit in the White House became the first president inaugurated in the new century. From the secure ground courageously won by his 19th-century predecessors – Hayes, Garfield, Arthur, and Cleveland – McKinley could fight 20th-century political battles.[68] He had found the tools to carve out a significant place for the president in domestic legislative affairs. Moreover, he reclaimed from the Senate the leading role in foreign policy and stretched the executive powers to fit the role. Indeed, much of what his more famous successor, Theodore Roosevelt, would do with loud self-reference, McKinley had done with tactful self-deprecation.

Notes

1. Quoted in Binkley, *American Political Parties*, 1958: 292.
2. Boller, Jr., 1981: 153.
3. White, 1958: 23.
4. Binkley, *American Political Parties*, 1958: 293–4.
5. Pious, 1979: 280.
6. In Pennsylvania, legislators 'sold their votes to grant privileges to corporations, then blackmailed the same corporations by threatening to rescind their privileges.' Hoogenboom, 1988:
7. Adams, 1870: 58.
8. Binkley, *American Political Parties*, 1958: 304; Hoogenboom, 1988: 5, 20–1.
9. Reichley, 1992: 153. As the governor of Indiana put it: 'While it may be true that not every Democrat is a traitor, every traitor is a Democrat.'
10. Hoogenboom, 1988: 25–31.
11. Reichley, 1992: 147–49.
12. Binkley, *American Political Parties*, 1958: 306–07.
13. Binkley, *American Political Parties*, 1958: 307–08.
14. Barnard, 1954: 187–93; Hoogenboom, 1988: 9–10. As president, and later in his life, Hayes promoted education for blacks as the key to economic prosperity and eventual political equality. See Rubin, Jr., 1959: xiii–iv.
15. Hoogenboom, 1988: 11–12, 36, 44, 48–49, 57, 60–62.
16. Ibid., 73.
17. Binkley, *President and Congress*, 1958: 173.
18. White, 1958: 31–32; Bryce, 1894: vol. I, pp. 61–62 and Chapter 60 ('The Machine'). Senators used this power to gain control over executive agencies and the subordinate federal jobs. These jobs were used as patronage to buy state party loyalty and, thereby, secure their own re-elections.
19. Binkley, *President and Congress*, 1959: 153.
20. Binkley, *American Political Parties*, 1958: 304.
21. White, 1958: 33.

22. Hoogenboom, 1988: 131–42.
23. White, 1958: 36.
24. Quoted in Hoogenboom, 1988: 226.
25. Morison, 1965: 735. The assassin thought he deserved a high diplomatic post as compensation for a speech, never delivered, which he nonetheless thought had swept Garfield into office.
26. Peskin, 1978: 13, 28.
27. Doenecke, 1981: 145–45.
28. Morison, 1965: 735.
29. Howe, 1934: 21; Doenecke, 1981: 77.
30. Doenecke, 1981: 78.
31. Howe, 1934: 51–75.
32. Boller, Jr., 1981: 165; Morison, 1965: 735–36.
33. Howe, 1934: Chapters 15–16.
34. Bryce, 1894: Chapter 45 ('Spoils'); White, 1958: Chapter 1.
35. White, 1958: 26–27.
36. Reichley, 1992: 189; Bryce, 1894: vol. II, pp. 847–8.
37. Nevins, 1932: Chapters 6, 8–9.
38. Welch, Jr., 1988: 61. Cleveland extended the reach of the merit system at the end of each term, but only, it seems, in order to protect Democratic officers from the incoming Republicans.
39. White, 1958: 31; Nevins, 1932: Chapters 14–15.
40. Welch, Jr., 1988: 205.
41. Binkley, *American Political Parties*, 1958: 311. See generally, Nevins, 1932: Chapter 21.
42. Binkley, 1958: 70.
43. Socolofsky and Spetter, 1987: 50–51, 102.
44. Binkley, 1947: 181–82.
45. White, 1958: 19–54, 60–67; Congressional Quarterly, 1976: Chapters 11, 20.
46. Socolofsky and Spetter, 1987: 30.
47. Socolofsky and Spetter, 1987: 54.
48. Welch, 1988: 116–17.

49. Nevins, 1932: 523–28, 533–48; Welch, 1988: 115–19, 122–24.
50. Welch, 1988: 81–83.
51. George Pullman, a particularly egregious industrialist, had driven the workers in his 'company town' to the brink with a series of wage cuts and by firing the delegates seeking to discuss their grievances. The ensuing strike grew rapidly in scope. Cleveland sent in troops against the wishes of the governor of Illinois and with the effect of increasing the violence. See Binkley, 1958: 313 and Nevins, 1932: Chapter 33.
52. See DiClerico, 1995: 338–39.
53. Indeed, Cleveland's most prominent biographer praises him as an example 'of the courage that never yields an inch in the cause of truth, and that never surrenders an iota of principle to expediency' (Nevins, 1932: 766). This is odd praise for a politician, praise that Jefferson, Lincoln, and Franklin Roosevelt do not merit.
54. Gould, 1980: 9; White, 1958: 43.
55. Gould, 1980: 6, 39.
56. Binkley, *American Political Parties*, 1958: 326–27.
57. Binkley, *President and Congress*, 1947: 188.
58. Binkley, *President and Congress*, 1947: 125–26.
59. Gould, 1980: 38.
60. Congressional Quarterly, 1976: 200.
61. Gould, 1980: 68–70, 88–89.
62. Gould, 1980: 91. See also Fisher, 1995: 41–44.
63. Gould, 1980: 150.
64. Gould, 1980: 201–05, 222–24
65. Leech, 1959: 575–76, 587–88, 590–603. Gould, 1980: 244–45.
66. Binkley, *American Political Parties*, 1958: 336.
67. Morison, 1965: 722–25. For example, the number of blacks registered to vote in Louisiana went from 130,334 in 1896 to a mere 1,342 in 1902.
68. Gould, 1980: Chapter 10.

Burton I. Kaufman

10
THE MODERN PRESIDENCY EMERGES

Theodore Roosevelt	**1901-1909**
William Howard Taft	**1909-1913**
Woodrow Wilson	**1913-1921**
Warren Harding	**1921-1923**
Calvin Coolidge	**1923-1929**
Herbert Hoover	**1929-1933**

In a new political, economic, and international climate, the modern
presidency took root as a powerful center of leadership.
As Roosevelt and Wilson showed, the redefined office offered great
opportunity for accomplishment. Hoover plumbed the
office's downside – blame for the nation's ills.

General Pershing's First Division marching in triumph
through Washington, D.C., in the Victory Parade of 1919.

The modern American presidency was born around the turn of the 20th century. Hitherto, the presidency had usually been the weakest of the three branches of the federal government. Generally, presidents did not set the national agenda or offer broad legislative programs. Most of what legislation was passed emanated from Congress. Nor did presidents have large staffs to assist or advise them. To a considerable extent the main role of presidents was ceremonial.

This situation began to change toward the end of the 19th century. The power of the presidency was strengthened and broadened. Presidents like Cleveland and McKinley took a more expansive view of their responsibilities, and as the United States became a world power, the president became the nation's chief diplomat.

During the first two decades of the 20th century, commonly known as the Progressive Era, the office became even more powerful. Although historians argue about the meaning of the Progressive Movement, they agree that it involved increased presidential authority in response to the stresses caused by America's transformation from an agrarian nation to an industrial, financial, and corporate behemoth. The United States' involvement in World War I had a similar effect on the presidency, so that by the time President Woodrow Wilson left office in 1921, many Americans were complaining that the office had become too powerful.

In many ways, William McKinley had been the nation's first modern president. What made his presidency significant were the measures he took to enhance the power of his office. He formalized the process of decision-making at the White House. He employed the cabinet as a sounding-board for policy and established a press operation in the White House that made it, and not Congress, the center for Washington news. Similarly, McKinley spotlighted the presidency by his carefully planned and orchestrated tours of the nation. And he helped turn the United States into a world power as a result of the Spanish–American War and the promulgation of the Open Door Notes of 1899 and 1900.[1]

THEODORE ROOSEVELT

The first 20th century president, Theodore Roosevelt, built on the legacy he inherited from McKinley. Roosevelt is widely recognized as one of the United States' most important presidents and certainly one of its most engaging personalities. Born on October 27, 1858, to a socially prominent New York family, Roosevelt was a sickly, nearsighted and asthmatic child who overcame his physical problems through strenuous physical activity. An avid reader, he became an amateur naturalist and an early exponent of the conservation movement in the United States.[2]

From his parents, Roosevelt developed a deep sense of duty and social responsibility, which naturally turned his interest to politics. In 1881, just two years out of Harvard, he was elected to the New York State Legislature where he quickly developed a reputation for exposing corruption and being an outspoken proponent of governmental reform. After running unsuccessfully for mayor of New York City in 1886, he was appointed to the United States Civil Service Commission and then, in 1894, to the New York City Board of Police Commissioners. In 1897, President McKinley appointed him an assistant

Above: Number 28 East 20th Street, New York, birthplace of Theodore Roosevelt. As a boy and young man, his struggle was not against poverty – as was that of many predecessors – but ill health.

secretary of the navy, but after war was declared against Spain in 1898, he resigned that position to form the legendary cavalry unit known as the Rough Riders.

Taking advantage of his wartime fame, Roosevelt ran successfully for governor of New York and then angered Republican leaders by his nonpartisanship and efforts at governmental reform, including increasing the regulatory power of the state over factories and sweatshops. Mostly as a way of removing him from the governorship, Republican leaders helped put him on the 1900 presidential ticket as McKinley's vice presidential running mate. When McKinley was killed less than a year later, Roosevelt suddenly found himself elevated to the White House. At age 42 he was the nation's youngest president.

In contrast to the common image of Roosevelt as a swashbuckling reformer, he proved to be a cautious and moderate chief executive. But, concerned about growing corporate power, he attacked those corporations that, in their quest for profits, engaged in questionable business practices. He brought a successful anti-trust suit against the Northern Securities Company, which was formed from the $400 million merger of the railroad interests of three of the richest men in the United States, E.H. Harriman, James J. Hill, and J.P. Morgan. In the bitter anthracite coal strike, he took the side of the United Mine Workers in demanding an eight-hour day and higher wages. He also established a Bureau of Corporations to examine business practices and supported the Elkins Act prohibiting railroad rebates.

Running for re-election in 1904 on a platform that promised all Americans a 'square deal,' Roosevelt easily defeated his Democratic opponent, Alton B. Parker. He used his political mandate to gain approval of some far-reaching legislation, including the Hepburn Act, which gave the Interstate Commerce Commission (ICC) authority to set shipping rates and monitor corporate records, and the Pure Food and Drug Act and Meat Inspection Act to regulate purveyors of food and drugs. The first American president to take an active interest in conservation, Roosevelt also supported the Newlands Reclamations Act providing federal funds to build dams, reservoirs, and canals in the West, and he named the conservationist Gifford Pinchot to head the newly established Forest Service.

In foreign policy, TR (the first president to be known by his initials) also struck out in new directions. Contrary to the now-popular image of Roosevelt as an imperialist and racist intrigued with power, he again moved cautiously and carefully. It is no coincidence, for example, that at the Portsmouth Conference of 1905 Roosevelt negotiated an end to the Russo–Japanese War, for which he won the Nobel Peace Prize, or that he played a similar role in reconciling differences between France and Germany over Morocco at the Algeciras Conference of 1906.

Roosevelt was most vulnerable to accusations of imperialism and racism for his actions in the Western Hemisphere. Referring to Latin Americans as 'Dagos', and determined to build an international waterway connecting the Atlantic and Pacific Oceans through the narrow Isthmus of Panama, Roosevelt intrigued with Panamanians in their successful revolt in 1903

Below: Both these Theodore Roosevelt campaign badges emphasize his 'Rough Rider' service in the Spanish-American War. Although he liked to quote the maxim 'speak softly and carry a big stick,' he was better known for tub-thumping oratory; in fact, the jaw of the badge seen here (left) is designed for the mouth to open and close.

Above: Roosevelt in classic war hero pose. The uniform was specially commissioned by him from Brooks Brothers in New York.

against Colombia after that country rejected a treaty giving the United States the right to build a canal through its province of Panama. He then negotiated an almost identical treaty with the new nation of Panama. To protect access to the canal, he issued the Roosevelt Corollary of 1904 giving the United States the right to intervene in Latin America to prevent intervention by foreign powers.

Even in Latin America, however, Roosevelt acted more on the basis of his perception of the national interest than because of any racial motivation. He used racial stereotypes in describing Latin Americans just as he did in describing Asians. But, whereas he viewed the Japanese as being racially advanced and willingly conceded that East Asia was within Japan's sphere of influence, he regarded Latin Americans as racially backward and the Western Hemisphere as distinctly within the United States' sphere of influence. Furthermore, he regarded construction of the Panama Canal as too important to countenance delay by supposedly greedy Latin American politicians.

Above: Photographed at San Juan Hill, Puerto Rico, in 1898 during the Spanish-American War, the then Colonel Roosevelt's (center) volunteer 'Rough Riders' was a curious mix of eastern Ivy League athletic types and western frontiersmen.

The key to understanding the Roosevelt presidency, therefore, is his strong sense of responsibility. He considered power and responsibility to be inseparable. But he was also a progressive who believed that government, guided by the president, had to play an expanded role in responding to the new problems of a complex corporate society. He did not reject the changes taking place in the United States. To the contrary, he accepted the existence of corporate power and distinguished between good and bad corporations on the basis of whether or not they served the national interest. Although he gained fame as a 'trust buster,' he initiated fewer anti-trust actions against American industry than his successor, William Howard Taft, and he accepted the notion of 'natural monopolies' in such industries as utilities, which he believed should be regulated, not broken up. A charismatic, vigorous, even hyperactive figure, he also used the office of the president as a 'bully pulpit' to promote the causes and programs he advocated. By force of personality alone, he made himself the nation's central political figure and his office a dynamic vehicle of change.

Right: For a sickly boy, Roosevelt emerged a remarkably strenuous man. As well as politics, he put much energy into conservation and some of his most enduring achievements were in this area.

WILLIAM HOWARD TAFT

Roosevelt's successor, William Howard Taft, had few of Roosevelt's qualities. Weighing over 330 pounds, he was neither charismatic nor vigorous. Instead, he had a contemplative, judicial frame of mind which would be valuable in his later role as chief justice of the Supreme Court but which did not serve him well as president. From a prominent Cincinnati family, he was born on September 15, 1857. After graduating from Yale in 1878 and the Cincinnati Law School in 1880, he spent the next 20 years in public service. In 1890 he was named by President Benjamin Harrison as United States solicitor general. This was followed by appointments as a United States circuit judge (1890) and

Above: A metal button for William Howard Taft's 1908 election campaign, a modern replacement for the by then outdated fabric ribbons of the previous century. Taft was chosen by Roosevelt, although he later regretted it.

Above: Music list and menu for the inaugural ball of President Taft, held on March 4, 1909. Pushed somewhat by his ambitious wife, Taft was not a happy president, later declaring, 'I am glad to be going. This is the lonesomest place in the world.'

Below: The early 20th century was an era of remarkable technological advances, and few were greater than powered flight. The Wright Type B was demonstrated at the White House in 1911, taking off from the lawn as Taft looked on.

high commissioner for the Philippine Islands (1900) before he was chosen by Roosevelt to be his secretary of war in 1904. In 1908 Roosevelt picked him as his successor, and in November he defeated his Democratic opponent, William Jennings Bryan, by more than a million votes.

It did not take long for Roosevelt to realize that Taft's concept of the presidency differed drastically from his own. Taft viewed the role as fundamentally that of an administrator. Accordingly, he was reluctant to mobilize public opinion behind programs of economic and social reform or otherwise provide the nation with vigorous leadership. In foreign affairs, too, Taft fol-

lowed a different direction than Roosevelt. Seeking to expand American markets and investments abroad, he was much more willing than his predecessor to challenge existing power relationships, especially in Asia.[3]

Taft's presidency had its achievements. The Payne–Aldrich Tariff of 1909, which Taft signed into law, provided for a new one percent tax on corporate income. The Mann–Elkins Act of

Below: Taft was a big man and had had a large build since childhood. His nicknames were 'Big Lub' and 'Big Bill.' In spite of his size (six feet tall and 300 pounds in weight) he was a good dancer.

1910 gave the ICC authority to suspend railroad rates and brought telephones and telegraphs within the Commission's jurisdiction. A system of postal savings banks, a parcel post system, and a Bureau of Mines were also established with Taft's support and influence. And he instituted more anti-trust suits against America's largest corporations than the much-fabled 'trust buster,' Roosevelt.

On the whole, however, the Taft administration was a failure. His support of the protectionist Payne–Aldrich Tariff, even though in many instances it violated his own campaign promises to lower tariffs, infuriated Midwestern Repub-

Below: Disappointed with his old friend and successor, William H. Taft, Theodore Roosevelt decided to campaign against him and established the Progressive Party for the purpose. Although he did not win, Roosevelt took enough votes from Taft to enable Woodrow Wilson to be elected.

"Look up, not down— Look out, not in— Look forward, not backward— And lend a hand."

Founders' Day
October 27, 1912
THE
Progressive
Party

ALLIED PRINTING
TRADES UNION LABEL COUNCIL 229
CHICAGO, ILL.

Above: On March 23, 1912, the American dead from the USS *Maine* were repatriated and a ceremony was held, attended by President Taft. This was the scene as the funeral procession passed along Pennsylvania Avenue on its way to the State, War & Navy Building for the ceremony.

licans who believed that the tariff would benefit Eastern corporate interests while raising their own cost of living. His dismissal of Gifford Pinchot, after Pinchot accused Secretary of the Interior Richard Ballinger of selling valuable coal land in Alaska to private interests, alienated conservationists including Roosevelt, who broke with Taft over the incident. His clumsy efforts at dollar diplomacy ('substituting dollars for bullets'), in which he tried to gain access to Asian markets by promoting American financing of railroad construction in Manchuria, alienated Japan and Russia, which regarded the United States as a threat to their interests.

In 1912 Roosevelt announced that he would oppose Taft for the Republican nomination. After narrowly losing to Taft at the Chicago convention in June, the former president and his followers bolted the GOP to form the Progressive Party. When Roosevelt proclaimed that he was 'as strong as a bull moose,' the Party adopted the

Left: President Taft and his chauffeur in an auto in about 1914. Mass production was creating a new world; Henry Ford declared, 'I am going to democratize the automobile,' and by 1917 there were five million of them on the nation's roads.

nickname 'Bull Moose Party.' With most rank-and-file Republicans backing Roosevelt, the only question was whether he or the Democratic candidate, New Jersey Governor Woodrow Wilson, would be elected in November.

WOODROW WILSON

A college president before entering politics, Wilson was born in Staunton, Virginia, on December 28, 1856. The son of a Presbyterian minister, he was devoutly religious and dogmatically self-righteous, characteristics that would pervade his entire political career. As the holder of a PhD in political science from Johns Hopkins University (1884) and the president of Princeton University from 1902 to 1910, when he ran for governor of New Jersey, Wilson had developed a national reputation as a scholar and educational leader. Active politics was considered an unlikely arena for professors.[4]

Yet Wilson was extremely self-confident and

Below: The inauguration of Woodrow Wilson as president in 1913. Four years later the United States was to enter the war in Europe, giving foreign policy a higher profile than ever before.

ambitious, and his ambition extended to holding high public office, which he considered almost a form of ministry. As president of Princeton, he had developed a reputation as a progressive leader who broke with tradition by revising the curriculum and trying, unsuccessfully, to abolish undergraduate eating and social clubs. In 1910 he was persuaded by a group of Democratic leaders, desperate to end 14 years of Republican control of the statehouse, to be their gubernatorial candidate. Sweeping into office, he pushed through a program of political and economic reform, which made him a leading candidate for the party's presidential nomination in 1912. At the convention, he won the nomination, which required a two-thirds vote, on the 46th ballot.

The 1912 election was one of the nation's most interesting. In a program known as the 'New Nationalism' Roosevelt emphasized the need to subordinate individual interests to the larger national welfare; in a program known as the 'New Freedom' Wilson stressed the importance of protecting individual freedoms. Yet the two programs were not as far apart as they seemed. Like Roosevelt, Wilson spoke in terms of serving the national interest and emphasized the importance of strong executive leadership. The major difference was that, in contrast to

Roosevelt, Wilson believed the national interest was best served by protecting and promoting individual opportunity. Despite an energetic campaign by Roosevelt, Wilson defeated him by more than two million votes. Taft ran a distant third.[5]

A month after he took office in March 1913, Wilson broke with tradition by appearing before Congress to deliver the annual State of the Union message in person (the first president to do so since John Adams) and by returning the next day to confer with Democratic leaders. In the months that followed he helped push three major pieces of legislation through Congress: the Underwood–Simmons Tariff Act (October 1913), which reduced tariffs to their lowest levels since before the Civil War; the Federal Reserve Act (December 1913), which reformed the nation's outmoded banking system by establishing a Federal Reserve Board and a nationwide system of 12 Federal Reserve banks to help regulate the availability and supply of money; and the Clayton Anti-Trust Act (October 1914), intended to strengthen the nation's anti-trust laws by defining monopolistic business practices. Even more important to Wilson than the Clayton Act, however, was another measure that Congress also passed establishing the Federal

Trade Commission (September 1914) to prevent unfair methods of competition in interstate commerce.

By the time Congress completed its work in 1914, Wilson had clearly established his ascendancy over the legislature. Although Congress helped shape all the legislation it enacted and the Federal Reserve Act in particular involved artful compromises worked out by the congressional leadership, Congress acted largely upon the president's existing programs. With good reason Wilson could claim in 1914 that his 'New Freedom' program was completed. But during the next two years he continued to demonstrate his leadership of Congress. Among the measures that the president sought and the House and Senate approved were bills to establish a Tariff Commission, a Shipping Board to regulate and aid merchant seamen, and a Federal Farm Loan Board to provide long-term loans to farmers. In addition Congress passed the Keating–Owen Act, prohibiting child labor in interstate commerce, and the Adamson Act, providing an eight-hour day for interstate railroad workers.

By the end of 1916 Wilson's attention had turned to the war in Europe, which had broken out in August 1914 and threatened to involve the United States. Wilson's diplomacy has often been characterized as 'missionary diplomacy' because the president felt he had a mission to bring about a 'New World Order' predicated on democratic and free trade principles. Early in his presidency he had intervened in the Mexican Revolution in an effort to guide the revolution along democratic lines. In 1916 he sent an expeditionary force of more than 11,000 troops, led

Above and below: Woodrow Wilson was a well educated man – this portrait (below) reflecting thoughtfulness. He was a graduate of Princeton, and subsequently was a professor and president there – leadership and organizational experience which launched his political career. The academic cap and president's medal are both from those Princeton days; as is the Hammond Typewriter upon which he did all his own correspondence. He wrote the book *George Washington* in 1897.

Left: This leather fob bearing Woodrow Wilson's image is a further example of the multitude of campaign memorabilia available. It could be attached to the button hole, watch strap, or briefcase in order to declare your allegiance.

Above: President Wilson addressing a crowd at Independence Hall, Philadelphia, on July 4, 1914. He believed in honest, democratic government and felt the president had to represent the people and not the special interest groups.

by General John Pershing, deep into Mexico in a vain effort to capture the Mexican bandit, Pancho Villa, after Villa's forces had burned down the border town of Columbus, New Mexico. But in January 1917 Wilson withdrew the Pershing expedition and granted formal recognition to the government of Venustiano Carranza, having failed, in his words, to teach the Mexican people 'to elect good men.'

By this time, Wilson was preoccupied with the war in Europe. In the two years following the outbreak of the war, Wilson had tried to be neutral. Although he greatly admired Britain's parliamentary form of government and strongly preferred the Allied powers (Britain, France, and their allies) to the Central Powers (Germany, Austria–Hungary, and their allies), he believed both sides were responsible for the war because of their military alliances and competing imperial interests. His first actions after war broke out were to issue a declaration of neutrality and a ban

on loans to the belligerent powers, and to ask both sides to abide by international law and respect the rights of neutral powers on the high seas.[6]

Wilson refused, however, to prohibit American trade with the warring powers. Because Britain controlled the high seas, this gave the British and French an advantage, especially since Wilson soon permitted the extension of commercial credits and in March, 1915 approved a $50 million loan to Britain from the banking house of J.P. Morgan. By 1917, the United States had loaned the Allies $2.25 billion and Germany only $27 million. Moreover, when Britain, in violation of American neutrality, seized American ships bound for the Central Powers, Wilson made only mild protests. But when in 1915 Germany, in an effort to starve Britain into submission, announced a campaign of submarine warfare against enemy shipping, Wilson warned that Germany would be held 'to strict accountability.' Following the sinking in May 1915 of the British passenger ship, *Lusitania*, in which almost 1,200 people, including 128 Americans, died, Wilson issued a series of notes to Germany so threatening in tone that William Jennings Bryan, the anti-war Secretary of State, resigned in protest. After the Germans sank the British channel steamer *Sussex* in March 1916 with further loss of American lives, Wilson warned Germany that he would sever relations unless it stopped its submarine attacks on merchant passenger ships. Germany responded with the so-called 'Sussex' pledge' promising not to sink ships without adequate warning and without attempting to save lives.

Throughout the remainder of 1916, Germany abided by the pledge. In November Wilson won a narrow re-election victory – the first Democrat to win a second consecutive term since Andrew

Left: President Wilson was a keen bridge player and these decks of cards with embossed leather storage cases – made by Arrco Playing Card Company in Chicago – were used for the purpose.

Jackson in 1832 – over his Republican opponent, Supreme Court Justice Charles Evans Hughes, on the basis of the slogan, 'He kept us out of war.' In January 1917, however, Germany announced that it was resuming submarine warfare, and on April 17, 1917, the United States declared war on Germany.

Significantly, Wilson took the country into the war as an 'associate power' rather than as an ally. In his view, both sides had been responsible for the war, and he wanted the freedom to establish his New World Order, which, he believed, would prevent any future wars. Thus he said he was entering the war 'to end all wars' and 'to make the world safe for democracy.' In January 1918 Wilson spelled out his plan for the postwar world in an address known as the Fourteen Points, which called for the establishment of a League of Nations to resolve international disputes.[7]

America's contribution of men and materiel to the Allies was crucial in the last months of the war, and on November 11, 1918, Germany agreed to an armistice ending the war. The next month peace talks began in Paris. From December 1918 to July 1919, Wilson spent almost all his time at the conference trying to forge an agreement based on his Fourteen Points. But although he got the Allies to agree to establish a League of Nations, the Treaty signed at Versailles was not the 'peace without victory' he envisioned. The agreement sacrificed the concept of self-determination to specific Allied war aims, forced Germany to agree to a 'war guilt' clause, and exacted heavy reparations from Germany.

Below: The flag and storage case from the USS *George Washington* – formerly a German luxury liner – that took President Wilson to Europe. The flag is embroidered along the hoist 'Presidents St'd. NY. NY. Mar' 1916'.

Above: President Wilson leading the Heroes' Parade in Washington, D.C., on February 27, 1919. More than 100,000 Americans had died in the war.

Although Wilson campaigned hard for Senate approval of the Treaty after he returned to the United States in July, it encountered strong opposition from the Republican-controlled Senate, which had been left out of the Treaty negotiations. The major objections to the Treaty were directed against the convenant of the League of Nations, which, it was claimed, unreasonably restrained America's freedom of action in the world. Wilson might have won Senate ratification of the agreement if he had accepted reservations meant to protect American interests, but he opposed every reservation that senators raised.

Instead, Wilson decided to take his case directly to the American people. While speaking at Pueblo, Colorado, he suffered a major stroke, which left him paralyzed and largely incapacitated for seven months. During this period, the Senate rejected an amended version of the Treaty three times after Wilson ordered Senate loyalists

PRESIDENT WOODROW WILSON

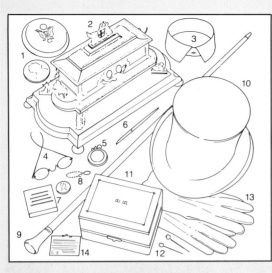

1. Gold medal with leather presentation case embossed with the Great Seal of the United States. Belgium presented it to Wilson; its King Albert is on the coin.
2. Silver and gilt Peace Casket and base presented to Wilson by the City of London.
3. The president's white detachable collar.
4. Rimless gold wire spectacles.
5. Cigarette lighter presented by Clemenceaux of France during the 1919 peace talks. One side bears the legend 'Je fais la guerre.'
6. Pen used by President Wilson to sign the proclamation of war against the Imperial German Government on April 6, 1917.
7. Verdun Medal awarded to Wilson by the city.
8. Gold watch fob engraved 'Woodrow Wilson.'
9. Gold-headed cane given by Dr. Howe to Wilson upon his becoming president.
10. Silk top hat with the gilt initials 'W.W.' in the crown.
11. Man's leather jewelry box, similarly initialed.
12. Two Californian gold stick pins bearing the presidential seal.
13. White dress gloves, made in Germany.
14. Gold nugget from California, given to the Wilsons to be made into a wedding band.

to join Republicans in opposing it. As a result, the United States did not enter the League of Nations. Still paralyzed on his left side, Wilson watched as voters in 1920 returned the Republicans to the White House, with Ohio Senator Warren Harding easily defeating his Democratic opponent, Governor James Cox of Ohio.

During his presidency, Wilson's self-righteousness and stubbornness had sometimes obstructed his better judgment, as in the case of his decision to intervene in the Mexican Revolution and his unwillingness to compromise with Senate Republicans over the Treaty of Versailles. A native Southerner, Wilson also shared the prevailing Southern attitudes on race, so that blacks were excluded from even those few government positions of any consequence that had been traditionally reserved for them. During the war, moreover, Wilson approved passage and enforcement of the Espionage Act (1917) and the Sedition Act (1918) to silence and imprison anti-war critics.

Despite Wilson's flaws, his eight years as president left an indelible mark on the office and the nation. He greatly expanded presidential power and government responsibilities. Not even his Republican successors would seek to repeal Wilson's major legislative accomplishments. Although he failed to win Senate approval of the Treaty of Versailles, the United States would continue to play a major role in world affairs. Even more important, Wilson's concept of a new, American-styled world order would remain the guiding objective of US foreign policy to the present day.

WARREN HARDING

By 1920 Americans were anxious to forget about the war and its aftermath and to return to normalcy. That meant putting Republicans back in power, and for the next 12 years, three Republicans – Wareen Harding, Calvin Coolidge, and Herbert Hoover – would occupy the White House. Although they rejected neither the new role of government established during the previous 20 years nor the Wilsonian call for a New World Order, they put their own twist on domestic and foreign policy. Opposed to the vast expansion of government power they had witnessed since the turn of the century, the Republican presidents supported a business–government partnership with government the junior partner. Without rejecting Wilsonian internationalism, they emphasized the need to build economic and financial bridges to Europe through cooperative ventures between American

Below: A metal campaign button for Warren G. Harding who vowed to return the country to 'normalcy' after the trauma of World War I – one unsavory aspect of this was renewed corruption.

Above: This gilt Great Seal of the United States was owned by President Woodrow Wilson and used to imprint government documents. It was made by the William H. Horstmann Company based in Philadelphia.

Below: President Warren Harding (his portrait in oils, right) with his wife at the National Horse Show in Washington, D.C., in 1921. His campaign promise was 'Less government in business and more business in government.'

CALVIN COOLIDGE

Harding's successor, Vice President Calvin Coolidge, was a former governor of Massachusetts who, in contrast to Harding, was best known for his moral rectitude, frugality, and cryptic language. Born in Plymouth, Vermont, on July 4, 1872, Coolidge practiced law in Massachusetts and then served in the state legislature and as lieutenant governor before being elected governor in 1919. He gained national notoriety and a place on the 1920 Republican ticket for his action in suppressing the Boston Police Strike of 1919, declaring 'There is no right to strike against the public safety by anybody, anywhere, anytime.'[9]

As president, Coolidge was enormously popular because he both symbolized traditional values and was a master in manipulating the mass media. Although Taft had been the first president to hold press conferences, Coolidge institutionalized the practice, meeting twice weekly with the press and answering pre-selected questions. He also was seen regularly on newsreels and was the first president to use the radio to speak to the American people.

During Coolidge's administration, government continued to be dominated by business interests and by the belief that less government was good government. Greatly influenced by Treasury Secretary Mellon, a wealthy banker and financier, Coolidge sought to cut federal expenditures, reduce taxes, and block any liberal legislative initiatives. Coolidge's overwhelming

Below: A Coolidge campaign button. He was known as 'Silent Cal' because of the brevity of his statements, and was also minimalist in terms of the work he undertook during his term of office.

and European business leaders. But although the role of the president was somewhat circumscribed during the Republicans' 12 years in office, the return to normalcy did not mean a return to the practices of the 19th century.

The first of the three Republicans, Warren Harding, was ill-suited to be president. Born in Ohio on November 2, 1865, he attended Ohio Central College and was owner-editor of the Marion, Ohio, *Daily Star* before entering politics. Elected to the US Senate in 1915, he was chosen as the Republican presidential nominee in 1920 after the party convention became hopelessly deadlocked. Handsome, distinguished-looking, and gregarious, he received 60.4 percent of the popular vote in the election, the largest ever cast for a Republican presidential nominee.[8] (His record stood until 1972, when Richard Nixon received 60.7 percent.)

Through a program of high tariffs and low taxes, Harding was able to combat America's post-war recession. He also supported legislation establishing the Bureau of the Budget and the General Accounting Office, and he was successful in getting Congress to approve measures to develop highways, hospital facilities, and aviation. His able Secretary of State, Charles Evans Hughes, presided over the Washington Naval Conference of 1921–22, which set limits on the construction of capital ships, replaced the old Anglo–Japanese Alliance with a four-power agreement to maintain the status quo in the Pacific, and guaranteed the administrative

Above: Calvin Coolidge, photographed when he was vice president. He had a reputation as a dour individual and had his image reinvented quite considerably by advertising associates. This program (above right) is from his inaugural ball.

integrity of China. Harding's Secretary of Commerce, Herbert Hoover, used his department to foster cooperation among American business leaders and to promote American exports.

Yet even Harding recognized his personal limitations, remarking at one time, 'I am a man of limited talents from a small town. I don't seem to grasp that I am President.' With the notable exceptions of Hughes, Hoover, and Treasury Secretary Andrew Mellon, he surrounded himself with political hacks, who used their positions for personal profit. The most notorious scandal of his administration involved Secretary of the Interior Albert Fall, who persuaded harding to transfer the rich naval oil reserves at Teapot Dome, Wyoming, from the Navy Department to the Department of the Interior. Fall then secretly leased them to two businessmen, Harry Sinclair and Edward Doheny, in return for millions of dollars in bribes.

Although most of the scandals of the Harding administration were not revealed until after Harding died, rumors of malfeasance circulated while he was still alive. Tired and depressed by these rumors, Harding suffered a heart attack in San Francisco while returning from a vacation to Alaska. He died on August 2, 1923.

Above: President Calvin Coolidge throwing out the first ball at the baseball World Series. Given his popularity it is highly likely he would have been re-elected in 1928; instead, he chose not to run again.

election victory in 1924 over his Democratic opponent John W. Davis signified the public's approval of business ascendancy in the 1920s.

However, business ascendancy did not mean a return to the laissez-faire economics of the 19th century. Businessmen wanted government to encourage private and corporate pursuits, and Coolidge obliged. Under Secretary Hoover, the Commerce Department continued to foster close private–public cooperation, especially by encouraging the establishment of trade associations and promoting American foreign commerce. The Federal Reserve Board kept interest rates low. The Federal Trade Commission became a friendly adviser to business. The Interstate Commerce Commission was staffed by railroad people. In short, many of the government agencies that had been established to regulate business became its allies, and the White House encouraged this process.[10]

In contrast to business, agriculture did not fare well under Coolidge. Farmers never recovered from the decline in agricultural prices that took place after World War I. In an effort to give

Right: Although not Coolidge's responsibility, during his term of office the nativist Ku Klux Klan reached a peak of membership and felt bold enough to stage mass marches down Pennsylvania Avenue in the shadow of the Capitol.

Above: These buttons are from the presidential campaign of Herbert Hoover (left) whose term of office included the stock market crash of 1929 and the Great Depression that followed.

Hoover's efforts to promote foreign trade, they also indicated the administration's commitment to a Wilsonian world order characterized by international cooperation, peaceful commercial competition, disarmament, and the end of war.

HERBERT HOOVER

Although Coolidge remained an immensely popular president, he announced in 1928 that he would not seek re-election. To replace him, the Republicans turned to Herbert Hoover. Born in West Branch, Iowa on August 10, 1874, Hoover's private and public careers personified the American success story. After putting himself through Stanford, where he earned a degree in engineering in 1895, he went on to become a wealthy and successful international businessman. Following the outbreak of World War I in 1914, Hoover began a new career of public service, first as director of food relief for Belgium, then as food administrator after the United States entered the war in 1917, and finally as

Below: Hoover addressing the electorate via an early radio transmission in 1928. He was painted as uncaring by his opponents, and was blamed by the public for the economic downturn.

them relief, Congress twice passed the McNary–Haugen Bill, a complex measure intended to stabilize agricultural prices through government purchases of surplus agricultural production. In his most serious confrontation with Congress, Coolidge twice vetoed the measure and twice had his veto upheld.

In foreign policy, the most significant developments of the Coolidge presidency were the Dawes Plan of 1924, that was arranged through the international banking community and that provided for a restructuring of Germany's finances and the establishment of a new reparations payments schedule for Germany; the Geneva Naval Conference of 1927, an unsuccessful effort by the major naval powers to limit the construction of noncapital ships (mostly cruisers); and the Kellog–Briand Pact of 1928, which outlawed war as an instrument of national policy. Although the Geneva Conference was a failure and the Kellog–Briand Pact came to seem naïve in the wake of World War II, the leading role the United States played at Geneva and in formulating the agreement outlawing war indicated America's continuing involvement in world affairs. Along with the Dawes Plan and

STRICTLY NOT TRANSFERABLE

Mrs Hoes

will please present this card at the
EAST ENTRANCE
of The White House, Thursday evening

JANUARY 30, 1930
9.00 O'CLOCK

The White House

Admit at **East** Gate

NOT TRANSFERABLE

Jan 30 1930

DISPLAY ON WIND SHIELD OF CAR

*The President and Mrs Hoover
request the pleasure of the company of*
Mrs Hoes
at a reception to be held at
The White House
*Thursday evening, January the thirtieth
nineteen hundred and thirty
at nine o'clock*

Above: An invitation to a White House reception, an admission ticket, and a car pass, all sent by President and Mrs Hoover to Mrs Hoes, the great granddaughter of President Monroe. Mrs Hoes was instrumental in establishing the First Ladies' Collection in the National Museum of American History, Smithsonian Institution.

director of American relief efforts in Europe after the 1918 armistice. By 1920, he had earned an international reputation as a successful businessman-turned-humanitarian.[11]

As secretary of commerce during both the Harding and Coolidge administrations, Hoover continued to add to his reputation by transforming his department into a beehive of activity for the promotion of public–private cooperation, good management practices, and business growth at home and abroad. As one of the most influential figures of the 1920s, Hoover was an obvious choice to head the Republican ticket in 1928. In the election that followed, in which religion proved a major influence on voting, he trounced his Democratic opponent, Governor Al Smith of New York, a Catholic and the son of Irish immigrants.

In October 1929, not yet eight months in office, Hoover was faced with the crash of the stock market and the ensuing Great Depression, which proved to be the nation's worst economic disaster. At the time, most economists believed that the depression was part of a natural economic cycle, and that as soon as there was general confidence in the economy, economic recovery would follow automatically. Classical theory suggested that in order to restore economic confi-

Right: Hoover pictured in readiness for his Armistice Day speech on November 11, 1929. He himself had headed the Food Administration during the war.

dence, government had to cut spending and do little else.

Hoover did not reject conventional economic theory insofar as it involved economic confidence-building. He believed that, in the final analysis, most of the burden for ending the depression had to fall on the private sector. But he was also convinced that the depression's magnitude was too great for government to stand by idly. Government, for example, could undertake necessary public works projects, such as building roads and dams. Even more important, it could promote cooperative ventures within the private sector and assist corporate enterprise in responding to the depression, much as Hoover had done as secretary of commerce.

This was the approach Hoover followed as president, bringing together business leaders in an effort to get them to cooperate in maintaining wages and levels of production. The effort was unsuccessful, and when the crisis worsened in 1932, he established the Reconstruction Finance Corporation (RFC) to make loans to faltering banks, railroads, and insurance companies. He also speeded up public works projects, such as construction of the enormous Hoover Dam, and encouraged states to do the same. In 1933, just before leaving office, he signed the Emergency Relief and Construction Act, which provided $1.8 billion in relief loans and self-liquidating public works. The problem with Hoover, therefore, was not that he was a cold and uncaring 'do-nothing' president, as his critics charged, but that he relied too heavily on the private sector to deal with the worst economic crisis in the nation's history. Although he did much to cope with the crisis, he did not do enough.[12]

Left and below: Exterior and interior views of Camp Hoover, a fishing and vacation retreat built by the Marines, and paid for and used by Hoover during his presidency. In 1933 he donated it to Shenandoah National Park for future presidents.

Above: President Hoover at his desk in the White House signing the bills passed by Congress authorizing loans to farmers in drought-stricken areas and a program of emergency construction to give relief to the unemployed.

Hoover's foreign policy was also beleaguered. His efforts to continue the commitment of his Republican predecessors to a Wilsonian world order were undermined by a new naval arms race, Japanese military expansion into Manchuria in 1931, and the worldwide depression. Efforts at the London Naval Conference of 1930 to stop the arms race failed. The Stimson Doctrine of nonrecognition, applied against the Japanese puppet state of Manchukuo by Secretary of State Henry Stimson, was also a failure; Japan refused to leave Manchuria. Although an international business committee headed by the industrialist Owen Young developed a new reparations plan for Germany in 1929, the Plan did not survive the onset of the Depression. The economic downturn brought a virtual end to both reparations and debt repayments and contributed to the rise of fascism in Germany. Viewed in terms of the goals he set forth in 1929, Hoover's foreign policy must be regarded as a failure.

In 1932, Hoover was resoundingly defeated in his bid for re-election by Governor Franklin D. Roosevelt of New York, whose New Deal policies would permanently change the character of the American presidency as well as the American nation. Yet the modern presidency, characterized by activist executive leadership on behalf of an expanded sense of the role and responsibilities of the US government both at home and abroad, was already in place by the time Roosevelt took office in 1933.

Notes

1. Gould, 1980: 231–53
2. Harbaugh, 1963: 149–423; Mowry, 1958: 106–225.
3. Mowry, 1958: 226–95.
4. Walworth, 1978: 1–394.

5. Cooper, Jr., 1983: 143–221.
6. Link, 965: 3–156; Smith, 1965: 1–201.
7. Mayer, 1964: 34–36, 161–62, 329–93.
8. Murray, 1969: passim; Murray, 1973: 1–129.

9. McCoy, 1967: passim; Hicks, 1960: 79–152.
10. Hawley, 1992: 66–110.
11. Wilson, 1975: 3–208.
12. Romasco, 1995: 10–234; Karl, 1983: 80–110.

Burton I. Kaufman

11
THE MODERN PRESIDENCY

Franklin D. Roosevelt   1933-1945
Harry S. Truman   1945-1953
Dwight D. Eisenhower   1953-1961
John F. Kennedy   1961-1963
Lyndon B. Johnson   1963-1969

The middle third of the 20th century was the apex of the presidency. Sparked by FDR's leadership in the Great Depression and World War II, the office was lifted to new heights of power and prestige, both domestically and on the world stage. Roosevelt's successors rose to the new standard: historians have rated each of the era's five presidents as 'great' or 'near-great.' Yet the modern presidency was darkened by Kennedy's assassination and Johnson's failed policies in Vietnam, thus setting the stage for a diminution of presidential power.

Crowds fill Times Square, New York, on
VJ Day to celebrate the end of World War II.

Between 1933 and 1969 the American presidency went through its most expansive and activist period. Beginning with Franklin D. Roosevelt's New Deal and ending with Lyndon Johnson's 'Great Society,' American presidents expanded the scope of government beyond anything imagined even by most Progressive reformers a generation earlier. During this period the United States also achieved a level of global supremacy unique in world history and, in a spirit of bipartisanship, Congress generally deferred to the executive branch in the formulation and execution of foreign policy. As a result, the American presidency was never as strong and powerful as in the 35 years following Roosevelt's inauguration as the nation's 32nd president.

FRANKLIN D. ROOSEVELT

A distant cousin of Theodore Roosevelt, Franklin D. Roosevelt was born in Hyde Park, New York on January 30, 1882. Graduating from Harvard in 1904, he attended Columbia Law School and briefly practiced law before being elected to the New York State Senate in 1911. In 1913, he was appointed by Woodrow Wilson as assistant secretary of the navy, and in the 1920 election he was James M. Cox's vice presidential running mate. A year later, Roosevelt was stricken with polio. Although partially paralyzed, he recovered sufficiently to return to politics. In 1928, he was elected governor of New York, and in 1932, he received the Democratic presidential nomination. In November, he crushed Hoover, gaining 57 percent of the popular vote.

Right: A fit and healthy Assistant Secretary of the Navy Roosevelt arriving at his office during Woodrow Wilson's administration. This was a post his cousin Theodore had also once held.

Taking office on March 4, 1933, Roosevelt immediately called Congress into special session and declared a bank holiday. During the next 100 days, he dazzled the nation with a program of legislation known as the New Deal that ranged from banking reform to jobs creation and development of electrical power in the Tennessee Valley. Washington became dotted with new agencies and programs having such acronyms as FDIC (Federal Deposit Insurance Corporation), CCC (Civilian Conservation Corps), and TVA (Tennessee Valley Authority).

The cornerstones of the first 100 days, however, were two measures intended to bring about the recovery of agriculture and industry. The Agricultural Adjustment Act (AAA) addressed the chronic plight of the nation's farmers by raising agricultural prices through curtailed production. In return for leaving land idle, farmers were given cash subsidies. The National Industrial Recovery Act (NIRA) provided for a system of industrial self-government in which business groups prepared fair-competition codes regulating production, prices, and wages. Once these codes were approved by a new federal agency, the National Recovery Administration (NRA), they

Below: Franklin D. Roosevelt as a candidate for the presidency in 1932, shaking hands from the rear platform of his train – the Roosevelt Special – in one of the most strenuous campaigns in American political history.

became law. Two other sections of the legislation acknowledged labor's right to collective bargaining and established the Public Works Administration (PWA), whose purpose was to provide jobs for the unemployed.[1]

By the time the special session of Congress adjourned in June, it had approved 15 major pieces of relief, recovery, and reform legislation. Never had the scope of government been expanded so fast or so dramatically. And presiding over this expansion was Franklin D. Roosevelt (FDR), who had rallied Congress and the country behind his programs, bringing the Oval Office into the homes of millions of Americans for the first time through his 'fireside chats,' which were broadcast over radio.

Yet much of the 'first New Deal' was experimental rather than well-conceived. Furthermore, it said almost as much about Roosevelt's inherent conservatism as his willingness to break from tradition. At a time when he could have assaulted big business, he chose instead to prop it up through a system of self-regulation. His farm

Above: The depression meant destitution for
thousands of citizens and their families and
shanty towns grew in the suburbs. This public
health nurse is trying to help such a family.

Below: A poster for the Social Security Board
whose pensions provisions enacted in 1935 were
among the most significant measures of the
'second New Deal's' legislation.

legislation benefited mostly landowning farmers
producing for market while driving off share-
croppers whose land was left idle so that its
owners could collect federal subsidies. Even the
most important of his work relief programs, the
PWA, was administered conservatively with
more attention paid to the value of the projects
being built than to the creation of new jobs.

In 1935, however, FDR pushed through
Congress a 'second New Deal' of reform legislation that represented a major departure from
the past. By this time, the president was being
attacked politically from both right and left.
From the right, business and farm leaders, experiencing the first signs of economic recovery,
chafed at the restrictions imposed upon them by
the AAA and NIRA and successfully challenged
the constitutionality of both measures before the
Supreme Court. From the left, national figures
with huge followings like Senator Huey Long of
Louisiana, the radio priest Father Charles
Coughlin, and the retired California physician
Dr Francis Townsend were calling for drastic
measures, including a national redistribution of
wealth, nationalization of the banking system,
and substantial old-age pensions. Senator Long
also seemed ready to challenge Roosevelt for the
1936 Democratic presidential nomination.[2]

Angered by his right-wing critics and concerned about his own chances for re-election in
1936, Roosevelt veered toward the left. The
result was another program of sweeping legislation and a new set of acronyms. The WPA
(Works Progress Administration) built play-
grounds, schools, and hospitals and employed
writers, musicians, and muralists in meaningful
jobs. The REA (Rural Electrification Administration) brought electric power for the first time
to remote areas of the nation. The NLRB
(National Labor Relations Board) conducted
collective bargaining elections and protected
employees from coercive employers. But the
most significant measure of the 'second New
Deal' was the Social Security Act, which for the
first time provided old-age pensions to retired
persons 65 years of age and older.[3]

Although Roosevelt was to serve in the office
for another decade, passage of the 'second New
Deal' was the high point of his legislative
achievements. In 1936, he won a resounding re-
election victory over his Republican challenger,
Governor Alfred P. Landon of Kansas, capturing
every state except Vermont and Maine. In Congress, Democrats also won the largest majorities
for any party since the mid-19th century. Yet
Roosevelt's second administration witnessed a
sharp decline in New Deal fortunes. Angered by
the Supreme Court decisions invalidating major
portions of his New Deal program, Roosevelt
tried to pack the court by legislation that would
have allowed him to add as many as six new

members to the court. This produced a backlash among the public who thought Roosevelt was trying to subvert the Constitution. A series of favorable decisions by the court on several pieces of New Deal legislation, including the Social Security Act, undermined the argument for re-organization, and in 1937 Congress killed the so-called 'court-packing' Bill. The fight over the legislation, however, had weakened Roosevelt's hold over Congress. A conservative coalition of Republicans and Southern Democrats became an effective barrier against further social legis-lation.[4]

By this time, moreover, Roosevelt was becoming increasingly preoccupied with the deteriorating world situation. Italy's seizure of Ethiopia in 1935, Nazi Germany's reoccupation of the Rhineland in 1936, the beginning of the Spanish Civil War a few months later, Japan's military advances in China (where it had been waging war since 1932), and Germany's annexation of Austria in 1938 caused him growing alarm. In October 1937 Roosevelt spoke about the need to 'quarantine' aggressors. But an isolationist mood pervaded the nation. In order to avoid foreign entanglements, Congress adopted a series of neutrality acts between 1935 and 1937 which prohibited arms sales to warring powers, travel on belligerent ships, and loans or credits to belligerents.

Although Roosevelt was reluctant to move much beyond what he thought public opinion would permit, he sought a substantial increase in military appropriations in 1938. The next year he urged Congress to repeal the neutrality laws, and when Germany's invasion of Poland in

Below: This cartoon by Clifford K. Berryman dates from February 1939 and refers to the multitude of opinions which existed about foreign policy in an officially neutral USA.

Above: President Roosevelt delivering his election eve message on November 4, 1938, for the midterm Congressional elections.

September 1939 led to the outbreak of World War II, he persuaded Congress to lift the arms embargo. This allowed Britain and France to buy munitions on a cash-and-carry basis. Following the fall of France in June 1940, Roosevelt provided aircraft to Britain, and in September, he concluded the 'destroyers-for-bases' deal; in exchange for leases of British bases in the Western Hemisphere, Britain received destroyers to protect its Atlantic convoys.

In November 1940 FDR was elected to an unprecedented third term despite a strong challenge from his Republican opponent, Wendell Willkie. During the campaign Roosevelt had promised American mothers that he would not send their boys to war, but in March 1941 he won congressional passage of the Lend Lease Act, which allowed the Allies to obtain military supplies from the United States without having to pay cash for them. The USA, he explained, needed to be 'the arsenal of democracy.'

Below: Campaign buttons from three of FDR's election victories, plus an anti-Roosevelt button from 1940. The Democratic donkey one is from the 1936 election, 'We Want F.D.R. Again' is from 1940, and the Roosevelt-Truman one is 1944.

MAYBE IT'S A CASE OF TOO MANY COOKS.

In June 1941 Germany invaded the Soviet Union. Alarmed by the specter of Nazi domination of the entire European continent, the president met with British Prime Minister Winston Churchill in August at Argentia Harbor, Newfoundland, where they signed the Atlantic Charter. Following a German submarine attack on the USS *Greer*, Roosevelt ordered American naval forces to 'shoot on sight' any German or Italian vessel in the Western Atlantic. After a German submarine sank the USS *Reuben James* in October, he authorized the arming of American merchant ships and permitted them to carry cargo to belligerent ports.

In time, undeclared naval war would probably have led to a formal state of war between the United States and Germany. What happened, however, was that Germany declared war against the United States following its ally Japan's attack on Pearl Harbor on December 7, 1941. Although the American people had been reluctant to wage war in Europe, they were more willing to engage the Japanese, whose interests in East Asia clashed directly with those of the United States. Desperately in need of oil and other raw materials in Southeast Asia, and convinced that Washington would not allow it to expand southward, Japan decided to attack and destroy the American fleet at Pearl Harbor. Japan hoped that this would give it time to consolidate its position before the United States could retaliate. Honoring a mutual assistance pact between the Axis powers, Germany, Japan, and Italy (the Tripartite Agreement of 1940), Hitler declared war against the United States on December 11, three days after the United States declared war against Japan.[5]

Still regarding Germany as a more serious threat than Japan, Roosevelt believed that the United States had to undertake an early military campaign against Germany. In 1942 he agreed to a plan favored by Churchill for an invasion of North Africa, even though this meant delaying

Above: Congressional leaders look on as President Roosevelt signs the bill that declared the United States as being in a state of war with the Japanese Empire on December 8, 1941.

an invasion of Europe across the English Channel until sometime in 1944. Launched in November 1942, Operation Torch succeeded by May in freeing all of North Africa from Axis control. Military operations against Sicily and Italy followed.

The long delay in opening a second front in Europe angered Soviet leader Joseph Stalin, whose forces along the Eastern front bore the brunt of the war. But with the launching on June 6, 1944, of Operation Overlord (the cross-channel invasion of Normandy), relations among the Allies improved markedly. By this time, the Soviets were moving into Eastern Europe. Despite a startling German counteroffensive in December 1944, known as the Battle of the Bulge, Allied forces were able to close a vise on the Nazis from East and West. By the time Churchill, Roosevelt, and Stalin met at the Yalta Conference in February 1945, the war leaders were turning their attention to the post-war settlement.

Roosevelt went to Yalta newly elected for yet a fourth term as president after defeating the Republican candidate, Governor Thomas Dewey of New York, by about 3.6 million votes, the narrowest of his four presidential victories. Pictures of the president at Yalta show a sick man – thin, drawn, tired, and haggard; in fact, he was suffering by this time from an enlarged heart and high blood pressure. Roosevelt's detractors later maintained that his ill-health affected his judgment at Yalta. They accused him of 'giving away' Poland and much of Eastern Europe to the Soviet Union. In truth, Roosevelt had nothing to give away; at the end of the war, Eastern Europe was already occupied by Soviet forces, and Moscow was determined to maintain control of the region.[6]

On April 12, 1945, while vacationing in Warm Springs, Georgia, Roosevelt suffered a stroke and died three hours later. Americans were shocked by the death of the president who had governed longer than any other, led them through a depression and a world war, and, in the process, changed the character of the Oval Office and the role of government. Crisis furnishes an opportunity for greatness, and Roosevelt responded to

Below: A joint press conference on December 23, 1941, at the White House featuring President Roosevelt and Britain's prime minister, Winston S. Churchill, now a close wartime ally.

crisis by making the presidency far more powerful and more central to the nation than ever before. More than that, his New Deal had shown the possibilities of government as an engine of social change during a period of economic and social upheaval. It also established the political and social agenda for the next 30 years.

HARRY S. TRUMAN

Upon the death of FDR, Vice President Harry S. Truman of Missouri was suddenly elevated to the Oval Office. Born in Lamar, Missouri, on May 8, 1884, Truman had operated a family farm until 1917 when he served as a World War I army captain in France. After the war, he opened a men's store in Kansas City. Although the business eventually failed, he became good friends with Tom Pendergast, the local political boss. With Pendergast's backing, Truman was made a county judge (the equivalent of a county executive). He remained in that post from 1922 until 1934, when he won election to the US Senate. After narrowly winning re-election in 1940, he gained national prominence for his

work as chairman of the Senate Committee to Investigate the National Defense Program, which exposed considerable mismanagement and corruption in war production. Looking for a compromise candidate to replace his controversial vice president, Henry Wallace, on the 1944 Democratic ticket, Roosevelt settled on Truman, who had close ties to conservative Southern Democrats but was also acceptable to Northern liberals.

The contrast between Truman and Roosevelt could not have been more striking. Whereas Roosevelt's charisma was acknowledged even by his detractors, the kindest description of Truman was that he was an unassuming midwestern politician who had been picked by Roosevelt to be his running mate largely because he was inoffensive. Certainly Truman felt unprepared to replace Roosevelt, and with good reason: Roosevelt had never taken his vice president into his confidence.

Immediately facing Truman was the post-war settlement of Europe. At the Yalta Conference, the Soviet Union had agreed to hold free elections in Eastern Europe. But Stalin was unwilling to allow non-communists to share power in Poland. Although Truman sought to carry out Roosevelt's plans for the post-war world, which were predicated on maintaining the wartime coalition, he was heavily influenced by the anti-Soviet views being expressed at the State

Above: Thomas E. Dewey was the losing Republican candidate in 1944 and 1948. He reduced FDR to his lowest winning margin in 1944 and unexpectedly lost to Truman in 1948.

Below: The funeral procession for Franklin D. Roosevelt in Washington, D.C., in 1944. In office he had confronted two of the nation's greatest crises, depression and world war.

Department, which he shared. At a meeting in April with Soviet Foreign Minister Vyacheslav Molotov, he berated the Soviets for not honoring their pledges in Eastern Europe.

Truman's most important decision in his first six months in office, however, was to use the atomic bomb against Japan. Although Germany surrendered to the Allies in May, the war in the Pacific continued. Since the battles of Midway Island and Guadalcanal in 1942 and early 1943, the United States had advanced steadily toward Japan, island-hopping across the South and Central Pacific. But the Japanese were tenacious fighters. In the battle for Okinawa, more than 11,000 Americans were killed before the island was captured in June 1945. The planned invasion of the Japanese islands was expected to result in enormous additional casualties. As vice president, Truman had not even been informed about the development of the atomic bomb. But once the weapon was successfully tested at the end of July, he never wavered in his decision to use it. On August 6 the first bomb was dropped on Hiroshima; three days later a second bomb was dropped on Nagasaki. On August 14, the Japanese surrender ended World War II.

Although Truman used the bomb to end the war, he believed that a combination of America's atomic monopoly and the Soviet Union's need for American economic assistance after the war might persuade the Soviets to behave as they had promised at Yalta. Instead, Stalin accused the West of intimidation and provocation and relied exclusively on Soviet resources to rebuild his war-devastated country.

Between 1946 and 1949 the Cold War escalated, as Soviet and American interests clashed in such places as Eastern Europe, Iran, Greece, Turkey, and Germany. In 1947, Britain announced that it could no longer be the defender

Below: The Japanese surrender document is handed to President Truman in the Oval Office by Colonel Bernard Thielen on September 7, 1945, as some of the leading American military figures look on. It had been signed five days earlier in Tokyo Bay aboard the warship USS *Missouri*.

Above: Truman was the first president to travel regularly by aircraft. He used an adapted Douglas DC-6 called 'The Independence' – a scale model of which is seen here, together with actual china and silverware used on board. The bone china is English, made by Royal Doulton.

Above: General Douglas MacArthur, the Supreme Commander of Allied Powers in Tokyo and Commander of U.N. Forces in Korea, was relieved of his command for criticizing Truman in 1951.

Above: President Truman on the campaign trail in Bridgeport, Pennsylvania, during the first week of October 1948. At that stage he lagged behind Governor Dewey of New York quite considerably.

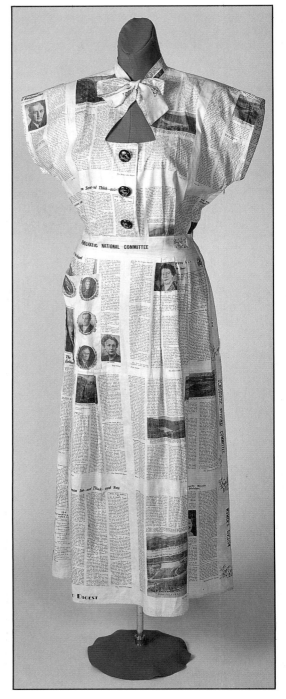

Left: Dresses such as this were worn by female pages at the 1948 Democratic Convention in Philadelphia. The cotton material is imprinted with copy from the *Democratic Digest*.

of Western interests in the Mediterranean region. The president responded with the Truman Doctrine, which provided $400 million in economic and military assistance to Greece and Turkey and included an open-ended pledge to protect friendly nations from subversion and aggression. In June, Secretary of State George C. Marshall proposed the Marshall Plan for the economic reconstruction of Western Europe. That same month, George Kennan, a high State Department official, published an article signed 'X' in the American journal *Foreign Affairs*, in which he outlined the doctrine of containment, America's strategy for waging the Cold War. In 1948, Truman ordered an airlift of supplies to Berlin after the Soviets imposed a blockade on that city. In 1949, he extended diplomatic recognition to West Germany (the Federal Republic of Germany) and approved American membership in NATO.[7]

The most serious foreign crisis that faced Truman as president, however, came in Korea during his second term. In one of the biggest political upsets in history, Truman in 1948 defeated his Republican opponent for president, former Governor Dewey of New York, who was making his second run for the office. In protest against a civil rights plank in the Democratic Party platform, Southern Democrats broke off to form their own 'Dixiecrat' Party. But by attacking the 'do-nothing' Republican-controlled 80th Congress and conducting a vigorous campaign while Dewey ran a deliberately cautious campaign, Truman won the election, receiving 24.1 million votes to Dewey's 22 million votes.

On June 25, 1950, North Korea invaded South Korea and advanced almost to the southernmost tip of the Korean Peninsula. The president responded by sending American armed forces under United Nations (UN) auspices to Korea. Following a brilliant amphibious operation at Inchon in September conceived by General Douglas MacArthur, the much-revered

Below: These chicken feed sacks were used in the unofficial straw ballot in Kansas City in 1948 that came to be known as the 'pullet poll' – the only poll that showed Truman in the lead. The bags carried either party's symbol and whichever was purchased was deemed to show voter preference.

Commander of UN Forces in Korea, the tide of battle was reversed. By November, UN forces had crossed the 38th parallel into North Korea and advanced to the Yalu River, the border separating North Korea from the People's Republic of China. At the end of November, the Chinese intervened in massive numbers. Before their offensive was stopped, they had driven back UN forces to South of the 38th parallel. Regaining the initiative, UN forces were then able to drive the Chinese back to a line approximating the 38th parallel. Chafing under orders that prevented him from expanding the war, MacArthur publicly criticized the administration's policy. In response, Truman relieved him of his command in April 1951. Although armistice negotiations began in July 1951, they became deadlocked over the issue of repatriation of prisoners of war. For the remainder of Truman's administration, both the war and the negotiations remained unresolved.[8]

Despite Truman's preoccupation with foreign affairs, he also devoted considerable time to domestic issues. While representing Missouri in the Senate, he had been a loyal supporter of the New Deal. As president, he sought to go beyond the New Deal with his 'Fair Deal,' which even provided for a program of universal health insurance. Although most of his programs were defeated by a conservative Congress, Truman was able to bring about modest gains in such areas as housing and Social Security, thereby expanding upon the legacy he inherited from Roosevelt. He also reorganized the federal government. The Atomic Energy Act of 1946 placed control of all fissionable material in a new civilian agency, the Atomic Energy Commission. The Presidential Succession Act placed the speaker of the House and the president *pro tempore* of the Senate ahead of cabinet secretaries in the line of succession should the president and vice president die or be disabled. The National Security Act of 1947 unified the military services under the new Department of Defense and created the National Security Council (NSC) and Central Intelligence Agency (CIA).[9]

In 1952, there was speculation that Truman might seek re-election, but by this time he had become extremely unpopular. Americans were tired of the Korean War. Senator Joseph McCarthy of Wisconsin and other right-wing Republicans were making wild but politically effective charges of internal communist subversion in government, and the administration had become tainted by revelations of corruption and influence-peddling in several federal agencies. On the defensive, Truman decided to withdraw from the race.

Although extremely unpopular when he left office in 1953, Truman is generally acknowledged by historians to have been one of

Left: Truman holding aloft the infamous *Chicago Daily Tribune* headline as his victory train rolls into the station at St. Louis, Missouri, on the morning of November 4, 1948.

PRESIDENT HARRY S. TRUMAN

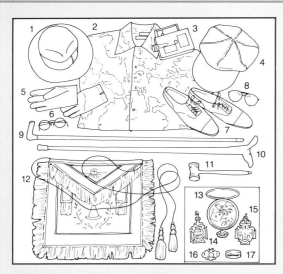

1. Gray felt borsalino hat with a black silk band.
2. Silk, patterned Hawaiian-style sport shirt made by Hoaloha, one of many Truman had.
3. Kodak cine camera given to Truman by 'Newsreel Friends,' and so engraved.
4. White twill and mesh cap with a visor, worn by Truman at Key West in 1951.
5. Unlined brown leather gloves.
6. Spectacles purchased on May 22, 1951.
7. White and tan Spectator shoes.
8. AN-G-22 Type II Flying Sun Glasses.
9. Presentation ebony cane with a gold head, given by his old World War I artillery unit.
10. Wood cane with a donkey-head handle, the symbol of the Democratic Party.
11. Wood gavel used when presiding over the opening of the 79th Congress in 1945.
12. Masonic apron made for Truman as Past Grand Master of the Missouri Grand Lodge.
13. Pocket watch with nickel case; the interior works are shaped as masonic implements.
14. Gold masonic jewel of the Knights Templar.
15. Gold masonic jewel of a Scottish Rite master.
16. Gold 32nd degree Master Mason ring.
17. Gold 33rd degree masonic ring – the only president to hold this rank of freemasonry.

Left: President Truman photographed aboard USS *Augusta* signing documentation. His period of office was a time of much American activity internationally, not least the creation of NATO.

The successful invasion of Europe and the victory over Germany less than a year later turned 'Ike' into a world celebrity. In 1948 he retired from the army to become president of Columbia University. Unhappy in that position, he assumed command in 1950 of NATO forces in Europe. By this time, a movement was underway in both major parties to draft Eisenhower for president. In 1952, he was persuaded by a group of moderate Republicans to head the Republican ticket. Winning the nomination on the first ballot, he then went on to an easy victory over his Democratic opponent, Governor Adlai Stevenson of Illinois.[10]

Although Eisenhower had been the candidate of moderate Republicans, once in office he proved to be a fiscal conservative. He also believed in limiting the role of the federal government. He turned over offshore oil rights to the seaboard states, opposed most federal public works projects, tried to overturn Democratic farm policy based on agricultural price supports, and opposed amendments to Social Security providing for medical insurance.

Yet Eisenhower accepted the basic outlines of the New Deal. Thus he signed into law a measure providing for the biggest single expansion of the Social Security system in history, fought successfully for an increase in the mini-

Below: Dwight D. Eisenhower, the military man. Command of the Allied invasions of North Africa and, later, Europe during World War II gave him organizational experience few could match.

America's better presidents. A feisty political figure who sometimes acted hastily and imprudently, he was, nevertheless, willing to make difficult decisions. His firing of General MacArthur in 1951, which led to calls in Congress for his impeachment, may have been the most courageous and unpopular decision of any president in the post-war period. But by his action, he reaffirmed the authority of the president as commander-in-chief. Similarly, he established the authority of the presidency in foreign policy at a time when the United States was thrust into the role of leader of the non-communist world. As president, this may have been his greatest legacy.

DWIGHT D. EISENHOWER

Truman's successor, Dwight D. Eisenhower, was born in Denison, Texas, on October 14, 1890. In 1911, he entered the United States Military Academy at West Point. Graduating in 1915, he spent most of the next 25 years in relative obscurity in the army. As late as 1941, he only held the rank of lieutenant-colonel. But that year he was promoted to colonel. During maneuvers in Louisiana, he displayed tactical skills which won him promotion to brigadier general and brought him to the attention of Army Chief of Staff George C. Marshall. In March 1942, Marshall promoted him to major general. During World War II Eisenhower commanded the Allied invasion of North Africa, and in 1944 he was given the plum assignment to head the invasion of Europe.

mum wage, and favored limited expansion of federal activity in housing, medical care, and education. In addition, his administration established the Department of Health, Education, and Welfare (HEW), and it obtained legislation providing for the construction with Canada of the Saint Lawrence Seaway and for the building of a 42,000-mile interstate highway system, the largest program of its kind in the nation's history.

On the least two critical domestic issues, McCarthyism and civil rights, Eisenhower's record was less than admirable. Although Eisenhower detested McCarthy personally, he shared the common belief that Soviet espionage in the United States had jeopardized national security, and he did little to stop McCarthy from making unsubstantiated charges about communist infiltration of government. Indeed, he issued an executive order permitting the firing of 7,000 federal employees considered to be security risks. In the end McCarthy brought about his own downfall by his unsubstantiated charges and boorish and bullyish behavior.

On the issue of civil rights, the administration's record was better, but not all that it might have been. Eisenhower believed that every American citizen was entitled to vote and to receive equal protection under the law. He signed into law a 1957 civil rights bill establishing an independent Civil Rights Commission and a Civil Rights Division within the Justice Department and a 1960 measure authorizing the appointment of federal referees to investigate voting rights violations. But the president also

Above: Dwight D. Eisenhower taking the oath of office as president in 1953. He had turned down both political parties in 1948, but agreed to the Republican overtures in 1952.

Below: A setting of the formal dinner service for state functions in the White House. The china plate is one of 120 given to Mrs Eisenhower in 1955. The silver knives are pearl-handled.

thought that responsibility for civil rights should be left to the individual states, and he did not believe that custom could be changed overnight by legislation. In the most serious civil rights crisis of his administration, involving the desegregation of Central High School in Little Rock, Arkansas, in 1957, he displayed a singular lack of leadership. Although Eisenhower eventually federalized the National Guard and sent in troops to protect the black children who were trying to

Below: Two framed miniature portraits which President Eisenhower kept on his desk during his term in office. At right is a photograph of Mamie, his wife; at left is a painting of his mother.

integrate the school, he did not act until rioting had broken out and the governor of Arkansas, Orval Faubus, had withdrawn the protection of the National Guard.

Eisenhower's foreign policy followed the internationalist lines of his Democratic predecessors. But believing that the Democrats had relied too heavily on the costly build-up of ground forces to contain Soviet expansion, he predicated his containment policy on the threatened use of 'massive retaliation' with nuclear weapons. In Korea in 1953, he let the Chinese know that he might use nuclear weapons if they did not conclude an armistice. In 1954, he considered using atomic weapons in Indochina where French troops, fighting the communist Vietminh forces, were on the verge of a major defeat at Dien Bien Phu. That same year, he considered bombing mainland China if the Chinese invaded the offshore islands of Quemoy and Matsu, which were under the control of Chinese Nationalists.

In none of these instances, however, were nuclear weapons used. In Korea the Chinese agreed to an armistice in June 1953. In Indochina, Eisenhower decided against intervention, and the French were forced to sue for peace after being defeated at Dien Bien Phu. In Quemoy and Matsu, Eisenhower again decided to avoid the risk of nuclear war, and the Chinese made it clear that they would not invade the islands.[11]

Above: The Eisenhower cabinet in May 1957; clockwise: Wilton Persons, Henry Cabot Lodge, Fred Seaton, George Humphrey, Richard Nixon, Herbert Brownell, Sinclair Weeks, Marion Folsom, Val Peterson, Percival Brundage, Gordon Gray, James P. Mitchell, Arthur Summerfield, John Foster Dulles, Eisenhower, C.E. Wilson, Ezra Taft Benson, Maxwell W. Rabb, and Sherman Adams.

The difficulty with massive retaliation was that by reducing conventional ground forces, it seriously limited US foreign policy options, leaving little but total war or inaction as policy choices. In 1956, for example, the United States could not have responded to the anti-communist revolution in Hungary even if it had wanted to because, short of a nuclear war, it lacked the military means. As presented to the American people by Secretary of State John Foster Dulles, moreover, massive retaliation was overly provocative and confrontational, raising the level of Cold War rhetoric several decibels.

Much to his credit, Eisenhower was the first American president to recognize the force of Third World nationalism. In 1956, when Britain and France invaded Egypt to prevent it from nationalizing the Suez Canal, thereby inflaming nationalist passions, the president forced the two European powers to withdraw their troops by applying economic pressure against them.

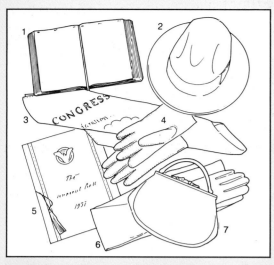

PRESIDENT DWIGHT D. EISENHOWER

1. The Holy Bible, American Standard Version, given to Dwight D. Eisenhower by his mother upon graduation from the United States Military Academy, West Point, in June 1915; he graduated with average grades. The front corner is embossed 'Dwight D. Eisenhower,' and the Bible was later used during the presidential inauguration.

2. Black homberg hat with grain ribbon; worn by Eisenhower during the inauguration. The interior label identifies the retailer as 'F.R. Tripler & Co., Madison Ave. at 46th Street.'

3. White silk scarf with the Declaration of Independence printed on it against a background of the Great Seal of the United States.

4. Pair of gray, fine-grained, soft leather men's gloves worn by President Eisenhower. The interior label states 'Chesterton/Genuine Mocha Gloves.'

5. Program for the inaugural ball.

6. Pair of women's long evening gloves worn by Mrs Eisenhower, possibly for the inaugural ball in 1957.

7. Beaded evening bag carried by Mrs Eisenhower. The bag has a date in it of 1957.

Above: President Eisenhower meeting black and civil rights leaders in June 1958. Truman had added the issue to the agenda but not until the 1950s and desegregation did it come to the fore.

Unfortunately, Eisenhower often failed to distinguish between nationalism and communism, as in 1958 when he sent 14,000 American troops into Lebanon to prevent a communist coup that never materialized.[12]

Eisenhower was the first American president who was barred from running for a third term by the Twenty-second (or 'two-term') Amendment to the Constitution (1951). Given his popularity, he probably could have won a third term in 1960 had he been allowed to run. Yet most presidential scholars at the time gave him low marks, claiming that he was not in control of his own administration and that he had failed to provide the nation with adequate leadership.

More recent scholarship has shown, however, that Eisenhower was very much in control and that although he delegated authority, much as he had as a military commander, he made all the crucial decisions. Moreover, scholars now look favorably upon his concerns about fiscal economy and the fact that, notwithstanding the rhetoric of his foreign policy, he was able to end the Korean War in 1953 and to avoid American involvement in any other war – something that neither his predecessor or successor could achieve. But the most important legacy of the Eisenhower presidency was that, as the first Republican to sit in the Oval Office since the the New Deal, Eisenhower accepted, and in some respects extended, the basic tenets of the social welfare state that had been established in the 1930s. At the same time, he was guided in his conduct of foreign affairs by the policy of containment with its burden of international responsibilities.

Left: Campaign memorabilia came in all shapes and sizes by the 1950s – neck tie, bracelet, compact, and so on – but a slogan was vital and 'I Like Ike' was simply a classic.

Above: This friendly meeting between Dwight Eisenhower and his young successor, John F. Kennedy, took place in California in early 1962.

JOHN F. KENNEDY

When Eisenhower left office in 1961, he was the oldest president in the nation's history. He was succeeded in office by John F. Kennedy, the nation's youngest elected president, after JFK narrowly defeated his Republican opponent, Vice President Richard Nixon, by less than 120,000 votes out of 68 million cast. The first Roman Catholic to be president, Kennedy was born in Boston on May 29, 1917. Raised in a family of great wealth, he was a frail and shy boy who suffered a series of illnesses as a youth. Graduating in 1940 from Harvard, where he wrote a senior thesis that was later turned into a best-selling book, *Why England Slept*, Kennedy served as a PT commander during World War II. Pushed to enter politics by his ambitious father, former ambassador Joseph Kennedy, the younger Kennedy ran successfully for the House of Representatives in 1946. After three terms in the lower chamber, he was elected in 1952 to the US Senate, defeating the incumbent, Henry Cabot Lodge. In 1956, Kennedy was vaulted into the national limelight when he almost gained the Democratic vice presidential nomination. In 1960, he defeated a number of candidates, including his eventual vice presidential nominee, Senator Lyndon B. Johnson of Texas, for the Democratic nomination.

Handsome and well-educated with a beautiful and sophisticated wife, Jacqueline, and two young children, Kennedy brought to the Oval Office youth, vigor, and culture. Despite a lacklustre career on Capitol Hill, he promised

Right: Kennedy's youth and religion helped the Republicans begin to close the gap on him but the public's doubts were overcome by his strong showing in the televised debates. This picture was taken during the second one on October 7, 1960.

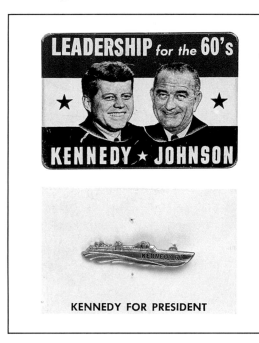

Above: Memorabilia from the victorious Kennedy-Johnson ticket. As well as emphasizing the two as the new leadership for a new era, JFK's wartime heroism was not forgotten and the sinking of his motor torpedo boat *PT 109* (pin at bottom) was a big factor in his favor during the campaign.

Left and below left: An invitation, ticket and program for John F. Kennedy's inauguration ceremony (below left) held on January 20, 1961. Five balls celebrated the event that evening. Kennedy's inaugural speech was one of the more memorable ones and included the line 'ask not what your country can do for you – ask what you can do for your country.'

dynamic leadership, and he was able to excite the American people with his charisma and public persona. Yet Kennedy's presidency was one more of style than of substance. During his administration, Congress passed modest increases in the minimum wage and in Social Security benefits. It also approved a $5 billion Housing Act. But Kennedy suffered major defeats in the areas of education, health, urban affairs, and youth unemployment. And for most of his administration, he was surprisingly indifferent to the growing civil rights movement in the United States.[13]

Indeed, Kennedy was far less interested in domestic legislation than he was in foreign affairs. But his conduct of foreign policy is also open to criticism. In an effort to overthrow the Cuban government of Fidel Castro, which had come to power in 1959 after a bloody revolution, he went along in April 1961 with a plan, conceived during the Eisenhower administration, to land 1,500 Cuban exiles at the Bay of Pigs in Cuba. The invasion turned into a fiasco and a humiliation for Kennedy when Castro's troops either killed or captured the exiles and then later released the prisoners in exchange for US-supplied tractors and medicine.

Later that year a major crisis developed when Soviet Premier Nikita Khrushchev announced that he was preparing to turn over control of

Below: President Kennedy meeting with Soviet Premier Khrushchev in June 1961. During these years the Cold War reached its tensest heights, most notably during the Cuban Missile Crisis.

Above: The large crowd of 200,000-plus which assembled for the civil rights march in Washington, D.C., on August 28, 1963, as viewed from the top of the Lincoln Memorial.

access routes to West Berlin to the communist East German government. In 1958, Khrushchev had made a similar threat, but Eisenhower defused the crisis through quiet diplomacy. In contrast, Kennedy mobilized reserve units and called for increased military appropriations. The crisis did not end until the Soviets built the Berlin Wall, cutting off the flow of East German refugees to the West.

The most serious crisis of the Kennedy administration and, probably, of the entire Cold War, occurred in October 1962, when a U-2 spy plane flying over Cuba revealed that the Soviets had placed offensive missiles on the island. For 13 days, the world hovered on the brink of a nuclear holocaust as the United States instituted a blockade of Cuba and prepared for an air strike and invasion of the island to eliminate the missiles. Finally, the Soviet Union announced that it would remove the missiles if the United States promised not to invade Cuba – a condition that the administration had already made clear was acceptable.

Defenders of Kennedy maintain that although he made some false starts as president, such as the Bay of Pigs fiasco, he learned from his mistakes

Left: President Kennedy addressing the nation on the evening of October 22, 1962. Following a week of tense deliberations Kennedy announced the existence of Soviet missiles in Cuba and the plans for a blockade and quarantine of the island.

and then successfully met the Soviet challenges in Berlin and Cuba. Critics contend that he was a conventional cold warrior who foresook diplomacy for confrontation over Berlin and led the world to the brink of nuclear war during the Cuban missile crisis. Although both sides have made good cases in support of their position, it is nevertheless true that the 13 days of the Cuban missile crisis were the most dangerous period of the Cold War. Moreover, Kennedy increased dramatically America's commitment to South Vietnam by sending 16,000 American troops to that country – the first significant contingent of American forces to be deployed there. Kennedy's defenders have argued that following the 1964 election, he planned to withdraw these forces. Critics maintain that there is insufficient evidence to substantiate that claim. Whoever is right, the fact remains that by the time Kennedy was suddenly killed in Dallas on November 22, 1963, the United States had made a commitment to Vietnam that, although not irreversible, increased the chances of an even greater commitment.[14]

Below: President Kennedy with his wife and Governor and Mrs John B. Connally at Brooks Air Force Base, Texas, on November 21, 1963. The very next day the president was assassinated.

LYNDON B. JOHNSON

Kennedy's assassination by Lee Harvey Oswald shocked the world and elevated to the Oval Office Vice President Lyndon B. Johnson (LBJ). Perhaps the adjective that best describes the Johnson presidency is 'ambitious.' Ambition drove LBJ as few presidents before him. He set out to be the greatest president in American history. His 'Great Society' programs were the

Above: Kennedy's flag-draped coffin in the Rotunda for a service on November 25, 1963. The late president was buried at Arlington National Cemetery, also the resting place of the former president, William Howard Taft.

most ambitious and far-reaching of any president. And ambition of a different sort – a determination not to be remembered as the only president in American history to lose a war – led

ultimately to the expansion of the Vietnam War.

Johnson was born in the hill country of Texas on August 27, 1908. After graduating from Southwest State Teachers College in 1930, he taught briefly in Houston before taking a job in

Below: Lyndon Johnson meeting in the Oval Office in January 1964 with civil rights leaders Martin Luther King, Jr. (left), Whitney Young (right), and James Farmer (far right).

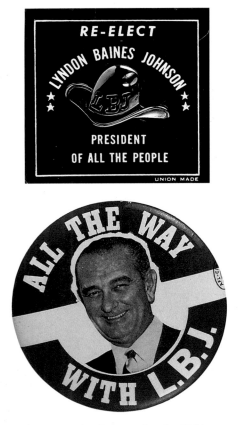

1931 as a congressional aide. Except for a two-year stint as director of the National Youth Administration in Texas, he remained in Washington until 1969, first as a member of the US House of Representatives (1936-1948), then as a member of the Senate (1949-1960), as Kennedy's vice president (1961-63), and, finally, as the president.

Johnson's personality was strewn with contradictions. A ruthless politician and a masterful political operator, he always sought public affection. A compassionate person deeply affected by the poverty he witnessed in South Texas, he rarely allowed sentimentality to interfere with his political wheeling and dealing. An insecure person, he had a towering ego and yearned for power. As a result of these contradictions, Johnson was always more feared than loved, more respected for his political skills than admired for the programs he championed.

Johnson's domestic program, known as the 'Great Society,' included the most sweeping reform legislation in the nation's history. Invoking Kennedy's memory, the new president quickly moved to win passage of two measures that Kennedy had failed to persuade Congress to approve – a $13.5 billion tax cut and a civil rights bill banning discrimination in public accomodations, establishing a Fair Employment Practices Commission, and authorizing federal suits in cases involving school segregation and violations of voting rights. In addition, Johnson used his political wizardry to gain congressional approval

of federal funds for mass transportation and an $800 million war on poverty.

In 1964, Johnson was elected to a full term as president by one of the greatest landslides in American history, gaining more than 61 percent of the vote against his Republican opponent, Senator Barry Goldwater of Arizona, an arch-conservative whose extreme views on most issues scared Americans. Now president in his own right, Johnson pushed through an overwhelmingly Democratic Congress a legislative agenda that included a $1.3 billion program of federal aid to primary and secondary education, national health insurance for the poor and elderly, an additional $1.6 billion for the war on poverty, a manpower training bill, college scholarships, environmental legislation, and measures to establish the Department of Housing and Urban Development and the National Endowments for the Arts and Humanities. But perhaps the greatest legacy of his 'Great Society' program was the Voting Rights Act of 1965, which authorized federal examiners to register voters and banned literacy tests for voting. Together with the Twenty-fourth Amendment to the Constitution prohibiting poll taxes (1964), the Act allowed blacks in the South to vote in large numbers for the first time.

Above: Two campaign buttons for the 1964 Johnson-Humphrey ticket. One (top) emphasizes the support of the unions for Johnson, the other has another classic slogan 'All the Way with LBJ.'

Below: President Johnson presents service medals to members of the 101st Airborne Division at Fort Campbell, Kentucky, in July 1966. By then there were more than 300,000 US troops in Vietnam.

Above: LBJ and his advisors (including General Westmoreland) during a private meeting with South Vietnamese leaders held on October 23, 1966, during the Manila conference of the South East Asia Treaty Organization (SEATO) nations.

Below: Taken during a passionate outburst, this photograph shows President Johnson as he defends his Vietnam policy in a press conference on November 17, 1967. The US commitment peaked the next year at 536,000 personnel.

About the same time that Congress was approving the Voting Rights Act, however, Johnson was taking a series of steps that would entrap the United States in the Vietnam War. During the 1964 election, he had portrayed himself as the peace candidate by depicting Goldwater as an irresponsible war hawk who, if elected president, might lead the United States into war. Yet in August 1964, after informing the nation that North Vietnam had attacked American warships in the Gulf of Tonkin, Johnson got Congress to approve a resolution authorizing him to wage a presidential war in Vietnam. Never an acute student of foreign policy, he blamed the civil war in Vietnam on North Vietnamese and Chinese aggression, which, if not stopped, would lead to further aggression.

Following an attack by Vietcong guerrillas on US military advisers at Pleiku in February 1965, Johnson instituted an air war against North Vietnam. He also decided to increase the number of American ground forces in South Vietnam. By July he had committed 100,000 American troops to the fighting. By the end of 1965 the number had grown to approximately 180,000. Three years later, the United States had more than 500,000 troops in Vietnam with no end of the war in sight.

The war destroyed Johnson's presidency. Despite the 'Great Society' programs that Johnson had pushed through Congress, he never won the trust of Democratic liberals, who disliked his

often crude behavior and his wheeling and dealing approach to politics. The war turned many of them openly against the administration. More important, as Johnson expanded America's commitment in Vietnam, opposition to the war grew, especially on college campuses.

The anti-war movement reached a crescendo in 1968 following the January Tet offensive, in which communist forces attacked all the major cities in South Vietnam and even penetrated the American Embassy in Saigon. Although the offensive was a military defeat for the North Vietnamese and Vietcong, who suffered enormous casualties during the fighting, the fact they had been able to launch such an extensive and well-coordinated attack seemed to belie the administration's claim that it was winning the war.

The political fallout of the Vietnam War was manifested in the New Hampshire presidential primary in March 1968 when a relatively obscure political figure, Senator Eugene McCarthy of Minnesota, almost upset the president. Four days later, a more formidable opponent, Senator Robert Kennedy of New York, brother of the slain president, entered the race. On March 31, Johnson went on national television to announce that he was restricting the bombing of North Vietnam to a small area and to invite the North Vietnamese to begin discussions on ending the war (an invitation they quickly accepted). Then Johnson startled the nation by declaring that he would not seek or accept the Democratic presidential nomination.

For all practical purposes, Johnson became a 'lame-duck' president. Although he did manage to win a few more victories on Capitol Hill,

Above: President Johnson announced during this address to the nation on March 31, 1968, that the bombing of North Vietnam would be restricted and that he would not seek re-election.

Below: Although Vietnam was a failure, at home Johnson did advance civil rights. This meeting with the movement's leaders was held on April 5, 1968 – the day after the King assassination.

Above: Appearing to sum up a president in despair, this July 31, 1968, image actually shows Lyndon Johnson listening to a tape recording made by his son-in-law, Captain Charles Robb, who was serving in Vietnam.

including an open housing law, a truth-in-lending measure, and a tax surcharge to pay for the war, even lawmakers of his own party were in open rebellion against him. Because of his unpopularity, the president declined to attend the riot-strewn Democratic convention in Chicago later that year, which nominated for president his vice president, Hubert Humphrey. But the Democrats had become so divided over the war that political pundits gave Humphrey little chance of defeating his Republican opponent, Richard Nixon.

In retrospect, the 1960s represented the unraveling of American liberalism, which had dominated politics in the United States since the New Deal. American liberalism was predicated on the existence of a strong chief executive who would provide the nation with a safety net of social programs and follow an internationalist foreign policy; the latter came to mean defending, with bipartisan congressional support, American values and interests against external threats, whether in Europe in the 1940s, South Korea in the 1950s, or Vietnam in the 1960s. In the aftermath of Vietnam, the very assumptions on which American liberalism rested, including presidential dominance, came into question.[15]

Notes

1. Freidel, 1973: 299-319 and 408-53.
2. Williams, 1969: 800-47.
3. Leuchtenberg, 1963: 143-96.
4. Leuchtenberg, 1963: 231-8.

5. Dallek, 1979: 23-313.
6. Dallek, 1973: 317-528.
7. The best book on Truman's foreign policy is Leffler, 1992: 25-360.
8. Kaufman, 1986: passim.
9. McCullough, 1992: 467-73.

10. Ambrose, 1983: passim.
11. Ambrose, 1984: 104-230.
12. Ambrose, 1984: 231-461.
13. Reeves, 1993: passim.
14. Kaufman, 1993: 447-69.
15. Matusow, 1984: passim.

Burton I. Kaufman

12

THE CONTEMPORARY PRESIDENCY

**Richard M. Nixon 1969-1974
Gerald R. Ford   1974-1977
Jimmy Carter   1977-1981
Ronald Reagan   1981-1989
George Bush   1989-1993
Bill Clinton   1993-**

Presidents in the late 20th century have served in an era of political difficulty reminiscent of a century ago. Nixon resigned to escape impeachment. His successor, Ford, lasted less than three years before losing to Carter, who in turn was defeated after one term by Reagan. Reagan served two full terms – the only contemporary president to do so – but Bush failed re-election at the hands of Clinton.

One president and four former presidents attend
the funeral of former president Richard Nixon in 1995.

Although the 1970s are still too recent to forecast how historians will view that decade, it will probably be seen as the period when the post-World War II presidency reached its nadir. Richard Nixon was forced out of office in disgrace; Gerald Ford, America's first non-elected president was defeated in 1976 by Jimmy Carter, who had been unknown to most Americans a year earlier; and Carter was in turn resoundingly defeated in his own bid for re-election in 1980 by Ronald Reagan. Although some of the prestige of the office was restored under Reagan, the history of American politics since the 1970s has increasingly been one of gridlock between a weakened presidency and a reinvigorated Congress.

RICHARD M. NIXON

If the 1970s were a watershed for the American presidency, the person most responsible for that development was Richard Milhous Nixon. Born in Yorba Linda, California, on January 9, 1913, Nixon was raised in Whittier, California. From a poor family, he worked his way through college, graduating from Whittier College in 1934 and Duke University Law School three years later.

From 1937 to 1943, Nixon practiced law in Whittier. During World War II he joined the navy and saw action in the South Pacific. After the war, he decided to enter politics, and in the Republican sweep of 1946, he was elected to Congress. As a member of the House Un-American Activities Committee (HUAC), Nixon spearheaded the investigation of Alger Hiss, a former State Department official who was later found guilty of perjury for denying under oath that he had been a Communist.[1]

In 1950, Nixon ran successfully for the Senate in a campaign tainted by his 'red-baiting' attacks against his Democratic opponent, Helen Gahagan Douglas. In 1952 Dwight Eisenhower, seeking to balance the ticket and mollify the right wing of the Republican Party, selected Nixon as his running mate. For the next eight years, Nixon served dutifully as Eisenhower's vice president. When Nixon narrowly lost to John F. Kennedy in the 1960 presidential election and then ran unsuccessfully for governor of California two years later, it seemed that his political career was finished. Instead, Nixon spent the next six years quietly cultivating the support of Republican leaders. In 1968 he was rewarded for his efforts with the Republican

Above: Nixon was keen to contrast his experience in foreign affairs with Kennedy's lack of it. Nixon had dealt with Khrushchev and dozens of other world leaders during his time in office.

presidential nomination. In the November election, he defeated his Democratic opponent, Vice President Hubert Humphrey, by less than 500,000 votes.

During the campaign, Nixon had indicated that he had a secret plan to get the United States out of Vietnam. In fact, he had no plan but, sensing the growing anti-war tide in the United States, he began a phased withdrawal of American forces from the country. Nixon was not abandoning Vietnam – at the same time that he announced the withdrawals, he intensified the bombing of North Vietnam and, in a policy known as Vietnamization, increased military aid to the South Vietnamese army. But he coupled Vietnamization with the Nixon Doctrine, which called for the reduced presence of American forces in Asia generally, and until 1970, when he appeared to widen the war by sending American forces into Cambodia, he was able to quell the anti-war movement in the United States.

Meanwhile, Nixon surprised many of his liberal critics by taking an advanced position on a number of important domestic issues. For example, he lobbied for the establishment of an Environmental Protection Agency (EPA) and a Department of Natural Resources. He supported a proposal that would have guaranteed a family of four an annual income of $1,600 plus $800 in food stamps. He adopted the 'Philadelphia Plan,' which set aside jobs for minorities in the construction industry. He also strengthened the Equal Employment Opportunity Commission (EEOC) and supported an Equal Rights Amendment (ERA) to the Constitution.

Nixon's main interest, however, was foreign affairs. Here he was heavily influenced by his brilliant national security adviser, Henry Kissinger, who shared his geopolitical approach to foreign policy. In 1971, Nixon surprised much of the world by announcing that he had secretly sent Kissinger to Beijing to lay the groundwork for a presidential visit to China early the next year. Embroiled in disputes with the Soviet Union, the Beijing government was anxious to improve relations with the United States. Nixon saw an opportunity to take advantage of the Sino-Soviet split by playing each side off against the other. In February 1972 he visited China, where he agreed to move forward on normalization of Sino-American relations. In May

Left: Vice President Nixon during the second debate with Kennedy on October 7, 1960, held in the NBC-TV studios in Washington, D.C. These debates were the first to be televised.

he went to Moscow, where he and Soviet leader Leonid Brezhnev signed the first Strategic Arms Limitation Treaty (SALT I), freezing the number of ballistic missiles and limiting the Soviet Union and the United States to two antiballistic missile (ABM) sites[2].

Nixon had his moments of crisis during his first term as president, such as in April 1970 when American forces went into Cambodia to try to disrupt enemy supply lines and destroy the suspected headquarters of the Vietcong. By appearing to widen the war in Vietnam, Nixon reignited the anti-war movement, setting off demonstrations on college campuses throughout the country and leading to the killing of four students at Kent State University by the Ohio National Guard. An invasion of Laos in February 1971 by South Vietnamese forces who were provided with American artillery and air support touched off a new wave of protests, but they were not of the same intensity as those in 1970[3].

Nixon also had difficulty controlling inflation and reducing unemployment, leading to the creation of a new term in the American political lexicon, 'stagflation.' In response to a weakened dollar and a run on American gold reserves by speculators cashing in dollars for gold, Nixon announced in 1971 his New Economic Policy (NEP). He ended gold convertibility and allowed the dollar to 'float' in international money markets. He also imposed a system of wage and price controls.

For the most part, Americans were satisfied with Nixon's performance as president. The NEP initially seemed to work as the rates of inflation and unemployment declined in 1972. On the eve of the November elections, the White House announced that peace was at hand in Vietnam. Consequently American voters saw no reason to vote Nixon out of office. In November he won an overwhelming victory against a weak Democratic candidate, Senator George McGovern of South Dakota, beating him by 61 percent to 38 percent. In casting their ballots, most Americans ignored news stories of White House involvement in the arrest of five persons linked to the Committee to Reelect the President (CREEP) for burglarizing the Democratic National Committee headquarters in Washington's Watergate complex.

In January 1973 Nixon was able to announce that after the heaviest bombing yet of North Vietnam, the Hanoi government had agreed to a cease-fire, allowing the North Vietnamese to keep their forces in South Vietnam but permitting the South Vietnamese government to remain in power. Unfortunately for Nixon, this was the last time he would be able to win public favor. Soon thereafter his administration began to unravel.

Nixon himself took a sharp turn toward the political right, even bringing in a hatchet man to dismantle the Office of Economic Opportunity. Balance of payment deficits led to a further weakening of the dollar in international markets. Together with increases in the price of oil charged by the Organization of Petroleum Exporting Countries (OPEC), a cartel of the major oil-producing nations, the deficits resulted in a re-emergence of stagflation. In the Yom Kippur War of October 1973, the Arab states launched a surprise attack on Israel, which nearly led to its defeat. When the United States rescued Israel with a massive resupply of military equipment, the Arab oil-producing states responded

Above: A styrofoam boater hat for the Nixon-Agnew campaign. Accessories such as these were distributed in large numbers at conventions and rallies during the 1968 political season. Nixon depicted himself as representing 'Middle America,' but secured only a narrow victory.

Below: Among this varied campaign memorabilia from 1968 is a button that highlights the increasing importance of the 'first lady factor' – the candidate's wife's popularity having a bearing on his chances of winning the election. Ironically, Pat Nixon preferred to stay out of the spotlight.

with an oil embargo resulting in a skyrocketing inflation rate, a stagnant economy, and a dramatic decline in the stock market.[4]

What led to Nixon's undoing as president, however, was the so-called 'Watergate affair.' It is now known that the president tried to cover up the involvement of his White House staff and re-election campaign with those arrested for the attempted Watergate burglary. On the recommendation of his closest White House advisers H.R. Haldeman and John Ehrlichman, his counsel John Dean, and his attorney general John Mitchell, Nixon agreed to provide hush money for the burglars. He also tried unsuccessfully to get the CIA to prevent an FBI investigation of the break-in on the false grounds of national security. Despite his denials of any cover-up, however, allegations persisted that the White House was involved with the burglary. The judge at the burglars' trial, John J. Sirica, used threats of heavy sentences to get two of the defendants to admit to receiving payoffs from the White House. The *Washington Post* and other news organizations published stories linking the White House to the burglary and exposing other illegal activities on the administration's behalf.

Amid rumors of scandal and political dirty tricks, the Senate established a Select Committee on Presidential Campaign Activities headed by North Carolina Senator Sam Ervin. During the hearings that followed, John Dean confessed to being part of the Watergate cover-up and implicated Haldeman, Ehrlichman, Mitchell, and acting director of the FBI L. Patrick Gray, as well as the president. On April 30, 1973, Dean, Haldeman, and Ehrlichman resigned under fire. At the hearings, it was also revealed that Nixon had been secretly tape-recording meetings in the Oval Office, and other White House locations. When the Ervin Committee demanded access to

Above: President Nixon taking the oath of office for the second time on January 20, 1973. First Lady Pat Nixon is holding two Bibles; Chief Justice Warren E. Burger is at her left.

Below: One of Nixon's best remembered accomplishments is the improvement of relations with communist China. In 1972 he became the first US president to visit the state.

the tapes, Nixon refused, claiming executive privilege. This touched off an extended legal battle that resulted in the October 20 firing by Nixon of Watergate Special Prosecutor Archibald Cox and the resignations of Attorney General Elliot Richardson and his deputy, William Ruckelshaus, after they refused to comply with Nixon's order to fire Cox.

The so-called 'Saturday night massacre' led to demands for Nixon's impeachment. Under mounting pressure to hand over the tapes, Nixon made available some edited transcripts in April 1974, but it took an order from the Supreme Court at the end of July before all the tapes were made available to the new special prosecutor, Leon Jaworski. One tape arrived with an 18.5-minute gap that experts determined had been deliberately erased. Other tapes showed the darker side of Nixon – conspiratorial, vulgar, even anti-semitic. But a tape of a June 23, 1972, meeting in the Oval office revealed clearly that Nixon had tried to use the CIA to cover up the Watergate burglary.

Once this 'smoking gun' became public, Nixon's impeachment or resignation was inevitable. During the last 12 months other misdeeds of the administration had surfaced, including the revelation of an 'enemies list' maintained by Nixon, which recorded the names of political foes he sought to punish through audits by the Internal Revenue Service. Also casting a shadow over the administration was the resignation in October 1973 of Nixon's vice president, Spiro Agnew, who was forced to resign or face prison for bribes he had taken while vice president.

The House Judiciary Committee had begun formal impeachment proceedings against Nixon

Below: These cuff links have the presidential seal on one side and Nixon's signature on the other. They were provided to secret service agents to give to others as a token of appreciation for their help in organizing security for a visit, and so on.

Above: A photograph recording Nixon's meeting with China's Mao Zedong in February 1972 that helped normalize Sino-American relations. Nixon's special assistant Henry Kissinger is on the right, Premier Chou En-Lai is on the far left.

before the June 23 tape was disclosed. Once the tape became public, even most Republicans gave up trying to save the president. On July 27 the Committee voted out articles of impeachment. Under pressure from the Republican leadership, and faced with an impeachment trial, Nixon announced on August 8, 1974, that he would resign the next day, thereby becoming the first American president ever to leave office voluntarily before the end of his term.

Even before the Watergate affair, the presidency had been under attack on Capitol Hill. In response to the Vietnam War, Congress in 1973 had passed over Nixon's veto the War Powers Act requiring the president to give an account of his action within 30 days after committing American troops to hostile situations abroad and to withdraw the forces after 60 days if the com-

mitment was not approved by Congress. Within academic and political circles, much concern was also being expressed about the development since the end of World War II of an 'imperial presidency' so powerful as to threaten basic democratic principles. By seeming to confirm these fears, Watergate compromised the power of the presidency even further and contributed to a wider revolt against Washington, which the American people accused of being too meddlesome and intrusive.

GERALD R. FORD

Nixon's successor, Vice President Gerald Ford, had replaced Agnew in December 1973. The former minority leader of the House had been selected by Nixon as his vice president because he

Below: Gerald R. Ford taking the presidential oath of office on August 9, 1974. The campaign badge stressed that 'experience counts,' but for many Americans 'elect' was the crucial word.

Above: President Gerald R. Ford holding a news conference in the East Room of the White House on August 28, 1974.

believed Ford would be easily confirmed by the Democratically-controlled Congress. Well liked even by Democrats, Ford appeared to have no presidential aspirations that might keep Democrats from voting for him.[5]

The first American president not to have faced a national electorate, Ford was born in Omaha, Nebraska, on July 14, 1913. He was raised in Grand Rapids, Michigan, by his mother and step-father, a local businessman who had married his mother following her divorce from his father and then adopted her only child. A star athlete, Ford played football at the University of Michigan, where he graduated in 1935. Turning down offers to play professionally, he accepted a position as assistant football coach at Yale. In 1938 he was admitted to the Yale Law School. He received his law degree in 1941.

Right: Soviet General Secretary Leonid Brezhnev jocularly chiding Secretary of State Henry Kissinger during a brief meeting outside the Soviet Embassy in Helsinki, Finland, on August 2, 1975, as President Ford looks on.

After serving in the navy during World War II, Ford returned to Grand Rapids, and practiced law until 1948, when he was elected to the House of Representatives. He was re-elected 12 times, always by majorities of more than 60 percent. Hard-working and well-liked, an internationalist on most foreign policy issues and a conservative on most domestic issues, Ford was elected House minority leader by his fellow Republicans in 1965. A Nixon loyalist, Ford stirred a hornet's nest when, acting for the administration, he tried unsuccessfully to impeach Supreme Court Justice William O. Douglas in retaliation for the Senate's rejection of two Nixon nominees to the court, Clement Haynsworth and G. Harrold Carswell. But this action was not characteristic of his service in the House.

For most of the eight months between Ford's appointment as vice president and Nixon's resignation, Ford remained in the background, continuing to believe in Nixon's innocence and thinking that the president would serve out his full term. When it became apparent that Nixon would be forced to resign or face impeachment, most political analysts anticipated that Ford would be a caretaker president, serving only until a new president was elected in 1976.

They were not entirely correct. In the two years he was president, Ford signed into law a $25 billion aid to education measure, a campaign reform act providing public funding for presidential campaigns, consumer protection legislation, an extension of unemployment benefits, and a $4.8 billion measure to improve mass transit facilities. He also used his veto power 66 times and had only 12 of them overturned by a two-thirds vote in Congress.

Yet the Ford presidency was characterized by generally indecisive leadership, political miscalculation, bad judgment, and lack of vision. In fairness to Ford, he lacked the three-month transition period a president-elect normally has between election and inauguration. He had no time to select a staff and cabinet of his own or to plan a coherent program. But by merely adding Nixon's senior staff to his own staff, he almost assured the administrative disarray that encumbered his presidency.

More important, though, was Ford's decision to offer clemency – but not amnesty – to Vietnam-era draft evaders and deserters and to grant Nixon a pardon from Watergate-related crimes. These decisions were part of Ford's effort to bring an end to two of the most nightmarish events in the nation's history. Despite later charges to the contrary, no political deal was involved in Ford's decision to pardon Nixon. Although Nixon's Chief of Staff, Alexander Haig, had floated the idea of a pardon with Ford just before Nixon resigned, Ford decided on the pardon for the reasons he later claimed: he felt Nixon had been punished enough, and he wanted to get on with the nation's other business.

Nevertheless, Ford handled the pardon issue poorly, failing even to insist that Nixon give up his presidential papers and tapes or issue a statement of contrition. The pardon, moreover, destroyed Ford's honeymoon with the American people, millions of whom were already infuriated by his decision to grant clemency to Vietnam-era draft evaders.

In a period of both high unemployment and high inflation, Ford also vacillated between a tax cut to promote economic growth and budgetary

Above: Ford continued Nixon's foreign policy of maintaining US power and prestige in the world, and to this end met Mao in December 1975. The latter's death in 1976 brought to power a more moderate regime keener for American ties.

Below: President Carter and First Lady Rosalynn wave to the crowds as they stroll back to the White House after his inauguration. The decision to walk suggested a touch of the 'common man.' Carter was the first to do it since Jefferson.

restraint to curb inflation.[6] In addition, he badly mishandled the so-called 'Mayaguez incident' in which fifteen marines were killed and eight U.S. helicopters downed in rescuing the crew of the merchant ship *Mayaguez*, which had been captured by the Khmer Rouge when it allegedly sailed in Cambodian waters. Not only were more lives lost in the rescue mission than the number of crew rescued, but the administration rejected the option of negotiations prior to the rescue mission. More generally, Ford failed to develop a coherent foreign policy.

In sum, Ford made a contribution to the American presidency by restoring some credibility to that much tarnished office. Overall, though, his record as president was mediocre.

JIMMY CARTER

Much the same can be said about Ford's successor, Jimmy Carter. Born in Plains, Georgia, on October 1, 1924, Carter graduated from the US Naval Academy in 1946. In 1953, he left the navy to return to Plains, where he became a successful businessman and community leader. In 1962, he was elected to the Georgia Senate. After serving two terms, he ran unsuccessfully for governor in 1966. Four years later, he made a second gubernatorial bid, this time winning by appeal-

Above: President Jimmy Carter shaking hands at the signing of the Panama Canal Treaty in 1977, negotiations for which had begun under Johnson. The treaty was not universally popular in the US.

Below: Carter giving a briefing to Congressional leaders, including Thomas P. O'Neill, Jr., on the subject of inflation, a recurrent economic problem of the 1970s.

ing to segregationist elements in the state. But after assuming office, Carter established a reputation as a racial moderate and reform leader. In 1974, he decided to run for president, believing that he could win by campaigning as a political outsider. Chalking up victories in the early primaries in 1976, he was able to gain the Democratic nomination and then to defeat Ford narrowly in November. He received 40.8 million votes to Ford's 39.1 million votes.[7]

Elected president mainly because he offered the American people new leadership, Carter almost immediately alienated Congress by cutting from the budget a series of water projects that had strong support on Capitol Hill. He also presented Congress with an overly ambitious legislative agenda, which included welfare reform, a comprehensive energy program, hospital cost containment legislation, tax reform, and Social Security reform. By August 1977 every one of these initiatives had become stalled on Capitol Hill. Meanwhile, a sluggish economy, which had begun to recover in the first half of 1977, started downward once more. The fact that Carter was more concerned with attacking inflation through budgetary restraint than with dealing with high unemployment through fiscal stimulus alienated many Democratic constituencies.

Besides domestic issues, Carter devoted considerable attention to foreign policy. In March

Above: President and First Lady Carter with Chinese leaders, including Deng Xiaoping, at a Sino-American signing ceremony to establish full diplomatic relations with the People's Republic.

Below: Carter shaking hands with Brezhnev in Vienna in 1979 following the signing of the SALT II arms control agreement, an accord soon to be threatened in the Senate.

1978 he won a major victory when, over strong opposition, the Senate ratified the Panama Canal agreements turning over ownership and control of the canal to Panama by the year 2000. Six months later, Egyptian President Anwar Sadat and Israeli Prime Minister Menachem Begin signed the Camp David Accords ending their nations' long conflict and providing the framework for a settlement of the entire Arab-Israeli dispute. Carter won plaudits worldwide for brokering the Camp David Accords. The next month he won an important legislative victory when lawmakers finally approved his energy program, which had been stalled in Congress for 18 months.

The political capital that Carter gained as a result of Camp David and his success on Capitol Hill was short-lived. As the nation experienced slow economic growth, high unemployment, and high inflation fed by dramatic increases in fuel costs, the president's approval ratings spiraled downward. Public discontent with Carter intensified in July 1979 when he fired five members of his cabinet after delivering a speech on energy in which he talked about a 'crisis of spirit' in America. Carter fell so low in the polls that many political observers thought the Democrats would turn to Senator Edward Kennedy of Massachusetts as their presidential nominee in 1980.

The political landscape was dramatically changed by two events: the taking in November 1979 of the American Embassy in Tehran, including 50 American hostages, by followers of the Ayatollah Ruhollah Khomeini, a fundamentalist Muslim cleric who had overthrown the

Above: Energy costs and the environment were issues of increasing importance from the 1970s onward; here, President Carter is signing a Synthetic Fuel Bill in June 1980.

Below: Former president Carter addressing the crowd assembled at Rhein-Main airbase, Germany, to greet the 52 hostages from Iran who had been freed during the final hours of his presidency.

Shah of Iran the previous January, and the Soviet invasion of Afghanistan in order to prop up a Marxist regime in that country. Carter responded to the seizure of the American hostages by trying to gain their release through diplomatic means. He responded to the Afghan invasion by imposing a grain embargo on the Soviet Union and asking the Senate to delay consideration of the SALT II agreement, which he had signed with Soviet leader Leonid Brezhnev on June 18, 1979. As a result of his handling of these two crises, Carter was able to fend off the Kennedy challenge and win the Democratic presidential nomination.

Yet the hostage crisis, together with the slumping economy, ultimately helped defeat Carter's bid for re-election. A failed military mission in April 1980 to rescue the hostages became another entry in the list of failures that many Americans attributed to the president. At the same time, the economy remained in the doldrums. Although Carter managed to stay even with his Republican opponent Ronald Reagan for most of the campaign by raising questions about Reagan's fitness to be president, Reagan was able to win an overwhelming victory after dispelling doubts about his presidential timber during a televised debate with Carter. The

Republicans then returned to the two issues – the economy and America's position in the world – that most concerned American voters. On November 4, they gave Reagan 51 percent of the vote to Carter's 41 percent. An independent candidate, Republican Congressman John Anderson of Illinois, received 7 percent of the vote.

RONALD REAGAN

A successful movie actor before starting a second career in politics in the 1960s, Reagan was born in Tampico, Illinois, on February 6, 1911. After graduating from Eureka College in 1932, he worked as a radio announcer and sports broadcaster in Iowa before signing an acting contract with Warner Brothers in 1937. During the next 25 years he played in more than 50 movies, and in 1940 Reagan married actress Jane Wyman. Following the outbreak of World War II he served as a captain in the US Army.[8]

Below: President Reagan and his wife, Nancy, waving from their armored limousine at the large numbers of spectators greeting the new Republican president following his inauguration on January 20, 1981.

Above: A metal campaign button from Reagan's first successful run for the presidency in 1980. He was to leave office eight years and two terms later as popular with most Americans as when he won.

Following his discharge from the army in 1945, Reagan returned to his acting career in Hollywood. In 1949, he and Wyman divorced, and three years later Reagan married actress Nancy Davis. From 1947 to 1952, and then again from 1959 to 1960, he served as president of the Screen Actors Guild. He also became a corporate spokesman for General Electric (GE). Around this time, his politics began to change. Throughout most of his adult life, Reagan had

Above: These leatherette document folders embossed with the presidential seal were used to categorize documents to be placed on President Reagan's White House desk.

been a New Deal Democrat. But, influenced by his new wife and the business executives with whom he frequently came into contact through his activities for GE, Reagan's political philosophy became increasingly conservative. He also became more politically active, delivering a nationally televised speech in support of Barry Goldwater in 1964, which, after Goldwater's defeat in November, made him the new hope of conservative Republicans. In 1966, Reagan shocked political analysts, winning the California governorship by a million votes.

Reagan served two terms as governor, during which he became widely regarded as the nation's leading conservative spokesman. Indeed, he became so popular within Republican circles that he nearly defeated Ford for the Republican presidential nomination in 1976. Four years later, he won the nomination after beating off challenges from a number of Republican candidates. His landslide over Carter followed in November.

Right: Ronald Reagan's two-term period in office marked a time of renewal for the United States following one of self-doubt in the post-Vietnam era. At the center of it stood Reagan's engaging and popular personality.

Throughout his political career, Reagan had always been underestimated by his rivals, who generally regarded him as an intellectual lightweight. This image has not changed. Even a number of former administration officials have commented on Reagan's lack of intellectual breadth, his inability to absorb details, and his delegation of authority to officials more knowledgeable than he. Yet Reagan compiled an impressive legislative record as president. Adopting the theory of supply-side economics – the view that tax cuts stimulate economic growth and actually lead to increased tax revenues – he got through Congress a five-year $750 billion tax cut. He also won congressional approval for reductions in domestic programs such as Medicare and Medicaid, school lunches, welfare, and food stamps. Aided by the Federal Reserve Board, which adopted a tight-money policy, he succeeded in bringing down the rate of inflation, although at a cost of higher unemployment. To 'unleash' private enterprise, Reagan instituted a program of federal deregulation in areas such as banking, natural gas, and environmental protection.

In foreign affairs, Reagan followed a firmer and more consistent policy than his predecessor. Taking a tough stand against the Soviet Union, which he once referred to as 'the Evil Empire,' he increased defense spending substantially and ordered the production of the B-1 bomber, which Carter had cancelled. He gave aid to anti-communist forces in Nicaragua (the Contras) and in El Salvador, and in 1983 he sent forces to the Caribbean island of Grenada to depose a left-

Above: A casually dressed president – in Michael K. Deaver's office – discussing the precarious situation in Beirut with Secretary of State Shultz during September 1982.

Below: President Reagan was especially popular with the military which benefited from increased defense spending during his terms. Here he is addressing troops at Camp Liberty Bell in 1983.

ist government. Finally, he took a strong stand against Israel following its invasion of Lebanon in 1982, and he sent marines into Beirut in an effort to restore peace to that city.

Reagan's decision on Lebanon proved to be a major blunder. In October 1983 a terrorist bomb exploded near the marine compound killing 241 American troops. As a result of the carnage, Reagan was forced to withdraw the remaining American forces to ships stationed off Lebanon's coast. Nevertheless, the president, who invariably was referred to in the media as 'the great communicator' because of his ability to relate to the American people, remained enormously popular. In November 1984 he was overwhelmingly re-elected to a second term, gaining 54.2 million votes to 37.5 million for his Democratic opponent, former vice president Walter Mondale of Minnesota.

During Reagan's second term, he succeeded in getting through Congress a major tax reform bill, which reduced the number of tax brackets from 14 to 2 and provided for the lowest tax rates since the 1920s. In December 1987 he and Soviet leader Mikhail Gorbachev, who had come to power in 1985, signed the Intermediate-range Nuclear Forces (INF) Treaty, in which they agreed to eliminate whole classes of nuclear weapons. A year later Gorbachev announced that he was reducing the size of the Soviet military as well as its presence in Eastern Europe. This thawing of the Cold War seemed to justify Reagan's earlier tough stance toward the Soviets.

Above: Reagan's second inauguration in 1985, mindful of William Henry Harrison, was held indoors at the Rotunda of the Capitol because of the extreme cold.

Below: In the 1980s the US became more deeply involved in counter-insurgency in Latin America and one result was casualties; the four marines being honored here were killed in San Salvador.

Yet much of Reagan's second term was dominated by the so-called 'Iran-Contra Affair,' involving the sale of arms to Iran in return for Iran's promise to help free American hostages held by Islamic fundamentalists in Lebanon. What made this arms-for-hostages agreement so embarrassing to the administration was Reagan's earlier vow never to deal with terrorists and his efforts to keep other nations from selling arms to Iran. What turned it into a scandal were the efforts by White House officials to cover up the swap by burning documents and preparing a false chronology of events, along with the revelation that the funds received from Iran had been secretly diverted, apparently without the president's knowledge, to the Contras in Nicaragua. A special commission appointed by the president and headed by former Texas Senator John Tower condemned the administration for secretly trading arms for hostages. Although it pinned the blame on Reagan's advisers rather than on the president, the Tower Commission criticized Reagan for his loose management style. Televised congressional hearings into the Iran-Contra affair confirmed what many people already suspected – that the president was not in control of his own administration.

Despite the Iran-Contra affair, Reagan had shown what a determined president with a well-defined legislative program and a mandate from the voters could accomplish. Taking office in 1981, he had faced the difficult task of reversing the decline in presidential authority that had occurred in the 1970s. To his credit, he enjoyed considerable success in achieving that goal.

Above: Ronald Reagan looks on as Secretary of Defense Caspar Weinberger administers the oath of office to Admiral William J. Crowe, Jr., Chairman of the Joint Chiefs of Staff, on October 1, 1985. Mrs Shirley Crowe, his wife, is assisting.

Below: George Bush served as Reagan's vice president, having built up an impressive record of government service. As UN ambassador in the early 1970s he accepted letters from a delegation concerned about missing servicemen in Vietnam.

Right: George Bush preferred foreign policy matters to domestic ones and as the recession bit from 1990 onward it cost him dear, and not even victory in the Gulf War could save him in 1992.

Yet the presidency remained much weakened from what it had been in the 25 years after World War II. The fact that the House and Senate, fearing a repeat of the Vietnam War. refused repeated requests by the White House for increased aid to anti-communist forces in Central America indicated the continued willingness of lawmakers to defy the president even in the realm of foreign policy. Major Democratic victories in the 1986 congressional elections also led to 'gridlock' between the administration and Congress. Revelations of corruption and cover-ups stemming from the Iran-Contra Affair resulted in indictments against former National Security Adviser Robert McFarlane and his successor, Admiral John Poindexter. Together with unrelated allegations of shady financial dealings by Attorney-General Edwin Meese, which eventually led to his resignation, these revelations further tarnished the Oval Office.

GEORGE BUSH

Replacing Reagan in the White House was his vice president for eight years, George Bush. The son of former senator Prescott Bush of Connecticut, Bush was born in Milton, Massachusetts, on June 12, 1924. He graduated from Yale in 1948 after interrupting his education to serve as a navy pilot during World War II. After graduation Bush moved to Texas, where he became a millionaire in the oil business. In 1966

Below: President Bush at a press conference in August 1990 with the first African American Chairman of the Joint Chiefs of Staff, General Colin Powell, in attendance.

he was elected to the House of Representatives after having run unsuccessfully as the Republican candidate for the US Senate two years earlier. He served two terms before running again for the Senate. Defeated a second time, he was subsequently appointed by President Richard Nixon as US Ambassador to the United Nations.[9]

During the 1970s, Bush held a number of appointed positions, including U.N. ambassador (1971-3), chairman of the Republican National Committee (1973-4), chief of the US Liaison Office in China (1974-5), and director of the CIA (1976-7). In 1980 he ran as a moderate for the Republican presidential nomination. After an upset victory in the Iowa caucuses, he emerged as Reagan's principal rival. Although he lost the nomination, Reagan chose him to be his running mate.

As vice president, Bush logged more than a million miles visiting foreign capitals. He also headed a number of task forces and, despite his later denials, was probably involved in the decision to sell weapons to the Iranians. For the most part, however, he maintained a low profile, biding his time until 1988 when a new president would be elected. Although he did poorly in the Iowa caucuses, Bush won the New Hampshire primary and then went on to a series of primary victories that left him without opposition at the Republican convention. Resorting to negative campaign tactics, he defeated his Democratic opponent, Governor Dukakis of Massachusetts, who ran a poorly conceived and desultory campaign, by a margin of 53 to 46 percent.

Three matters dominated the Bush administration: the economy, the collapse of communism, and the Persian Gulf War. Although inflation declined to less than three percent during the Bush administration, the economy remained stagnant. Unemployment and bankruptcies rose, while the number of newly-created

Above: This handshake across the table marks the second meeting between President Bush and Soviet General Secretary Mikhail Gorbachev. It took place aboard the *Maxim Gorky* at Malta in 1990 during far-reaching arms reduction talks.

Below: The US-led military operation to liberate Kuwait marked the high point of the Bush presidency. Here, the president and his wife, Barbara, are seen visiting some of the thousands of American troops on November 22, 1990.

jobs declined. The annual federal debt doubled to about $350 billion. To combat the growing deficit, Bush reversed a pledge he had made throughout the campaign not to raise taxes by agreeing to a series of tax hikes on everything from boats and luxury automobiles to gasoline and cigarettes. His broken promises on taxes caused backlash within Republican ranks, which contributed to his re-election defeat in 1992.

As president, Bush also had to deal with a major crisis in the savings and loan industry. Hundreds of savings and loan institutions became insolvent as a result of their involvement in risky real estate ventures and generally poor lending practices. To bail out the industry, Bush signed into law a package of reforms that included the establishment of a new federal agency, the Resolution Trust Corporation, to close failed institutions and sell their assets at a cost to the federal treasury that was expected to reach $500 billion by the year 2030.

For much of Bush's administration, however, domestic concerns were overshadowed by events abroad. In Eastern Europe, one communist government after another fell after Soviet leader Gorbachev made it clear that these governments could no longer look to Soviet military force to save them. In the spring of 1990, Gorbachev came to Washington, where he and Bush signed an agreement promising a reduction by both sides in their long-range nuclear weapons and chemical stockpiles. Later that year, the two leaders met in Paris to sign a mutual non-aggression pledge. Afterwards Bush declared that the Cold War was over. But even more dramatic than this pronouncement was the sudden disintegration of the Soviet Union following an unsuccessful coup in August 1991 against Gorbachev, whose policies of *glasnost* (openness) and *perestroika* (eco-

Above: President Bush accompanied by General Norman Schwarzkopf, American commander of the allied forces, during the November 1990 tour of US troops in the Gulf. With the subsequent victory, Bush's popularity reached a record high.

Below: After decades of Cold War, the liberation of eastern Europe and then the collapse of the Soviet Union were nothing short of revolutionary. The Russian Republic emerged led by Boris Yeltsin with whom a cautious Bush met in February 1992.

nomic restructuring) had set in motion the tidal wave now enveloping much of the communist world.[10]

While the communist governments were falling in Eastern Europe and the Soviet Union, in the Middle East events were in motion that led to Bush's finest hour as president. In August 1990, Iraq invaded Kuwait. Iraq's leader, Saddam Hussein, wanted the tiny but oil-rich sheikhdom to pay for a greater share of Iraq's recent war with Iran. Although Saddam had been marshalling his forces along Iraq's border with Kuwait, the invasion took the administration by surprise. Nevertheless, Bush responded by mobilizing a major international operation, known as 'Desert Shield,' to prevent Iraq from moving into Saudi Arabia and to pressure Iraq to withdraw its forces from Kuwait. When Saddam refused to leave Kuwait, Bush approved a two-stage military operation against Iraq known as 'Desert Storm.' It began on January 17, 1991, with the bombing of Iraq's military infrastructure, and culminated on February 24 with a ground offensive against Iraqi forces in Kuwait and Iraq.

Below: Governor Bill Clinton of Arkansas after accepting the nomination at the Democratic National Convention at Madison Square Garden on 16 July 1992. Bush's high ratings in 1991 had scared off some better known Democrats.

Although many military and political analysts had predicted a costly war with heavy casualties on both sides, Iraqi forces were routed in less than five days at a cost of fewer than 150 Americans killed in action. Because Bush had been responsible for creating the multinational coalition that defeated Hussein, he received overwhelming acclaim for the victory in the Persian Gulf War. His public approval rating rose so high, reaching 89 percent in one Gallup poll in the summer of 1991, that few Democrats were willing to challenge him in 1992.[11]

Yet Bush's popularity quickly began to fall. One reason for this drop was that he allowed Saddam to stay in power. Many Americans felt he should have ordered the coalition forces to march to Baghdad and depose Saddam instead of

Above: Campaign buttons and an inaugural button for Bill Clinton, the former appealing to voters on a domestic level. Note the prominent presence of Hillary Clinton, further increasing the importance of the first lady.

ordering a cessation of hostilities. But a more fundamental reason for the decline in Bush's approval rating was the economy, which continued to be plagued by high unemployment and huge budget deficits. In a three-way race for the

Above: President-elect Clinton reaching out to an ecstatic crowd gathered to greet him for his victory speech at Little Rock, Arkansas, on November 3, 1992. In winning the election he became the first president from his state.

presidency in 1992, which included the independent candidacy of Texas billionaire Ross Perot, Bush's Democratic opponent, Arkansas Governor Bill Clinton, was able to use the economy to defeat him.

BILL CLINTON

At age 46, Clinton was one of the nation's youngest presidents. Born in Hope, Arkansas, on August 19, 1946, he graduated from Georgetown University in 1968 and Yale Law School in 1973. Between Georgetown and Yale, he spent two years as a Rhodes Scholar at Oxford University, where be became involved in demonstrations against the Vietnam War. After graduating from Yale, Clinton taught law at the University of Arkansas before successfully running for Arkansas attorney general in 1967.[12]

Always interested in a political career, Clinton used the office of attorney general as a stepping stone to the governorship in 1978. At age 32, he was the youngest governor in the nation. Defeated in his bid for re-election two years later, largely because he had raised taxes and offended the trucking industry, Clinton was returned to office in 1982 and then re-elected three times (beginning in 1986 the gubernatorial term was extended from two to four years) before deciding to seek the Democratic presidential nomination in 1992. As governor, he made education his highest priority, raising teachers' salaries, but also insisting on teacher-competency tests.

In deciding to run for president, Clinton had

Above: A plastic-tasseled parade pom-pom and an automobile bumper sticker, both used in President Clinton's inaugural parade in 1993.

the advantage that Bush's high approval ratings had scared off some of his strongest potential opponents. Even before his campaign had started, Clinton was nearly forced out of the race by allegations of extra-marital affairs. But winning important primaries in the South and elsewhere, Clinton was able to gain the Democratic nomination in July. Although starting the presidential campaign with a substantial lead over Bush, he saw his margin dwindle as questions were raised about his draft deferment during the Vietnam War, his opposition to the war, and his general character. But helped by the candidacy of Ross Perot, which appealed to disaffected Republicans, and by making the economy his major campaign issue, Clinton was able to defeat Bush by a margin of 43 percent to 37 percent, with Perot winning 19 percent of the vote, the highest vote for any independent candidate since Theodore Roosevelt in 1912.

As president, Clinton has had a difficult time. For much of his term, he has found himself on the defensive, fending off Republican attacks on both his domestic and foreign policies. In 1994 he suffered a major setback when his highest leg-

Left: A good view of the vast crowd of hundreds of thousands assembled at the Capitol for Bill Clinton's inauguration on January 20, 1993. The oath is being administered by Chief Justice William H. Rehnquist.

Below: A major problem facing President Clinton has been attempting to deal with the Republican Party's control of both houses of Congress. He is seen here meeting with Republican leaders Bob Dole and Newt Gingrich.

Above: Hillary Clinton greeting local residents in Jakarta during her husband's visit to Indonesia in 1994. Her role, however, has been far more than simply accompanying the president: she has been one of the most powerful first ladies ever.

islative priority, a comprehensive program of national health insurance, was defeated on Capitol Hill. Making the failures of the Clinton administration a major campaign issue and proposing a 'Contract with America' that included major budget cuts, reduced taxes, and a balanced budget amendment to the Constitution, Republicans were able to make major gains in the congressional elections in 1994, capturing both houses of Congress for the first time since the Eisenhower administration.

In foreign policy, Clinton has also been roundly criticized for a lack of consistency or for having no policy at all. He has even been charged with allowing rhetoric to drive policy, as in the case of Bosnia, where he has been accused of embracing themes of high morality but of failing to back them up with military power, leading to diminished US influence in world affairs.[13]

In many ways, however, the Clinton administration merely mirrors the weakened status of the American presidency since the 1970s. A number of major historical developments have taken place during the last 25 years. These have included a more conservative electorate; the end of the Cold War; the reassertion of congressional prerogatives; and the seeming intractability of many of the social issues that have concerned the nation since the 1930s. Together, these developments make it highly unlikely that Clinton or any president in the near future will be able to set the national agenda in the same way that the post-World War II presidents prior to the 1970s were able to do.

Notes

1. Unless otherwise noted, this section on Richard Nixon is based on Ambrose, 1987, 1989 and 1991; Aiken, 1993; Wicker, 1991.

2. Kissinger, 1979: 112-94, 522-57, 684-841, 1049-96, 1124-64, and 1202-57.

3. Herring, 1986: 238-39.

4. Kaufman, 1995: 65-85.

5. Unless otherwise noted, this section on Gerald Ford is based on Greene, 1995.

6. Kellerman, 1984: 156-84.

7. This section on Carter is based on Kaufman, 1993.

8. This section on Ronald Reagan is based on Cannon, 1991; Scheiffer and Gates, 1989.

9. Unless otherwise noted, this section on Bush is based on Duffy and Goodgame, 1992; King, 1980.

10. Beschloss and Talbot, 1993: 19-464.

11. Kaufman, 1995: 149-73; Smith, 1992; Woodward, 1991.

12. Except where otherwise noted, this section on Clinton is based on Drew, 1994; Maraniss, 1995; Brumnett, 1994.

13. Clarke, 1995: 2-7.

Stephen L. Robertson

13
THE FIRST LADIES

What should the president's spouse – known since Julia Grant's
era as the 'First Lady' – do with her time ? History offers
numerous answers to this question, none of them satisfactory.
Changing public expectations mean that the purely domestic life
led by some early first ladies is no longer an option. Nor is the
sort of 'co-presidency' offered for a time by Bill Clinton and
Hillary Rodham Clinton. Modern first ladies have struggled
to find the golden mean – sometimes helped,
sometimes hurt by their husbands.

Suffragettes march to demand
the vote at the turn of the century.

The modern 'first ladyship' is the product of custom and history. The Constitution does not mention the president's wife; it gives her no role, no title, no power, no authority. Her glory is merely a reflection of his, and, more than any other person around the president, any power she may have is bestowed upon her, and can be removed, by him. In a real sense, she can be no more than he permits.

At the same time, broader forces have been at work upon the institution. At any given moment, the role of the first lady has tended to reflect the role of – and limits on – women in American society. As opportunities for women in American public life have increased, so too has the first lady become more visible and prominent. Today, it is not sufficient to tend to household affairs; the first lady is expected to be involved prominently in social causes. In this sense, if the first lady cannot be as much as she might like, neither can she be as little.

A wide variety of women have been first lady. Depending on the circumstances and their individual personalities, they have had a varied influence on the office. Some were very influential, either publicly or privately, in their husband's administration; others, not at all. Some proved to be tremendous assets to their husband's political fortunes, while others were of no help or were even a detriment to him. Many influenced public policy; others helped pave the way for women's advance in society. Almost all contributed in some way to shaping the institution of the first lady.

THE CREATION OF THE INSTITUTION

When Martha Washington (first lady, 1789–1797) arrived in the new nation's temporary capital of New York City in May 1789, the first ladyship was a blank slate. Indeed, there was not even any agreement about what to call the position. The term 'first lady' would not come into use for around 70 years; in its place was everything from the simple 'Mrs Washington' to 'Lady Washington' and the 'Republican Queen.'

As the initial first lady, Martha established numerous precedents, large and small, for her successors. She set standards for social life that were followed in the capital for years. She began the custom, followed for around 140 years, of opening the executive residence to all visitors on New Year's Day. Martha also set precedents by limiting herself to social matters, avoiding politics and political opinions. Her quiet, reserved dignity became the standard that placed the first lady firmly in a separate sphere from the president and in his shadow. Like her husband, she was respected and popular, and her social skills helped cement support for his administration.

Martha Washington's immediate successor as first lady was a very different sort of person. Abigail Adams (1797–1801) did not particularly enjoy being first lady. The social demands strained her budget and left her very little time for herself. In her letters (she was a prolific correspondent), Abigail complained bitterly on both counts. Intelligent, self-educated, outspoken, and witty, she was an early feminist who pleaded with her husband to 'remember the ladies' when the Declaration of Independence was being written in 1776. She took a keen interest in politics and personalities. John respected Abigail's intelligence and political insight and consulted her often on political questions. Consequently, Abigail had a lot of influence on her husband, a

fact that was well-known in the capital and may have hurt John politically. She strongly encouraged the passing of the Alien and Sedition Act of 1798, which gave the Adams administration a black eye. Many regarded her advice-giving as extremely inappropriate, preferring the apolitical example set by Martha Washington.

Abigail was the first first lady to occupy the White House. In the fall of 1800, she moved from Philadelphia to the new mansion, only to find it barely habitable. Just six rooms were finished, the house was so drafty that she needed more than a dozen fires to keep it warm, and she had to hang laundry in the stately East Room.

Thomas Jefferson was a widower when he reached the White House in 1801. During his two terms in office, either his daughter or Dolley Madison, the wife of his secretary of state, served as hostess.

When James Madison ascended to the presidency in 1809, his wife Dolley (1807–17) became first lady. Few first ladies have had such a far-reaching influence on the institution. Although she had little political clout, Dolley defined the social role of the first lady and showed how it could be employed to help the president. For years to come, she was the model for what a first lady ought to be.

Dolley Madison was born into a Quaker family but was expelled from the Friends when she married non-Quaker James Madison. She

responded by discarding her sedate Quaker garb for bright clothes and feathered turbans, which became her trademark. Outgoing and vivacious, she loved parties and crowds. Under her stewardship, the White House became the social center of Washington. Her weekly receptions and lavish dinner parties were immensely popular.

Dolley's social skills were a tremendous asset to her husband's administration. She had a considerable ability to put people at ease, could mix aristocratic manners with the common touch, was extremely good at remembering names, and so made everyone feel wanted and important. Aware of the criticism that had befallen Abigail Adams for her partisanship, Dolley expressed no political opinions publicly. Yet she had natural political instincts, knowing when and how to soothe ruffled feathers. This became very important because James lacked these qualities, often seeming distant and aloof in social settings. It was Dolley who played a major role in winning and keeping friends for her husband. Some have gone so far as to argue that she was crucial in James's narrow re-election win in 1812.[1]

Below: This daguerreotype of James K. Polk and his wife, Sarah, taken in the White House in 1847 or 1848 is the only known image of the couple alone. Sarah was an intelligent, politically inclined woman who encouraged and assisted her husband's political career.

Because she was raised a Quaker, Dolley was far better educated than most of the women of her day and was a skillful manager of the White House. She was also strong-willed and courageous. When the British army sacked Washington and burned the White House during the War of 1812, Dolley was one of the last to leave the mansion, staying long enough to salvage documents and several historically valuable artifacts. Among these was Gilbert Stuart's portrait of George Washington (which, contrary to common belief, was not cut down; the frame was broken and the portrait rolled up).

In retirement, Dolley was the first former first lady to receive a pension from Congress. She remained for years the Grande Dame of Washington, and was even granted an honorary seat on the floor of the House of Representatives. Immensely popular, Dolley Madison defined the ideal of the first lady for years to come.

THE RECLUSIVE FIRST LADY

By 1817, the role of first lady included social but not political responsibilities; she was to be seen in appropriate settings, but not heard. The outgoing first lady, as defined by Dolley Madison, was an example generally not followed by her successors. The view of women as weak and frail was common, and many of the first ladies reflected it. For various reasons, several of them prior to Reconstruction preferred to withdraw into the White House. With a few exceptions, the years 1817 to 1869 are the period of the reclusive first lady.

Not a recluse but much more withdrawn than her predecessor, Elizabeth Monroe (1817–25) marks the transition to the new period in the first lady's development. Between 1784 and 1817, the Monroes had spent much time representing the United States abroad. To better deal with the royalty of Europe, the Monroes had adopted European court manners. When James became president, they tried to bring a similar style to the White House, believing it suited the dignity of the office. It also suited Elizabeth, who was more aloof than her predecessor, may have suffered from ill health, and in any case did not relish non-stop entertainment. Social gatherings were smaller and less frequent than under Dolley Madison, and sometimes Elizabeth refused to attend White House functions. (Her absence meant that, according to the custom of the day, no other woman could attend, either.) The exhausting and time-consuming custom of making house calls on all the wives of congressmen, diplomats, and other Washington luminaries, was discarded – to the relief, no doubt, of future first ladies.

None of these changes went over well in Washington, particularly when contrasted with the just-departed Dolley Madison. Elizabeth Monroe and her daughters were criticized as being antisocial, haughty, and excessively European in taste and manner; for a time, the first lady's receptions were boycotted by Washington society. Whereas Dolley had used her social graces to help her husband politically, Elizabeth did not. Nowhere is this more obvious than in the marriage of their younger daughter Maria in 1820. With most of official Washington awaiting an invitation, Elizabeth had an opportunity to win allies for her husband; instead, she invited only the family's closest friends and resisted every effort to enlarge the guest list. In so doing, she set a precedent that later White House residents may have appreci-

ated, but which cost James much support.

Born in London, Louisa Adams (1825–29) was raised in England and France. She was 26 before she saw the United States, and spent much of her early marriage abroad, leading some to call her 'the most travelled woman of her time.' She may have played a key role in John Quincy Adams's election to the presidency; in 1824 she held numerous parties and dinners and won favor among the congressmen who would eventually elect him.[2] But Louisa did not enjoy her time as first lady. Her influence in the White House was limited to social events, for despite her intelligence, Louisa never interfered in politics and her husband did not include her in his work. On the rare occasions when she tried to give John political advice, as on his re-election campaign in 1828, he ignored her.[3] She found entertaining to be a strain. Living with a man who was totally immersed in a job that he would not share with her, shy and with few friends, and troubled by recurrent migraines, Louisa Adams was lonely and depressed in the White House.

The next two presidents, Andrew Jackson and Martin Van Buren, were both widowers when they became president. Jackson's wife Rachel, who had wanted no part of Washington, died of a heart attack a few months before he took office in 1829. During Jackson's term, his primary hostess was his niece, Emily Donelson. Van Buren's wife Hannah had been dead for 19 years when he was elected; his daughter-in-law, Angelica, served as his hostess.

William Henry Harrison was president for so short a time that his wife never made it to Washington. Anna Harrison (1841), who had been unenthusiastic about William's run for the presidency, was too ill to travel with him to his inauguration; he died a month into his term, before she could leave Indiana. It is one of the ironies of presidential history that the woman who was wife to one president and grandmother to another (Benjamin Harrison) never saw the White House.

When Vice President John Tyler became president upon Harrison's death, his wife was still on

their Virginia estate. Letitia Tyler (1841–42) had no formal schooling but was a skillful plantation manager and businesswoman. She apparently had no interest in politics; she had previously refused to accompany John to Washington when he was elected senator and vice president. By the time he became president, Letitia was an invalid, for she had suffered a serious stroke in 1839 and never completely recovered. She eventually came to the White House but did not take on the social duties of the first lady. Quiet and devout, and still partially paralyzed, she stayed out of sight except for her daughter's White House wedding in January 1842. In September 1842, Letitia suffered another stroke and died.

The bereaved president was devastated and ordered the White House hung in black. The period of mourning lasted several months, but eventually the first White House funeral gave way to the first presidential wedding: Tyler married Julia Gardiner, a women 30 years his junior, in June 1844, in New York City. The wedding was so secret that even Tyler's children did not know of it in advance.

Beautiful, vivacious, headstrong, and impulsive, Julia at 19 had scandalized her family by posing for a department store advertisement. Her time in the White House (1844–45) was brief but notable. Unlike many other first ladies, Julia enjoyed both the spotlight and the pomp. She entertained lavishly, held her own 'court,' and received guests seated on a throne of sorts. She began the custom of playing 'Hail to the Chief' upon the president's entry. Sensitive to the newspapers' stories about her, Julia was the first to hire her own press agent. She was also well aware of the political value of socializing; by some accounts, her informal lobbying helped win votes in Congress for the annexation of Texas.[4]

Julia's successor in the White House offered Washington a great contrast. Sarah Polk (1845–49) was a no-nonsense, politically inclined woman who was a major influence on her husband. Intelligent and ambitious, Sarah actively encouraged and helped James's political career. As first lady, she enjoyed an unprecedented degree of visibility and influence. Austere and religious, she banned drinking and dancing at the White House. Indeed, although Sarah recognized the political need for entertaining, she preferred to talk politics and tried to keep receptions as short as possible, in order not to interrupt other work. She labored side-by-side with her husband, often late into the night, never taking a vacation. She was his personal secretary; she read and marked papers for his review; and she gave him advice on issues of the day, notably on Westward expansion. So obvious was Sarah's role that many observers wondered openly if she were the president and not he.

Margaret Taylor (1849–50), perhaps the most reluctant of first ladies, had looked forward to retirement with her husband Zachary. Instead, she was forced to move to Washington when he was elected president. Once there, citing poor health, she retired to her quarters in the White House and rarely emerged, leaving entertaining to her daughter. Margaret was so reclusive that false rumors circulated that she was a pipe-smoking simpleton; many people were not even aware that President Taylor had a wife. Upon Zachary's sudden death, Margaret moved to Pascagoula, Mississippi, and died there without ever referring to her days as first lady. She is the only first lady whose portrait does not hang in the White House; indeed, no portrait of her exists.

Abigail Fillmore (1850–53) deferred much of the first lady's entertaining duties to her daughter, for she had an old ankle injury that made prolonged standing painful and, in any event, she did not enjoy large gatherings. She limited herself to smaller, less formal receptions. Her importance lay in her role as adviser to Millard. Abigail had good political instincts, and he consulted her on every matter of importance. On one crucial piece of legislation, he ignored her, however; he signed the Fugitive Slave Bill and, as she had warned him, it cost him any chance of being elected in 1852. A former teacher and an acknowledged bookworm, Abigail was appalled to find no books in the mansion and managed to obtain a congressional appropriation to start the White House library – perhaps her most lasting contribution.

Jane Pierce (1853–57) never wanted to be first lady; in fact, she hated Washington and did not want her husband to be in politics at all. She prayed that Franklin would lose in 1852, and when her only son was killed in a train wreck in January 1853, she took it as a divine judgment on his victory. Morbid and depressed, Jane came to the White House after her husband took office and retired to the second floor, where she wrote letters to her dead son. She did not make a public appearance until New Year's Day 1855, and although she carried out her social responsibilities thereafter, it was without enthusiasm or joy. Jane became known as 'the shadow in the White House,' and the mansion itself was considered a gloomy place during her time as first lady.

The only bachelor president, James Bucahanan, had his niece and ward, Harriet Lane, serve as first lady. Pretty and vivacious, Harriet restored dancing and entertainment to the White House; her time was referred to by some as 'the gayest administration.' She also had political influence, for her uncle had taught her politics and frequently listened to her opinions on political issues. Harriet's influence upon him was noted, but not always favorably; critics used it to attack Buchanan's 'manhood' and his fitness to be president.

Mary Todd Lincoln (1860–65) ranks as one of the most controversial and tragic of first ladies. Mary was ambitious and encouraged her husband's political career. Skilled as a hostess, she looked forward to being first lady, but her time in the White House proved to be a nightmare. She became first lady at a moment of bitter political division, and because no previous first lady had tried to be so visible a part of her husband's administration, much savage criticism came her way. Indeed, nothing she did satisfied her critics. Mary was attacked for entertaining too much and for entertaining too little, for over-dressing and for under-dressing, for her origins, her outspokenness, and almost everything else. When her brothers from Kentucky joined the Confederacy, even her loyalty to the Union was questioned, and some accused her of being a spy. She received so much hate mail that the White House mail clerk screened her letters, and she was the target of vitriolic newspaper attacks in Abraham's 1864 re-election campaign.

The relentless criticism and pressure, combined with the death of her son Willie in 1862, left Mary emotionally unstable. (She would be briefly confined to a mental institution in 1875.) She suffered blinding headaches, violent and unpredictable mood swings, fits of overwhelming grief and irrational jealousy, and moments of paranoia. She also became a compulsive shopper, ruining her family's finances. Instead of the help that she had hoped to be, Mary was a tremendous burden for Lincoln, who had to cope with her unpredictable behavior and the criticism it engendered, even as the war progressed. Following Lincoln's assassination, Mary remained in mourning in the White House for five weeks.

Eliza Johnson (1865–69) was a self-educated woman who taught her husband Andrew to read and write. Andrew Johnson embarked on a political career that would eventually take him to the presidency, but Eliza, his wife, preferred to stay in the background. Describing herself as 'simple folk,' she avoided the social rounds and continued to manage the family and the farm. By the time Johnson became president, she had suffered for several years from tuberculosis and was a semi-invalid. As first lady, she stayed upstairs and appeared at only two public functions, leaving entertaining to her daughter, Martha Patterson. Eliza's unflinching loyalty to her husband sustained him through his battles with Congress, but she took no interest in political issues.

THE FIRST LADY IN THE GILDED AGE

The first ladies from Monroe to Johnson were, as a group, retiring and relatively uninfluential. A few were political advisers to their husbands, but that role was behind the scenes; to speak out publicly on issues was unacceptable. Two first ladies, Harriet Lane and Julia Tyler, were especially prominent socially, while one (Mary Lincoln) sought a visible role in her husband's administration, with disastrous results. Most remained in the shadows.

The first ladyship was transformed in the 'Gilded Age'. The role of women in American society was beginning to change, and suffragettes had begun to campaign. Both in response to and leading the trend, first ladies began to move on to the public stage. As a group, they were more politically involved and more prominent than their predecessors. The emerging mass media

Below: President Ulysses S. Grant and his wife and their children. During Julia Grant's period at the White House the term 'first lady' came into use and it was she that made it into a truly national institution.

also helped to give new prominence to the first lady.

Julia Grant (1869–77) loved being first lady and later said that it 'was like a bright and beautiful dream.' Her political influence on Grant was limited, for she knew and cared little about most issues, but she did have a hand in removing cabinet officials she felt were harmful to her husband.[5] Socially, Julia was a major success. In an extravagant age, she entertained lavishly and often; her formal dinners had as many as 21 courses. She sought the spotlight, and the press eagerly gave it to her. It was during her reign that the term 'first lady' was permanently attached to the office. Julia made the first ladyship into a truly national institution, and as such she represents a turning point in its development.[6]

Lucy Webb Hayes (1877–81) was serious, deeply but quietly religious, intelligent, and the first first lady to have a college degree. Simple and frugal, Lucy was a stark contrast to Julia Grant. Her political influence is unclear. Many thought she was the power behind the president, but there is no real proof of this. The decision most widely attributed to her – the banning of alcohol in the White House, which earned her the nickname of 'Lemonade Lucy' – was actually Rutherford's, made to win the temperance vote. On political issues, she was generally silent, much to the dismay of those who hoped she would be the advocate for the 'New Woman.' Although Lucy had shown some feminist leanings when younger, her few statements as first lady were strictly traditional. Her cross-country travel helped push the first lady further forward on the national stage, and she was the first to give prepared speeches.[7] The first lady was becoming such a public figure that Lucy had to retain family members to help with her correspondence. She also initiated the annual custom of the White House Easter egg hunt.

Lucretia Rudolph Garfield's (1881) time as first lady was very short. She was planning to redecorate the White House in a historical style, and was undertaking research for the project, when she contracted malaria and had to leave Washington to recover. While at the train station on his way to visit her, James was shot by a deranged office-seeker. Despite her care, he died 80 days later. Thus, tragically, Lucretia was the first first lady to plan and attend a president's funeral.

Chester Arthur, who followed Garfield, was a widower when he became president and, during his term, his sister Mary McElroy served as White House hostess. When Grover Cleveland followed Arthur into office in 1885, he was still a bachelor and had to recruit his sister Rose to serve as hostess. This situation changed on June 2, 1886, when Cleveland married Frances Folsom, the daughter of his law partner, in the first White House wedding.

Frances Cleveland (1886–89 and 1893–97) was more than a first lady – she elevated the position to the status of celebrity. The national press was coming into its own, and Frances was its centerpiece. Everywhere she went, onlookers crowded to see her; every reception and receiving line was swamped with people. Everything she did was news – she was unprecedentedly popular. Her clothing and hairstyle were copied by women everywhere, and her picture was used (without permission) in advertisements. The attention was so great that she and Grover had to rent a second residence in Washington to get any privacy at all.

Above: Lucretia Garfield's time at the White House was short and tragic. She became ill with malaria and went away to recuperate. Her husband was on his way to visit her when he was shot by an assassin.

Frances showed some interest in charities but little in politics. However, she was to have an important political influence. Her grace and charm helped win friends for Grover, who could be rude and boorish. Her picture was displayed prominently on the Democratic campaign posters in the 1892 race, and some think she was a major reason Cleveland was returned to the White House.

Between Cleveland's two terms came Caroline Harrison's tenure as first lady. Caroline (1889–92) came to the White House with plans to rebuild the mansion, but Congress refused to agree and so a more modest yet thorough remodeling was done. (It was at this time that electricity was installed in the White House.) Caroline was a warm entertainer and helped offset her dour husband. An artist, she painted many decorations around the White House and donated many crafts to charity. Having feminist leanings, she helped ensure that the new Johns Hopkins University Medical School in Baltimore, Maryland, would be coeducational and helped found the Daughters of the American Revolution. She also started the White House china collection and decorated the first White House Christmas tree.

Caroline's health, which had been frail for years, deteriorated rapidly as Benjamin's term wore on. By 1892 she was so seriously ill with tuberculosis that her husband did not actively campaign for his re-election. (His opponent, Grover Cleveland, also declined to campaign.) She died in the White House a few days before the 1892 election.

Ida McKinley (1897–1901) came to the White House an invalid. As a young woman, she received an excellent education that included a knowledge of the banking industry and had a happy early marriage to William. But the deaths of her mother and of both her children within two years drove her to the brink of a nervous breakdown; she was left suffering from epilepsy, phlebitis, migraines, and depression.

photographs and stories about her children to reduce the media crush. Overseeing a renovation of the mansion, she carefully separated the living and working quarters. She also began the first lady portrait collection in the White House.

William Howard Taft did not particularly want to be president, but Helen Taft (1909–13) was determined to be first lady, and her relentless ambition drove him to seek and win the White House. After his inaugural address, she became the first first lady to ride back to the White House with a new president. Intelligent and politically engaged, Helen avoided social events whenever possible to focus on policy discussions. She discussed every appointment and issue with Taft; her influence with him was widely known. However, in May 1909, Helen suffered a serious stroke that left her partially paralyzed and mute. Although she eventually recovered, she was never as politically active again. Her most enduring legacy is Washington's famous cherry trees, which were planted at her request.

Ellen Wilson (1913–14) was an intelligent, independently-minded woman whose clear thinking and management skills were a great help to her husband. As first lady, Ellen was one of Woodrow's closest advisers. She was a quiet suffragette, no doubt encouraging her husband in that direction, and she took an interest in a number of charities. A talented artist, in 1913 Ellen donated the proceeds from her one-woman art show to the poor. She became concerned about the problem of substandard housing in Washington and pressed Congress to pass a housing bill to aid poor neighborhoods. Such public involvement by a first lady on a legislative issue was unprecedented. Congress eventually passed what was popularly known as 'Ellen Wilson's Bill,' but by then the first lady was dying. After suffering from kidney disease, she died in Washington in 1914.

Wilson was distraught at his wife's death, but he soon remarried. A few months after Ellen died, he met Edith Galt, a 42-year-old widowed businesswoman, and married her in December 1915.

Self-assured and decisive, Edith (1915–21) immediately stepped in as Wilson's personal secretary and common-sense adviser. When the United States entered World War I in 1917, she led by example, getting sheep to graze the White House lawn and donating the wool to the war effort.

Although at first not particularly interested in politics, Edith became more politically important than any first lady in history. In October 1919, Wilson suffered a massive stroke and, at least for a time, was rendered a total invalid. Edith took over the White House and protected the sick president. No one saw Wilson except with her consent; all papers and business went through her. Precisely how much power she exercised at this time has never been determined. Edith always claimed that she was merely a messenger and that Woodrow made all the important decisions. Others believed, however, that he was incapacitated and that Edith essentially *was* the president of the United States, at least for a few months. If true, no first lady before or since has had such power; even if exaggerated, few have been so important.

None of the three first ladies who followed Edith Wilson were as politically involved as she, but all appeared on the public stage. Florence Harding (1921–23) wanted to be the 'people's'

Unlike previous sickly first ladies, Ida refused to withdraw into the family quarters of the White House. Despite being temperamental and subject to sudden violent seizures, she was determined to play a public role and attend formal dinners and receptions. She tolerated no stand-ins for herself, and when her health worsened in 1901, she cancelled the entire social season. The constant need to have special arrangements in case Ida had seizures, combined with her erratic behavior, was a great burden for the president, but his devotion to his wife proved to be a political asset for him. To everyone's surprise, Ida showed great strength when William was assassinated in 1901. She attended his funeral and, back in Ohio, oversaw the building of his mausoleum.

THE FIRST LADY RESURGENT

The first ladies from Julia Grant to Ida McKinley gave the position a national prominence that it had not previously enjoyed. There were no more reclusive invalids; even the seriously ill Ida McKinley insisted on taking the public stage. During the next 30 years, succeeding first ladies

Above: Frances Cleveland writing a letter in the White House. She was highly popular with the public and elevated the first ladyship into a celebrity position, leading to it becoming a feature of political campaigning.

would, in various ways, institutionalize the role, expand its scope and visibility, and give it greater influence than ever before.

As first lady, Edith Roosevelt (1901–09) had a definite if discrete influence on her husband Theodore's policies. She sorted his mail, marked newspapers for him, reviewed position papers, and often spent time in the evenings working alone with him. She was pragmatic and level-headed, and Theodore consulted her on many issues. She was considered a restraining influence on the often impetuous president.

Edith also began institutionalizing the first ladyship. She hired the first personal secretary paid by government funds, thus beginning the first lady's staff. She held weekly meetings with the wives of cabinet members to coordinate official entertainment. Recognizing the public interest in the 'first family,' Edith released posed

guages. Her marriage to Herbert Hoover on February 10, 1899, was the start of frequent travels around the world on business and humanitarian missions. Lou also accompanied Herbert on the campaign trail when he ran for president in 1928. In the White House, she urged that women join the workforce and become politically active. She was the first first lady to make a speech on radio from the White House. She was very involved with the Girl Scouts, serving as honorary president. When the Depression hit in October 1929, Lou headed efforts to mobilize private relief and gave generously (and anonymously) of her own funds to help the destitute. Even her husband did not realize how many people she had helped until he discovered a pile of uncashed checks – repayment for money she had given to needy people – in her desk after her death.

THE MODERN FIRST LADY

The first ladies who occupied the White House for the first third of the 20th century were far more prominent than their predecessors. The first lady was now enshrined as a celebrity, a national figure with a larger role to play in American politics. Reflecting the increasing importance of women in public life, subsequent first ladies have greatly expanded that role.

Often called the greatest of the first ladies, Eleanor Roosevelt (1933–45) largely created the modern first ladyship. Drab and insecure in her youth, she was a retiring woman until her husband Franklin's contraction of polio in 1921 forced her into the public arena.

Before becoming first lady, Eleanor had been teaching, lecturing, writing, running a business, and participating in New York politics. When she moved to the White House, her pace increased. No first lady before or since has been so publicly engaged. She wrote an autobiography and a daily newspaper column (donating the royalties to charity), answered thousands of letters, held press conferences for women reporters, and gave radio broadcasts, speeches, and public lectures. She travelled across the country and around the world. She flew on airplanes and visited coal mines. In fact her busy schedule did not include time for the careful management of the White House itself, which led one visitor to complain of soiling her gloves on a dirty bannister.

Eleanor was heard as well as seen. Unlike most previous first ladies, she was vociferous in support of social causes. Attacking racism, she publicly resigned from the Daughters of the American Revolution when the group discriminated against a black opera singer. She supported women's rights and helped secure the first female cabinet appointment for Frances Perkins. She also advocated programs to assist the young and the poor.

Eleanor's political influence within the Roosevelt administration is difficult to measure, because Franklin sought so many opinions and amalgamated them all in the policies he pursued. But there is no question that her influence was extensive. Eleanor served in the National Youth Administration and the Office of Civilian Defense. More significantly, she was incessantly advocating ideas and policies to her husband, leaving materials for him to read, and arranging for him to meet people with new ideas. For Franklin, she was both eyes and ears, due to her constant travel, and sounding board, off whom

first lady. She reopened the White House after the war years and spent hours greeting guests, sometimes giving spontaneous tours. She held numerous receptions. Having been in the newspaper business with her husband Warren, she talked with reporters more than previous first ladies. Florence was particularly concerned about the wounded veterans from World War I and spent much time visiting them. She was also an avowed feminist and did not hesitate to speak out for women's rights, although she was careful not to outrun public opinion. Because observers said Florence dominated her husband, her political influence is often assumed to have been extensive, but she destroyed many of his papers after leaving the White House, and so no evidence for this claim remains.

Although Grace Coolidge (1923–29) showed almost no interest in politics during her time in the White House, she was far from reclusive. She was a teacher of the deaf; when she married Calvin Coolidge, friends joked that perhaps now she could teach the mute to speak. A more

Above: Edith Wilson photographed in about 1899. She was Woodrow's second wife and, just like his first wife, she became a close adviser of his. When he suffered a stroke she wielded great influence.

unlikely couple would be hard to find. She was outgoing, effervescent, witty, and charming; he was close-mouthed, reserved, and often glum.

Grace never gave political advice to her husband, who strongly discouraged her from getting involved in politics, and she never expressed political opinions publicly. Yet Calvin owed much of his popularity to Grace. Her happy vitality won friends daily for her husband. She seemed always to be in the public eye: she held receptions, went to luncheons and state dinners, helped raise money for the Red Cross and the deaf, rode in parades, sat with children, planted trees. She was, some said, '90 percent of the administration;'[8] certainly, she was its most visible part.

Lou Hoover (1929–33) took her geology degree from Stanford and was fluent in five lan-

he could bounce ideas. Sometimes he would take her arguments and repeat them as his own; she never knew if she had persuaded him or simply helped him clarify his thoughts.

Eleanor Roosevelt was more publicly and politically engaged than any previous first lady. She 'experimented with the role of president's wife and changed it, opening up what had been hidden and breaking down barriers that had stood firm for a century and a half.'[9] In so doing, she created new possibilities for her successors.

Bess Truman (1945–53), who followed the frenetic Mrs Roosevelt, thought that publicity was unbecoming for a lady, and so she had always attempted to stay in the background as Harry pursued his political career. As first lady, Bess refused to hold press conferences or otherwise comment on issues; her public statements were limited to charitable appeals and calls to renovate the White House. Although quiet, her influence was nonetheless significant. She was Harry's partner and assistant, reviewing his speeches, giving him practical advice on even the largest questions, and working on his papers and correspondence. Harry valued her help immensely and once noted that she had been his 'chief adviser' and 'a full partner in all my transactions – politically and otherwise.'[10] Bess also helped keep Harry's temper under control. Her rebuke, 'you didn't have to say that,' was legendary among the White House staff.

Mamie Eisenhower (1953–61) was more visible than Bess Truman but less political. She apparently took little interest in politics and was content to be an excellent hostess and a firm manager of the White House. A perfect fit for her times, effervescent Mamie was immensely popular. Her frills, lace, and domesticity were the standard for 1950s femininity. Women copied her hairstyle, her clothes, her pink decor, and even her fudge recipe. She was also the first first lady of the television era, giving her more exposure than any of her predecessors.

Jacqueline Kennedy (1961–63) was perhaps the most glamorous of all the first ladies. Young,

Above: Eleanor Roosevelt visiting a Works Progress Administration project in Des Moines, Iowa, in June 1936, which was converting a city dump into a waterfront park. Of all the first ladies she is one of the best known, principally because of her advocacy of social causes.

Below: Harry S. Truman with his wife, Bess, and daughter, Margaret, alongside Senator Barkley at the 1948 Democratic National Convention in Philadelphia. Bess kept a low profile as first lady, preferring to use her influence with her husband in private.

beautiful, vibrant, and intelligent, she as much as anyone embodied the ideal of 'Camelot' that many associate with the Kennedy administration. Although not very interested in government policies, she became her husband's goodwill ambassador and as such was often more popular than the president. On a state visit to France, she so charmed President Charles de Gaulle and the French people that John Kennedy introduced himself as 'the man who accompanied Jacqueline Kennedy to France.' She tried to elevate America's cultural awareness, inviting artists to perform at the White House, conducting a televised tour of the mansion, and seeking period pieces for its redecoration. A media 'darling' during and after her first ladyship, Jackie thrust the office firmly into the forefront of the new world of television and gave it (in the words of a British newspaper) a 'majesty' that it had not previously had.[11]

Lady Bird Johnson (1963–69) was not as glamorous as Jackie Kennedy, but she too expanded the horizons of the first ladyship. Lady Bird had no political experience when she married Lyndon Johnson, but she quickly learned the art of entertaining for her husband's benefit. As first lady, she had to entertain constantly because of LBJ's tendency to issue spur-of-the-moment invitations (sometimes to the entire Congress). Lady Bird travelled constantly around the country, frequently checking on the progress of LBJ's 'Great Society' programs. She adopted as her personal project the beautification of America, worked tirelessly to promote cleaning the environment, and lobbied Congress to pass the Highway Beautification Act of 1965. She campaigned on her own for Lyndon's re-election in 1964. Her political savvy was such that LBJ frequently solicited her thoughts on public policy.

Pat Nixon (1969–74) was one of the least active of the recent first ladies, initially because her husband's staff preferred to keep her out of sight and later because of Watergate. A charming, lively woman in private, Pat was uncomfortable in the spotlight. Nonetheless, despite her dislike for politics, she made the required public appearances and campaigned for Richard's election. She travelled more than any first lady, visiting 83 countries, often as the president's representative. Her major concern as first lady was to make the White House more accessible to the public, especially to the disabled; she also began Christmas candlelight tours and seasonal garden tours and introduced multilingual guidebooks to the mansion. Pat worked to acquire antiques to refurnish the White House. There is no indication that she ever gave her husband political advice, except when she urged him to destroy the Watergate tapes – advice that he ignored.

Betty Ford (1974–77) was neither quiet nor invisible as first lady. Trained by Martha Graham to dance professionally, she strongly supported the fine arts. She was an advocate for the elderly and the handicapped. Outspokenly tolerant on issues such as premarital sex, she was both harshly criticized and lavishly praised for her honesty and candor. Her willingness to dis-

Above: President Eisenhower and his wife, Mamie, pictured outside the White House on the occasion of their 38th wedding anniversary in 1954. They met when he was stationed in Texas as a second lieutenant. Mamie was a normal 1950's housewife and hostess, becoming immensely popular.

Left: Jacqueline Kennedy was a contrast to Mamie, representing a new, younger generation. The Kennedy campaign badge (above) referred specifically to the women, but they were not rivals as this friendly meeting in 1960 shows.

cuss the mastectomy she had in 1974 focussed national attention on breast cancer and may have saved many lives. She was perhaps the most outspoken feminist of any first lady; she strongly and publicly supported the proposed Equal Rights Amendment, spoke frequently on the need for women's rights, and pressured Jerry to appoint more women to office. Betty was also known to be a valued adviser to her husband; their 'pillow talks' covered many of the issues of the day. Despite the occasional controversy she created, Betty was so popular that when Jerry ran for the presidency in 1976, a common campaign button read 'Keep Betty's Husband President.'

Unfortunately for Betty, Gerald Ford was not elected in 1976, and Rosalynn Carter (1977–81) became first lady. Although many first ladies had causes, none since Eleanor Roosevelt were as politically active as Rosalynn. As the wife of candidate Jimmy Carter, she had stumped the country alone, allowing the campaign to reach twice as many voters; Jimmy admitted she was crucial to his victory. As first lady, she was constantly on the go; according to one source, in her first 14 months, she visited 18 nations and 27 American cities; held 259 private and 50 public meetings; made 15 major speeches; held 22 press conferences; gave 32 interviews; attended 83 receptions; and held 25 meetings with special groups in the White House.[12]

Rosalynn headed a drive to improve the nation's policy on mental illness; chaired the Commission on Aging to help senior citizens; extended the renovation of the White House begun by Jacqueline Kennedy and Pat Nixon; and pressed for women's rights. Although holding no official position, she attended cabinet

Above: This photograph of Lady Bird Johnson was taken in 1967 in Austin, Texas, just after she had become a proud grandmother and the president a grandfather. Their daughter, Luci, had given birth to a healthy baby boy.

Below: Richard and Pat Nixon meeting with the widow of China's late premier, Chou En-Lai. Pat did not care much for the spotlight, nevertheless she traveled more than any other first lady so far, visiting dozens of countries as first lady.

Above: Betty Ford addressing the Republican Women Candidate's lunch in Chicago on September 23, 1974. She had a high profile as a strong female figure and an advocate of sexual equality.

Above: This picture of Rosalynn and Jimmy Carter was taken on January 20, 1981, as they prepared to fly to Plains, Georgia, following the ceremony to inaugurate President Reagan.

Below: It took some time for the public to like Nancy Reagan and one factor which helped was the anti-drug abuse campaign she headed. Here, she is speaking at a 'Just Say No' rally in 1987.

meetings, discussed policy initiatives in her areas of interest with appropriate officials, and sometimes represented the administration abroad. She was Jimmy's closest adviser, reviewing his speeches, receiving briefing papers, discussing issues with him daily, and even sharing a working lunch with him once a week. He called her invaluable, and her influence was so visible and extensive that she was criticized by some who thought she had overstepped her role.

Rosalynn Carter was followed as first lady by Nancy Reagan (1981–89). Declaring that her only interest was her husband, Nancy became first lady with a very limited agenda. Combined with a public perception that she was insensitive to the poor, this made Nancy very unpopular at first. She responded to the criticism by becoming active in the Foster Grandparents program and by taking a prominent role in the fight against drug abuse with her 'Just Say No' program. She eventually became as popular as the president; a January 1985 poll placed her public approval rating at 72 percent, compared with her husband's 64 percent. Political issues did not interest her, but her husband did, and she protected him fiercely. It was well known that Nancy manipulated appointments and dismissals of people whom she felt had helped or harmed the president.

Barbara Bush (1989–93) devoted much of her time as first lady to helping the less fortunate. She made literacy her primary interest, working to eradicate illiteracy and devoting the proceeds of her bestselling book, *C. Fred's Story*, to that cause. She worked to assist the homeless, AIDS victims, and impoverished single parents, and served in the Leukemia Society of America (one of her own children had suffered from the disease). This work, combined with her grandmotherly appearance and demeanor, made her immensely popular. In the political realm, she was a quiet but important part of the Bush administration. Called by some 'the key element' of the Bush team, Barbara worked closely with George, sharing her thoughts on issues. She

Above: The wives of the world's two most powerful men, Barbara Bush and Raisa Gorbachev, in June 1990. Barbara was popular with Americans because of her good works and also thanks to her grandmotherly appearance.

Below: Hillary Rodham Clinton came to the White House having had an important legal career of her own. She is addressing medical students in 1993 to promote her health reform plan – a reflection of her active role in the administration.

reviewed papers for and discussed policy questions with him.

A successful lawyer in her own right, Hillary Rodham Clinton (1993–) became one of the most visible and active first ladies in history. She was a major force in Bill Clinton's 1992 campaign. As first lady, she took the lead in devising and promoting the administration's ill-fated health care reform plan; she headed the commission that created the plan and then lobbied on its behalf and appeared before five different congressional committees to explain and defend it. These appearances made her only the third first lady – after Eleanor Roosevelt and Rosalynn Carter – to appear before Congress. Hillary also was publicly active in children's and women's issues, attending the controversial United Nations Conference on Women in Beijing, China, in 1995. Within the administration, she was a major influence on policy. She weighed in on almost every issue and was one of Bill's closest advisers. Everyone knew to 'ask Hillary' before decisions were made. She had her own White House powerbase and her influence was so obvious that she was criticized for being too powerful. Hostile bumper stickers read 'Impeach the president – and Bill, too.' In one respect, Hilary was unique: no first lady had ever been granted so much authority, along with the resources needed to carry out her wishes.

CONCLUSION

The years since 1789 have witnessed the evolution of the first ladyship into an integral part of the modern presidency. Long undefined, the office has grown by practice and custom, never statute, into its present prominence. Along the way, different first ladies have enlarged the office and increased its importance.

Today, the first lady has her own staff housed in the East Wing of the White House and her own agenda. She is a public figure who is expected to be at the forefront of causes to improve America. The case of Nancy Reagan, who came under attack for her desire to stay out of the limelight, shows that first ladies have to be active or risk hurting the president politically. At the same time, their activity is limited by public expectations. Hillary Rodham Clinton is merely the latest of many first ladies to be criticized for being 'too involved in politics.'

Although the first lady derives her authority from the president and so, to some degree, shines with a reflected light, it is also true that she has acquired independent expectations. The frontiers of the office continue to be pushed back and first ladies continue to accrue new responsibilities: they campaign, they advocate, they lobby. Yet many things remain unchanged. By putting a human face on the administration, a first lady today can win friends for her husband just as Dolley Madison did. She can serve as a surrogate for the president, an *alter ego* to be there when he cannot. Because she is the person closest to the president – and because the two adjectives that describe most first ladies best are 'intelligent' and 'strong' – she is often among his closest advisers. In these ways, the first lady is one of the most important parts of the modern presidency.

Notes
1. Caroli, 1987: 17.
2. Anthony, 1990: 107.
3. Anthony, 1990: 110.
4. Anthony, 1990: 132.
5. Anthony, 1990: 215.
6. Caroli, 1987: 83.
7. Anthony, 1990: 233.
8. Boller, 1988: 260.
9. Carol , 1987: 200.
10. Boller, 1988: 321.
11. Boller, 1988: 364.
12. Boller, 1988: 443.

Michael Nelson

14

THE CHANGING OFFICE

Presidents come and go – 41 in little more than two centuries, an average of one every five years. Each of their personalities and policies leaves a mark on the office, some more enduring than others. But change in the presidency flows within channels created by the Constitution of 1787, a plan of government little changed since then by amendment. The combination of change and continuity is one of the hallmarks of the American political system, as embodied in the president.

George Bush, with a record of life-long government service, takes the vice presidential oath in 1981.

The presidential election of 1988 occurred squarely in the middle of the three-year bicentennial of the US Constitution, which was written at the Constitutional Convention of 1787, ratified by the states in 1788, and implemented in 1789. The bicentennial was, of course, an occasion for celebration: the announced theme of George Bush's post-election inauguration was 'From George to George' – Washington in 1789, Bush in 1989. It also was an occasion to begin reflecting on the enduring significance of the Constitution. To the extent that a consensus has emerged from nearly a decade of scholarly symposia, articles, and books on the Constitution's continuing influence, it is simply stated: the modern presidency and the postwar political system cannot be understood apart from their constitutional design. Presidents come and go, but the Constitution endures.

The point is obvious for the early presidents. But, even at a glance, the contemporary importance of the Constitution is also apparent in the administrations of all of Bush's recent predecessors, as well as his successor, Bill Clinton. As the political scientist Fred Greenstein showed in his book *The Hidden-Hand President*, the political success of Dwight D. Eisenhower, who served as chief executive from 1953 to 1961, is best explained by his mastery of the office's constitutional role as chief of state, the living symbol of national unity and, as such, the rough equivalent of the British monarch. The stability of both the presidency and the larger scheme of constitutional government that it inhabits was confirmed when the assassination of Eisenhower's successor, John F. Kennedy, on November 22, 1963, led not to a coup or to chaos but to a smooth transfer of power from the slain president to his vice president, Lyndon B. Johnson. The Johnson administration, initially successful because of the president's skill as the Constitution's 'chief legislator,' foundered politically on his disputed and unsuccessful use in the Vietnam War of the office's constitutional power as commander-in-chief.

Richard Nixon, whose tenure as president lasted from 1969 to 1974, stretched the Constitution beyond recognizable bounds by secretly bombing Cambodia and by impounding – that is, refusing to spend – billions of dollars of funds that had been appropriated by Congress for domestic programs that he disliked. Yet the document's resilience was demonstrated with a vengeance when Nixon was forced to resign in 1974 in order to avoid the constitutional processes of impeachment and removal for obstructing justice in the Watergate affair. The political fate of Nixon's successor, Gerald R. Ford, was sealed when he used the president's only unrestricted constitutional power to pardon the former president from criminal prosecution.

Ford had become president because of the recent enactment of the Twenty-fifth Amendment to the Constitution, part of which empowered the president (pending congressional confirmation) to fill sudden vacancies in the vice presidency. The first exercise of this power occurred when Vice President Spiro T. Agnew, in fulfilling a plea bargain to escape imprisonment for accepting bribes, resigned in 1973 and was replaced by Ford. When Ford succeeded to the presidency after Nixon resigned on August 9, 1974, he in turn nominated former New York governor Nelson A. Rockefeller to be vice president. Thus, in 1976, without controversy, the United States was led into the bicentennial celebration of its independence by a president and vice president who were unelected but still constitutionally legitimate.

Jimmy Carter, a Democrat, defeated Ford in the 1976 election but learned soon after that even the presence of an overwhelmingly Democratic Congress was not enough to assure the cooperation of the constitutionally independent legislative branch. Ronald Reagan, who was elected to replace Carter in 1980, was more successful in this regard, at least at first. But Reagan's most enduring mark on government may have been his exercise of the president's constitutional appointment power to pack the federal judiciary with conservative Republicans enjoying lifetime tenure on the bench. In 1989, like Eisenhower before him, Reagan was forced to leave office by the Twenty-second Amendment, which was enacted in 1951 to restrict presidents to two elected terms.

Bush, who served as Reagan's vice president and was elected to succeed him in 1988, leaned heavily on his constitutional powers. In 1991, for example, Bush welcomed Congress's endorsement of his plan to attack Iraq in the Gulf War but said that, even without such an endorsement, he would have fought the war on the basis of his authority as commander-in-chief. Bush also vetoed 46 pieces of legislation, and only once was Congress able to muster the two-thirds majority needed to override a veto under the Constitution. As for Clinton, even though the military did not respect him for evading service as a young man in the Vietnam War, they obeyed him as commander-in-chief when he sent them into harm's way in Somalia, Haiti, Iraq, Bosnia, and elsewhere.

Eisenhower and the constitutional chief of state role; Kennedy, Johnson and peaceful succession; Nixon's near-impeachment; Ford's pardon; Bush and Clinton's military leadership – these recent examples are but manifestations of an underlying truth about modern US government revealed by this book: because of the Constitution, the presidency is more an office of constancy than of change.

This is not to say that the office never changes or that presidents do not change it. But such changes are more like waves on an ocean's surface than like the ocean itself. Waves are visible and superficially dramatic, just as changes in presidents or intense political quarrels are visible and seem dramatic. But underneath the political turbulence, as with the enduring, slowly moving ocean, lies the constitutional office that the Framers invented more than two centuries ago.

Below: Democratic candidate Governor Bill Clinton appealing to the crowd and, crucially, the millions watching television, as President Bush (background) and Ross Perot (out of shot) listen during the second presidential debate in 1992.

Chronological Table of the Presidential Elections of the United States

Year	Winning Candidate and Party	Principal Opponent and Party
1789	George Washington (no party)	John Adams (no party)
1792	George Washington (no party)	George Clinton (Democratic-Republican)
1796	John Adams (Federalist)	Thomas Jefferson (Democratic-Republican)
1800	Thomas Jefferson (Democratic-Republican)	John Adams (Federalist)
1804	Thomas Jefferson (Democratic-Republican)	C.C. Pinckney (Federalist)
1808	James Madison (Democratic-Republican)	C.C. Pinckney (Federalist)
1812	James Madison (Democratic-Republican)	De Witt Clinton (Anti-war Republican/Federalist)
1816	James Monroe (Democratic-Republican)	Rufus King (Federalist)
1820	James Monroe (Democratic-Republican)	*Effectively uncontested*
1824	John Quincy Adams (Democratic-Republican)	Andrew Jackson (Democratic-Republican)
1828	Andrew Jackson (Democratic)	John Quincy Adams (National Republican)
1832	Andrew Jackson (Democratic)	Henry Clay (National Republican)
1836	Martin Van Buren (Democratic)	William Henry Harrison (Whig)
1840	William Henry Harrison (Whig)	Martin Van Buren (Democratic)
1844	James K. Polk (Democratic)	Henry Clay (Whig)
1848	Zachary Taylor (Whig)	Lewis Cass (Democratic)
1852	Franklin Pierce (Democratic)	Winfield Scott (Whig)
1856	James Buchanan (Democratic)	John C. Fremont (Republican)
1860	Abraham Lincoln (Republican)	Stephen A. Douglas (Democratic)
1864	Abraham Lincoln (Republican)	George B. McClellan (Democratic)
1868	Ulysses S. Grant (Republican)	Horatio Seymour (Democratic)
1872	Ulysses S. Grant (Republican)	Horace Greeley (Democratic and Liberal Republican)
1876	Rutherford B. Hayes (Republican)	Samuel J. Tilden (Democratic)
1880	James A. Garfield (Republican)	Winfield S. Hancock (Democratic)
1884	Grover Cleveland (Democratic)	James G. Blaine (Republican)
1888	Benjamin Harrison (Republican)	Grover Cleveland (Democratic)
1892	Grover Cleveland (Democratic)	Benjamin Harrison (Republican)
1896	William McKinley (Republican)	William Jennings Bryan (Democratic-Populist, and National Silver)
1900	William McKinley (Republican)	William Jennings Bryan (Democratic-Populist)
1904	Theodore Roosevelt (Republican)	Alton B. Parker (Democratic)
1908	William Howard Taft (Republican)	William Jennings Bryan (Democratic)
1912	Woodrow Wilson (Democratic)	Theodore Roosevelt (Progressive)
1916	Woodrow Wilson (Democratic)	Charles E. Hughes (Republican)
1920	Warren Harding (Republican)	James M. Cox (Democratic)
1924	Calvin Coolidge (Republican)	John W. Davis (Democratic)
1928	Herbert Hoover (Republican)	Alfred E. Smith (Democratic)
1932	Franklin D. Roosevelt (Democratic)	Herbert Hoover (Republican)
1936	Franklin D. Roosevelt (Democratic)	Alfred M. Landon (Republican)
1940	Franklin D. Roosevelt (Democratic)	Wendell L. Willkie (Republican)
1944	Franklin D. Roosevelt (Democratic)	Thomas E. Dewey (Republican)
1948	Harry S. Truman (Democratic)	Thomas E. Dewey (Republican)
1952	Dwight D. Eisenhower (Republican)	Adlai E. Stevenson (Democratic)
1956	Dwight D. Eisenhower (Republican)	Adlai E. Stevenson (Democratic)
1960	John F. Kennedy (Democratic)	Richard M. Nixon (Republican)
1964	Lyndon B. Johnson (Democratic)	Barry M. Goldwater (Republican)
1968	Richard M. Nixon (Republican)	Hubert H. Humphrey (Democratic)
1972	Richard M. Nixon (Republican)	George S. McGovern (Democratic)
1976	Jimmy Carter (Democratic)	Gerald R. Ford (Republican)
1980	Ronald Reagan (Republican)	Jimmy Carter (Democratic)
1984	Ronald Reagan (Republican)	Walter Mondale (Democratic)
1988	George Bush (Republican)	Michael Dukakis (Democratic)
1992	Bill Clinton (Democratic)	George Bush (Republican)
1996		
2000		

Chronological Table of the Presidents of the United States

	Years of office	*State of birth*	
George WASHINGTON	1789 - 1797	Virginia	
John ADAMS	1797 - 1801	Massachusetts	
Thomas JEFFERSON	1801 - 1809	Virginia	
James MADISON	1809 - 1817	Virginia	
James MONROE	1817 - 1825	Virginia	
John Quincy ADAMS	1825 - 1829	Massachusetts	
Andrew JACKSON	1829 - 1837	South Carolina	
Martin VAN BUREN	1837 - 1841	New York	
William Henry HARRISON	1841	Virginia	Died in office, April 4, 1841
John TYLER	1841 - 1845	Virginia	
James K. POLK	1845 - 1849	North Carolina	
Zachary TAYLOR	1849 - 1850	Virginia	Died in office, July 9, 1850
Millard FILLMORE	1850 - 1853	New York	
Franklin PIERCE	1853 - 1857	New Hampshire	
James BUCHANAN	1857 - 1861	Pennsylvania	
Abraham LINCOLN	1861 - 1865	Kentucky	Assassinated April 14, 1865
Andrew JOHNSON	1865 - 1869	North Carolina	
Ulysses S. GRANT	1869 - 1877	Ohio	
Rutherford B. HAYES	1877 - 1881	Ohio	
James A. GARFIELD	1881	Ohio	Assassinated July 2, 1881 (died September 19)
Chester A. ARTHUR	1881 - 1885	Vermont	
Grover CLEVELAND	1885 - 1889	New Jersey	
Benjamin HARRISON	1889 - 1893	Ohio	
Grover CLEVELAND	1893 - 1897	New Jersey	Second period of office
William McKINLEY	1897 - 1901	Ohio	Assassinated September 6, 1901 (died Sept 14)
Theodore ROOSEVELT	1901 - 1909	New York	
William Howard TAFT	1909 - 1913	Ohio	
Woodrow WILSON	1913 - 1921	Virginia	
Warren HARDING	1921 - 1923	Ohio	Died in office, August 2, 1923
Calvin COOLIDGE	1923 - 1929	Vermont	
Herbert HOOVER	1929 - 1933	Iowa	
Franklin D. ROOSEVELT	1933 - 1945	New York	Died in office, April 12, 1945
Harry S. TRUMAN	1945 - 1953	Missouri	
Dwight D. EISENHOWER	1953 - 1961	Texas	
John F. KENNEDY	1961 - 1963	Massachusetts	Assassinated November 22, 1963
Lyndon B. JOHNSON	1963 - 1969	Texas	
Richard M. NIXON	1969 - 1974	California	Resigned from office, August 14, 1974
Gerald R. FORD	1974 - 1977	Nebraska	
Jimmy CARTER	1977 - 1981	Georgia	
Ronald REAGAN	1981 - 1989	Illinois	
George BUSH	1989 - 1993	Massachusetts	
Bill CLINTON	1993 -	Arkansas	

BIBLIOGRAPHY

Chapter 1 The Constitutional Presidency

Bailey, H.A. (ed.) *Classics of the American Presidency*, Oak Park, Illinois, 1980.

Bessette, J.M. and Tulis, J.K. (eds.) *The Presidency in the Constitution*, Baton Rouge, Louisiana, 1981.

Buchanan, B. *The Presidential Experience*, Englewood Cliffs, New Jersey, 1978.

Corwin, E.S. *The President: Office and Powers*, 4th edition, New York, 1957.

Farrand, M. *The Framing of the Constitution of the United States*, New Haven, Connecticut, 1913.

Farrand, M. (ed.) *The Records of the Federal Convention of 1787*, 4 Vols., New Haven, Connecticut, 1966 and 1987.

de Grazia, A. *Republic in Crisis*, New York, 1965.

Greenstein, F. 'The Benevolent Leader Revisited: Children's Images of Political Leaders in Three Democracies' in *American Political Science Review*, December 1975.

Greenstein, F. *The Hidden Hand Presidency: Eisenhower as Leader*, Baltimore, 1994.

Hargrove, E.C. and Nelson, M. *Presidents, Politics, and Policy*, Baltimore, 1984.

Light, P.C. *The President's Agenda*, Baltimore, 1982.

Lipset, S.M. *The First New Nation: The United States in Historical and Comparative Perspective*, New York, 1979.

McPherson, H. *A Political Education*, Boston, 1972.

Milkis, S.M. and Nelson, M. *The American Presidency: Origins and Development, 1776-1993*, Washington, D.C., 1994.

Nelson, M. *A Heartbeat Away*, Washington, D.C., 1988.

Nelson, M. (ed.) *Historic Documents on the Presidency, 1776-1989*, Washington, D.C., 1989.

Nelson, M. (ed.) *The Elections of 1988*, Washington, D.C., 1989.

Neustadt, R.E. *Presidential Power*, New York, 1960.

Pious, R.M. *The American Presidency*, New York, 1978.

Roche, J.P. 'The Founding Fathers: A Reform Caucus in Action' in *American Political Science Review*, December 1961.

Rossiter, C. *The American Presidency*, Baltimore, 1984.

Sheatsley, P.B. and Feldman, J.J. 'The Assassination of President Kennedy: Public Reactions' in *Public Opinion Quarterly*, Summer 1964.

Tufte, E.R. *Political Control of the Economy*, Princeton, New Jersey, 1978.

Chapter 2 The American System

Abbot, W.W. (ed.) *The Papers of George Washington*, Charlottesville, Virginia, 1989.

Allen, C. *Eisenhower and the Mass Media: Peace, Prosperity, and Prime-Time Television*, Chapel Hill, North Carolina, 1993.

Bowles, N. *The White House and Capitol Hill: The Politics of Presidential Persuasion*, Oxford, 1987.

Edwards, G.C. *The Public Presidency: The Pursuit of Popular Support*, New York, 1983.

Galambos, L. (ed.) *The New American State*, Baltimore, 1987.

Gauch, J.E. 'The Intended Role of the Senate in Supreme Court Appointments' in *University of Chicago Law Review*, 1989.

Goldman, S. 'Bush's Judicial Legacy: The Final Imprint' in *Judicature*, 1993.

Grossman, M.B. and Kumar, M.J. *Portraying the President*, Baltimore, 1981.

Hargrove, E.C. and Nelson, M. *Presidents, Politics, and Policy*, Baltimore, 1984.

Hart, J. *The Presidential Branch*, 2nd edition, Chatham, New Jersey, 1995.

Heclo, H. and Salamon, L.M. (eds.) *The Illusion of Presidential Government*, Boulder, Colorado, 1981.

Hertsgaard, M. *On Bended Knee: The Press and the Reagan Presidency*, New York, 1988.

Iglehart, J. 'Major HEW Legislation Tailored by White House "Working Groups"' in *National Journal*, March 7, 1970.

Kernell, S. *Going Public: New Strategies of Presidential Leadership*, Washington, D.C., 1986.

King, G. and Ragsdale, L. (eds.) *The Elusive Executive*, Washington, D.C., 1988.

Klein, H. *Making it Perfectly Clear*, New York, 1980.

Levy, L.W. and Fisher, L. (eds.) *Encyclopedia of the American Presidency*, New York, 1994.

Maltese, J.A. *Spin Control: The White House Office of Communications and the Management of Presidential News*, 2nd edition, Chapel Hill, North Carolina, 1994.

Maltese, J.A. *The Selling of Supreme Court Nominees*, Baltimore, 1995.

Minow, N.N., Martin, J.B., and Mitchell, L.N. *Presidential Television*, New York, 1973.

Nathan, R.P. *The Plot that Failed: Nixon and the Administrative Presidency*, New York, 1975.

Nelson, M. (ed.) *The Presidency and the Political System*, 4th edition, Washington, D.C., 1995.

Neustadt, R.E. 'Presidency and Legislation: Planning the President's Program' in *American Political Science Review*, December 1955.

Oudes, B. (ed.) *From: The President – Richard Nixon's Secret Files*, New York, 1989.

Pfiffner, J.P. *The Modern Presidency*, New York, 1994.

Rosenbaum, D.E. 'Push for Line-Item Veto Runs Out of G.O.P. Steam' in *New York Times*, July 20, 1995.

Ruckman, P.S., Jr. 'The Supreme Court, Critical Nominations, and the Senate Confirmation Process' in *Journal of Politics*, 1993.

Safire, W. *Before the Fall*, New York, 1975.

Seidman, H. *Politics, Position, and Power*, 3rd edition, New York, 1980.

Solomon, B. 'How a Leak-Loathing White House is Putting the Press in its Place' in *National Journal*, February 13, 1993.

Sundquist, J.L. *The Decline and Resurgence of Congress*, Washington, D.C., 1981.

Tulis, J.K. *The Rhetorical Presidency*, Princeton, New Jersey, 1987.

Williams, R. *The Modern Presidency*, New York, 1987.

Witt, E. (ed.) *Guide to the Supreme Court*, Washington, D.C., 1979.

Chapter 3 The Vice Presidency

Goldstein, J.K. *The Modern American Vice Presidency*, Princeton, New Jersey, 1982.

Light, P.C. *Vice-Presidential Power: Advice and Influence in the White House*, Baltimore, 1984.

Milkis, S.M. and Nelson, M. *The American Presidency: Origins and Development, 1776-1993*, Washington, D.C., 1994.

Nelson, M. *A Heartbeat Away*, Washington, D.C., 1988.

Nelson, M. (ed.) *The Presidency and the Political System*, 4th edition, Washington, D.C., 1995.

Williams, I.G. *The Rise of the Vice Presidency*, Washington, D.C., 1956.

Chapter 4 Electing the President

Agranoff, R. (ed.) *The New Style in Election Campaigns*, Boston, 1976.

Anderson, K. *Creation of a Democratic Majority, 1928–1936*, Chicago, 1979.

Binkley, W.E. *American Political Parties: Their Natural History*, 2nd edition, New York, 1947.

Burnham, W.D. *Critical Elections and the Mainsprings of American Politics*, New York, 1970.

Campbell,A., Converse, P.E., Miller, W.E., and Stokes, D.E. (eds.), *Elections and the Political Order*, New York, 1966.

Carmines, E., McIver, J., and Stimson, J.A. 'Unrealized Partisanship: A Theory of Dealignment' in *Journal of Politics* 49, May 1987.

Carroll, E.M. *Origins of the Whig Party*, New York, 1970.

Ceaser, J.W. *Presidential Selection: Theory and Practice*, Princeton, New Jersey, 1979.

Ceaser, J.W., *Reforming the Reforms: A Critical Analysis of the Presidential Selection Process*, Cambridge, Massachusetts, 1982.

Chambers, W.N. *Political Parties in a New Nation: The American Experience*, London, 1963.

Charles, J. *The Origins of the American Party System*, Williamsburg, Virginia, 1956.

Chase, J.S. *Emergence of the Presidential Nominating System: 1789–1832*, Urbana, Illinois, 1973.

Clubb, J.M., Flanigan, W.H., and Zingale, N.H. *Partisan Realignment: Voters, Parties, and Government in American History*, Beverly Hills, California, 1980.

Cunningham, N., Jr. *The Jeffersonian Republicans: The Formation of Party Organization, 1789–1801*, Chapel Hill, North Carolina, 1957.

Dauer, M.J., *The Adams Federalists*, Baltimore, 1953.

David, P.T., R.M. Goldman, and R.C. Bain. *The Politics of National Party Conventions*, Washington, D.C., 1960.

Dolce, P.C and G.H. Skau (eds.), *Power and the Presidency*, New York, 1976.

Gienapp, W. *The Origins of the Republican Party: 1852–1856*, New York, 1987.

Haworth, P.L. *The Hayes–Tilden Disputed Election of 1876*, Cleveland, Ohio, 1906.

Hofstadter, R. *The Idea of a Party System: The Rise of Legitimate Opposition in the United States, 1780–1840*, Berkeley, California, 1969.

Holt, M.F. *The Political Crisis of the 1850s*, New York, 1978.

Key, V.O. 'A Theory of Critical Elections' in *Journal of Politics* 17, February 1955.

Key, V.O. 'Secular Realignment and the Party System' in *Journal of Politics* 21, May 1959.

Kleppner, P. *The Third Electoral System: 1853–1892: Parties, Voters, and Political Cultures*, Chapel Hill, North Carolina, 1979.

Kleppner,P., Burnham, W.D., Formisano, R.P., Hays, S.P., Jensen, R., and Shade, W.G. (eds.), *The Evolution of American Electoral Systems*, Westport, Conn., 1981.

McCormick, R.P. *The Second American Party System: Party Formation in the Jacksonian Era*, Chapel Hill, North Carolina, 1966.

McCormick, R.P. *The Presidential Game: The Origins of American Presidential Politics*, New York, 1982.

Moos, M. *The Republicans: A History of Their Party*, New York, 1956.

Morgan, H.W., *From Hayes to McKinley: National Party Politics, 1877–1896*, Syracuse, New York, 1969.

Morgan, W.G. 'The Origins and Development of the Congressional Nominating Caucus' in *Proceedings of the American Philosophical Society*, 1969.

Nelson, M. (ed.), *Guide to the Presidency*, Washington, D.C., 1989.

Nichols, R.F. *The Invention of American Political Parties*, New York, 1967.

Ostrogorski, M. 'The Rise and Fall of the Nominating Caucus, Legislative and Congressional' in *American Historical Review*, 2, December 1899.

Patterson, T. *The Mass Media Election: How Americans Choose Their President*, New York, 1980.

Peirce, N.R., and L.D. Longley. *The People's President: the Electoral College in American History and the Direct Vote Alternative*, revised edition, New Haven, Connecticut, 1981.

Polsby, N.W. *The Consequences of Party Reform*, New York, 1983.

Polsby, N.W., and A. Wildavsky. *Presidential Elections: Contemporary Strategies of American Electoral Politics*, 9th edition, Chatham, New Jersey, 1995.

Remini, R.V. *Martin Van Buren and the Making of the Democratic Party*, New York, 1959.

Sayre, W., and J.H. Parris. *The Electoral College and the American Political System*, Washington, D.C., 1970.

Schlesinger, Jr., A.S. (ed.), *History of U.S. Political Parties*, 4 vols, New York, 1973.

Schlesinger, Jr., A.S., and F.L. Israel (eds.), *History of American Presidential Elections*, 10 vols, New York, 1986.

Shafer, B.E. *Quiet Revolution: The Struggle for the Democratic Party and the Shaping of Post-Reform Politics*, New York, 1983.

Shafer, B.E. *Bifurcated Politics: Evolution and Reform in the National Party Convention*, New York, 1988.

Silbey, J.H. and McSeveney, S.T. (eds.), *Voters, Parties, and Elections*, Lexington, Mass., 1972.

Smallwood, F. *The Other Candidates: Third Parties in Presidential Elections*, Hanover, New Hampshire, 1983.

Sundquist, J.L. *Dynamics of the Party System: Alignment and Realignment of Political Parties in the United States*, revised edition, Washington, D.C., 1983.

Thach, C.C., Jr. *The Creation of the Presidency, 1775–1789: A Study in Constitutional History*, Baltimore, 1922.

Thompson, C. *The Rise and Fall of the Nominating Caucus*, New Haven, Connecticut, 1902.

Chapter 5 The Seat of Presidential Power

Carter, R. *First Lady from Plains*, Boston, 1984.

Hess, S. *Organizing the Presidency*, Washington, D.C., 1976

President's Committee on Administrative Management. *Report of the Committee*, Washington, D.C., 1937.

Rather, D. and Gates, G. P. *The Palace Guard*, New York, 1974.

Wayne, S.J. *The Legislative Presidency*, New York, 1978.

Woll, P. (ed.), *American Government: Readings and Cases*, Boston, 1987.

Chapter 6 The Early Presidents

Beard, C.A. *Mr President: The Presidents in American History, 1789–1980*, New York, 1977.

Boller, P. F., Jr. *Presidential Anecdotes*, New York, 1981.

Bowman, J. *Pictorial History of the American Presidency*, New York, 1986.

Degregorio, W. A. *The Complete Book of U.S. Presidents*. 4th edition, New York, 1993.

Ellis, J.J. *Passionate Sage: The Character and Legacy of John Adams*, New York, 1993.

Flexner, J. *Washington: The Indispensable Man*, Boston, 1974.

Frank, S. and Melick A. D., *The Presidents: Tidbits and Trivia*, New York, 1984.

Friedel, F. *Our Country's Presidents*, Washington, D.C., 1966.

Friedel, F. *The Presidents of the United States of America*, Washington, D.C., 1987.

Leish, K. W. (ed.). *George Washington through Rutherford B. Hayes*, Vol. I. of *The American Heritage Pictorial History of the Presidents*, New York 1968.

Mason, A.T. and Baker, G.E., *Free Government in the Making: Readings in American Political Thought*, 4th edition, New York, 1985.

Nelson, M. (ed.). *Guide to the Presidency*, Washington, D.C., 1989.

Peabody, J.B. (ed.). *The Founding Fathers: John Adams, A Biography in His Own Words*, New York, 1973.

Post, R.C. (ed.). *Every Four Years: The American Presidency*, revised edition, 1989.

Ross, G.E. *Know Your Presidents and Their Wives*, Chicago, 1960.

Smith, C. (ed.). *A Sourcebook on the U.S. Presidency: The Founding Presidents*, Brookfield, Connecticut, 1993.

Urofsky, M.I. *A March of Liberty*, New York, 1988.

Voss, F.S. *The Smithsonian Treasury: The Presidents*, Washington, D.C., 1991.

Chapter 7 The Jacksonian Era

Boller, P.F., Jr. *Presidential Anecdotes*, New York, 1981.

DeGregorio, W.A. *The Complete Book of US Presidents*, 4th edition, New York, 1993.

Freidel, F. *Our Country's Presidents*, Washington, D.C., 1977.

Milkis, S.M. and Nelson, M. *The American Presidency: Origins and Development, 1776-1993*, Washington, D.C., 1994.
Nelson, M. (ed.). *Guide to the Presidency*, Washington, D.C., 1989.
Safire, W. *Safire's New Political Dictionary*, New York, 1993.
Voss, F.S. *The Presidents*, Washington, D.C., 1991.
The World Book Encyclopedia, Chicago, 1994.

Chapter 8 The Civil War Presidents
Anderson, D.D. (ed.). *The Literary Works of Abraham Lincoln*. Columbus, Ohio, 1970.
DeGregorio, W.A. *The Complete Book of U.S. Presidents*. 4th edition, New York, 1993.
Donald, D.H. *Lincoln*, New York, 1995.
Freidel, F. *Our Country's Presidents*, Washington, D.C., 1977.
Milkis, S.M., and Nelson, M. *The American Presidency: Origins and Development, 1776–1993*, Washington, D.C., 1994.
Nelson, M. (ed.). *Guide to the Presidency*, Washington D.C., 1989.
Voss, F.S. *The Presidents*, Washington, D.C., 1991.
Ward, G.C., with Burns, R. and Burns, K. *The Civil War*, New York, 1991.
The World Book Encyclopedia, Chicago, 1994.

Chapter 9 The 'Gilded' Age
Adams, H. 'The Session' in *North American Review*, July 1870.
Barnard, H. *Rutherford B. Hayes and His America*, New York, 1954.
Binkley, W.E. *President and Congress*, New York, 1947.
Binkley, W.E. *American Political Parties*, New York, 1958.
Binkley, W.E. *The Man in the White House*, New Baltimore 1958.
Boller, P.F., Jr. *Presidential Anecdotes*, New York, 1981.
Bryce, J. *The American Commonwealth*, New York, 1894.
Congressional Quarterly, *The Origins and Development of Congress*, Washington, D.C., 1976.
DiClerico, R.E. *The American President*, 4th edition, Englewood Cliffs, New Jersey, 1995.
Doenecke, J.D. *The Presidencies of James A. Garfield and Chester A. Arthur*, Lawrence, Kansas, 1981.
Fisher, L. *Presidential War Power*, Lawrence, Kansas, 1995.
Gould, L.L. *The Presidency of William McKinley*, Lawrence, Kansas, 1980.
Hoogenboom, A. *Outlawing the Spoils: A History of the Civil Service Reform Movement*, Urbana, Illinois, 1961.
Hoogenboom, A. *The Presidency of Rutherford B. Hayes*, Lawrence, Kansas, 1988.
Howe, G.F. *Chester A. Arthur: A Quarter Century of Machine Politics*, New York, 1934.
Leech, M. *In the Days of McKinley*, New York, 1959.
Morison, S.E. *The Oxford History of the American People*, New York, 1965.
Nevins, A. *Grover Cleveland: A Study in Change*, New York, 1932.
Peskin, A. *Garfield*, Kent State University, 1978.
Pious, R. *The American Presidency*, New York, 1979.
Reichley, J. *The Life of the Parties: A History of American Political Parties*, New York, 1992.
Rubin, L.D., Jr., (ed.) *To Teach the Freeman: The Correspondence of*

Rutherford B. Hayes and the Slater Fund for Negro Education, Baton Rouge, Louisiana, 1959.
Socolofsky, H.E. and Spetter, A.B. *The Presidency of Benjamin Harrison*, Lawrence, Kansas, 1987.
Welch, R.E., Jr., *The Presidencies of Grover Cleveland*, Lawrence, Kansas, 1988.
White, L.D. *The Republican Era: 1869–1901*, New York, 1958.
Woodward, C.V. *The Strange Career of Jim Crow*, 3rd edition, New York, 1974.

Chapter 10 The Modern Presidency Emerges
Cooper, J.M., Jr. *The Warrior and the Priest: Woodrow Wilson and Theodore Roosevelt*, Cambridge, Massachussetts, 1983.
Gould, L.L. *The Presidency of William McKinley*, Lawrence, Kansas, 1980.
Harbaugh, W.H. *The Life and Times of Theodore Roosevelt*, New York, 1963.
Hawley, E.W. *The Great War and the Search for a Modern Order: A History of the American People and Their Institutions 1917-1933*, 2nd edition., New York, 1992.
Hicks, J.D. *Republican Ascendancy, 1921–1933*, New York, 1960.
Karl, B. *The Uneasy State: The United States from 1915 to 1945*, Chicago, 1983.
Link, A.S. *Wilson the Diplomatist: A Look at His Major Foreign Policies*, Chicago, 1965.
Mayer, A.J. *Wilson vs. Lenin: Political Origins of the New Diplomacy, 1917–1918*, New York, 1964.
McCoy, D.B. *Calvin Coolidge: The Quiet President*, New York, 1967.
Mowry, G.E. *The Era of Theodore Roosevelt*, New York, 1958.
Murray, R.K *The Harding Era: Warren G. Harding and His Administration*, Minneapolis, 1969.
Murray, R.K *The Politics of Normalcy: Governmental Theory and Practice in the Harding–Coolidge Era*, New York, 1973.
Romasco, A.U. *The Poverty of Abundance: Hoover, the Nation, the Depression*, New York, 1995.
Smith, D.M. *The Great Departure: The United States and World War I, 1914–1920*, New York, 1965.
Walworth, A. *Woodrow Wilson*, 3rd edition, New York, 1978.
Wilson, J.F. *Herbert Hoover: Forgotten Progressive*, Boston, 1975.

Chapter 11 The Modern Presidency
Ambrose, S.E. *Eisenhower: Soldier, General of the Army, President-Elect 1890-1952*, New York, 1983.
Ambrose, S.E. *Eisenhower: The President*, New York, 1984.
Dallek, R. *Franklin D. Roosevelt and American Foreign Policy, 1932-1945*, New York, 1979.
Freidel, F. *Franklin D. Roosevelt: Launching the New Deal*, Boston, 1973.
Kaufman, B.I. *The Korean War: Challenges in Crisis, Credibility, and Command*, New York, 1986.
Kaufman, B.I. 'John F. Kennedy as World Leader: A Perspective on the Literature' in *Diplomatic History*, 17, Summer 1993.

Leffler, M.P. *A Preponderance of Power: National Security, the Truman Administration, and the Cold War*, Stanford, California, 1992.
Leuchtenberg, W.E. *Franklin Roosevelt and the New Deal*, New York, 1963.
Matusow, A.J *The Unraveling of America: A History of Liberalism in the 1960s*, New York, 1984.
McCullough, D. *Truman*, New York, 1992.
Reeves, R. *President Kennedy: Profile of Power*, New York, 1993.
Williams, T.F. *Huey Long*, New York, 1969.

Chapter 12 The Contemporary Presidency
Aiken, J. *Nixon: A Life*, Washington, D.C., 1993.
Ambrose, S. *Nixon: The Education of a Politician, 1913-1952*, New York, 1987.
Ambrose, S. *Nixon: The Triumph of a Politician, 1962-1972*, New York, 1989.
Ambrose, S. *Nixon: Ruin and Recovery, 1973-1990*, New York, 1991.
Beschloss, M. and Talbott, S. *At the Highest Levels: The Inside Story of the End of the Cold War*, 1993.
Brumnett, J. *Highwire: From the Backgrounds to the Beltway – The Education of Bill Clinton*, 1994.
Cannon, L. *President Reagan: The Role of a Lifetime*, New York, 1991.
Clarke, J. 'Rhetoric Before Reality' in *Foreign Affairs*, 74, September/October 1995.
Drew, E. *On the Edge: The Clinton Presidency*, New York, 1994.
Duffy, M. and Goodgame, D. *Marching in Place: The Status Quo Presidency of George Bush*, New York, 1992.
Greene, J.R. *The Presidency of Gerald R. Ford*, Lawrence, Kansas, 1995.
Herring, G. *America's Longest War: The United States and Vietnam*, New York, 1986.
Kaufman, B.. *The Presidency of James Earl Carter, Jr.*, Lawrence, Kansas, 1993.
Kaufman, B.. *The Arab Middle East and the United States: Inter-Arab Rivalry and Superpower Diplomacy*, New York, 1995.
Kellerman, B. *The Political Presidency: Practice of Leadership from Kennedy through Reagan*, New York, 1984.
King, N. *George Bush: A Biography*, New York, 1980.
Kissinger, H. *White House Years*, Boston, 1979.
Maraniss, D. *First In His Class: A Biography of Bill Clinton*, New York, 1995.
Schieffer, B. and Gates, G.P. *The Acting President*, New York, 1989.
Smith, J.E. *George Bush's War*, New York, 1992.
Wicker, T. *One of Us: Richard Nixon and the American Dream*, New York, 1991.
Woodward, B. *The Commanders*, New York, 1991.

Chapter 13 The First Ladies
Anthony, C.S. *First Ladies: The Saga of the Presidents' Wives and Their Power, 1789–1961*, New York, 1990.
Boller, Jr., P.F. *Presidential Wives: An Anecdotal History*, New York, 1988.
Caroli, B.B. *First Ladies*, New York, 1987.

ACKNOWLEDGMENTS

The publishers are grateful to and would like to thank the numerous museums and collectors for the opportunity to photograph artifacts. Also thanks go to the various picture sources and individuals in the United States and the United Kingdom for their help in the preparation of this book and for granting permission to publish their images. All artifact and picture sources are listed overleaf by page; artist's names are given where appropriate. Every effort has been made to trace the copyright holders where known.

The Technical Consultant on the project was Russ A. Pritchard, a principal of the American Ordnance Preservation Association, Inc. (AOPA), and formerly Executive Director of the Civil War Library and Museum, Philadelphia, for 20 years. He now serves on the Board of Governors of the Civil War Library and Museum, and is a consultant for the Museum of the Confederacy, Richmond, Virginia. He is a member of the American Society of Arms Collectors, Fellow of the Company of Military Historians, and life member of the National Rifle Association. He graduated from the Choate School and Washington and Lee University.

A special thank you goes to the following institutional collections and individuals:

Daughters of the American Revolution Museum:
Anne D. Ruta, Registrar
Cricket Bauer, Assistant
Gretchen Bulova, Assistant

Dwight D. Eisenhower Library and Museum:
John E. Wickman, Director
Dennis H.J. Medina, Curator
Marion M. Kamm, Registrar
Gary W. Holman, Exhibits Specialist
Steve James, Museum Technician

Rutherford B. Hayes Presidential Center:
Dr. Roger D. Bridges, Director
James B. Snider, Chief Curator
Mary Lou Rendon, Curatorial Assistant
Barbara Paff, Co-Librarian

The Hermitage:
Marsha A. Mullin, Curator of Collections
Courtney A. Bradsby, Curatorial Assistant

Kensmore Association:
Stacia Norman, Curator

Lincoln Memorial University:
Stephen Hague, Director and Curator
Frank B. Coburn, Curatorial Assistant

The James Madison Memorial Foundation:
Olive W. Foran, President
Judy Ramsden, Administrator
Ken Clark, Museum Technician

James Monroe Museum and Memorial Library:
Lee A. Langston-Harrison, Curator

Monticello:
Dr. Daniel P. Jordan, Director
Suzanne Olson, Assistant Curator
Mindy Keyes Black, Communications Officer

James K. Polk Ancestral Home:
John C. Holtzapple, Director
Kristine P. Brvan, Curator of Collections
Jeff K. Walters, Education Officer

Harry S. Truman Library:
Dr. Benedict K. Zobrist, Director
Mark L. Beveridge, Curator

Tudor Place Foundation, Inc.:
Eleanor C. Preston, Curator

Washington and Lee University:
Dr. Thomas V. Litzenburg, Jr., Director
Reeves Center

George Washington Masonic National Memorial:
Donald Robey, Executive Secretary

The Woodrow Wilson House:
Frank Aucella, Curator and Assistant Director

Private Collections:
Mr and Mrs James A. Tyler, Charles City, Virginia
Mr Kevin Hofman, Bethlehem, Pennsylvania
Mr John Griffiths, Fredericksburg, Virginia
Mr Tony Hall, London, England

PICTURE CREDITS

With the exception of any items listed below, all the artifact photography reproduced in this book is the work of Don Eiler's Custom Photography, Richmond, Virginia, with the kind cooperation of the many institutions listed.

All the organizations and individuals that supplied photographs or artifacts are credited here by page number and position, with any reference numbers where known. The positions are indicated as follows: (T): Top; (B): Bottom; (C): Center; (TR): Top Right; (BR): Bottom Right; (TL): Top Left; and (BL): Bottom Left.

Endpapers: Jim Winkley; **Page 1:** (all) courtesy Dwight D. Eisenhower Library and Museum; **3:** (all) courtesy Dwight D. Eisenhower Library and Museum; **4:** courtesy Harry S. Truman Library; **5:** courtesy Harry S. Truman Library; **6:** © Tony Stone Worldwide Images, Greg Pease; **8:** © Tony Stone Worldwide Images, Reza Estakhrian; **9:** Courtesy, The Henry Francis du Pont Winterthur Museum, accession number 57.1261; **10:** The Library Company of Philadelphia; **11:** The National Portrait Gallery, Smithsonian Institute/Art Resource, New York, ref NPG.79.216; **12:** (TL) Courtesy, The Henry Francis du Pont Winterthur Museum, registration number 60.0570A, (BR) The Library Company of Philadelphia; **13:** Delaware Art Museum, Museum Purchase, 1912, Acc. No. 2026; **14:** The National Portrait Gallery, Smithsonian Institute/Art Resource, New York, ref NPG.80.129; **15:** National Graphic Center/The Architect of the Capitol, ref neg 70222; **16:** (T) National Graphic Center/The Architect of the Capitol, ref neg 70228,(B) National Graphic Center/The Architect of the Capitol, ref neg 70225; **17:** Virginia Museum of Fine Arts, Gift of Edgar William and Bernice Chrysler Garbisch, Acc. No. 50.2.1, Photo No. 51988.5; **18:** Range/Bettmann/UPI, ref 10015449; **19:** Bush Presidential Materials Project, ref P17675-11; **20:** (T) Library of Congress, ref LCUSZ62 7622, (B) Library of Congress, ref 49-3457; **21:** (T) Jimmy Carter Library, ref C10017-35, (B) Courtesy of Reagan Library, ref C33193-34; **22:** Library of Congress, ref LCUSZ62 5379; **23:** Range/Bettmann/UPI, ref 10016696; **24:** US Navy Photo, SDAN: K-116301; **25:** (T) Range/Bettmann/UPI, ref 10023534, (B) Range/Bettmann/UPI, ref 10023554; **26:** (T) Library of Congress, ref LCUSZ62 1306, (BL) Franklin D. Roosevelt Library, ref 48–22:4291, (BR) US Naval Historical Center, ref NH 57395; **27:** (T) Range/Bettmann/UPI, ref 10023522, (B) courtesy Dwight D. Eisenhower Library, ref 72-1447-1 National Park Service; **28:** (T) courtesy Dwight D. Eisenhower Library, ref 72-3205-1 National Park Service, (B) Range/IME, ref 10023567; **29:** (T) courtesy Franklin D. Roosevelt Library, ref 48–22:3713 (92), (B) Range/Bettmann/UPI, ref 10023542; **30:** (T) courtesy Dwight D. Eisenhower Library, ref 72-1629-2 National Park Service, (B) courtesy Franklin D. Roosevelt Library, ref 47–96:1838; **31:** (T) Range/Bettmann/UPI, ref 10023550, (B) Range/Bettmann/IME, ref 10023562; **32:** (T) The White House, Pete Souza, (B) Range/Bettmann/UPI, ref 10023530; **33:** (T) Range/Reuter/Bettmann, ref 10023541, (B) Range/Reuter/Bettmann, ref 10023574; **34:** Range/Bettmann/UPI, ref 10023527; **35:** Range/Bettmann/UPI, ref 10023539; **36:** LBJ Library Collection/Cecil Stoughton, ref 1A1; **37:** Library of Congress, ref LCUSZ62 74108; **38:** (L) Range/Bettmann, ref 10015485, (R) Range/Bettmann, ref 10015453; **39:** (T) Range/Bettmann/UPI, ref 10015445, (BL, badge) courtesy Tony Hall Collection, (BR) Range/Bettmann/UPI, ref 10015450; **40:** (T) The White House, Cynthia Johnson, (BL, badge) courtesy Tony Hall Collection, (B) Bush Presidential Materials Project, ref P26579-6; **41:** (T) Range/Bettmann/UPI, ref 10015454, (B) Range/Reuter/Bettmann, ref 10015442; **42:** Courtesy, The Henry Francis du Pont Winterthur Museum, accession number 57. 816; **43:** Courtesy, The Henry Francis du Pont Winterthur Museum, accession number 59.131A; **44:** Samuel Finley Breese Morse, The Old House of Representatives, 1822, oil on canvas, 86 1/2 x 130 3/4 in (219.71 x 332.11 cm) In the Collection of the Corcoran Gallery of Art, Museum Purchase, Gallery Fund; **45:** The National Portrait Gallery, Smithsonian Institute/Art Resource, New York, ref NPG.82.10; **46:** (L) Library of Congress, ref LCUSZ62 13699, (R) Library of Congress, ref LCUSZ62 34717; **47:** National Portrait Gallery, Smithsonian Institute/Art Resource, New York, ref NPG.83.5; **48:** (T) Lithograph by Britton & Rey, San Francisco, designed and drawn by Henry Clay Donnell, published by US Election Map Co., courtesy Rutherford B. Hayes Presidential Center, (B) courtesy James Monroe Museum and Memorial Library; **49:** courtesy of Truman Library, ref 64-491D; **50:** courtesy Geral R. Ford Library; **51:** Range/Reuter/Bettmann, ref 10016692; **52:** John F. Kennedy Library, ref KN–C19364; **53:** Range/Reuter/Bettmann, ref 10015517; **54:** Library of Congress, ref LCUSZ62 13226; **55:** (T) courtesy James Monroe Museum and Memorial Library, (B) Library of Congress, ref LCUSZ62 22336; **56:** (T) Library of Congress, ref LCJ698 81254, (B) Library of Congress, ref LCJ698 81329; **57:** Library of Congress, ref LCUSZ62 16483; **58:** Public Relations, Boeing Defense & Space Group, Military Airplanes, Wichita Branch, KS 67277-7730; **59:** (T) Library of Congress, ref LCUSZ62 91315, (B) MacArthur Archives, ref ph 2244; **60:** (T) Library of Congress, ref LCUSZ62 76095, (B) John F. Kennedy Library, ref AR 6287-D; **61:** (T) LBJ Library Collection, ref A-4231-4, (B) The White House, Mary Anne Fackelman; **62:** (T) Library of Congress, ref LCH216 24394, (B) John F. Kennedy Library, ref C63-11-WH63; **63:** © Tony Stone Images, Robert Shafer; **64:** National Graphic Center/The Architect of the Capitol, ref neg 70242; **65:** (BL) courtesy The Reeves Collection, Washington and Lee University, (T & BR) courtesy Tudor Place Foundation; **66:** (T) George Washington by Thomas Sully, Permanent Collection of the University of Delaware, (BL) courtesy James Monroe Museum and Memorial Library; **67:** (1 & 8) courtesy Tudor Place Foundation, (2, 3, 5 & 7) courtesy Daughters of the American Revolution Museum, (4) courtesy George Washington Masonic National Memorial Association, (6) courtesy Kenmore Association; **68:** (T) Library of Congress, ref LCUSZ62 3992, (B) courtesy James Monroe Museum and Memorial Library; **69:** (T) US Department of the Interior, National Park Service, Adams National Historic Site, Quincy, Massachusetts, (BL) courtesy The Reeves Collection, Washington and Lee University, (BR) courtesy James Monroe Museum and Memorial Library; **70:** (T) The National Portrait Gallery, Smithsonian Institute/Art Resource, New York, ref NPG.82.97, (BL & BR) courtesy James Monroe Museum and Memorial Library; **71:** (all) courtesy Monticello, The Thomas Jefferson Memorial Foundation, Inc.; **72:** © Tony Stone Worldwide, Robert Shafer; **73:** (T) In the Collection of The Corcoran Gallery of Art, Acc. No. 75.16 mn, (B) Salamander Books Ltd; **74:** (T) Thomas Sully, James Madison, 1809, oil on panel, 27 1/2 x 19 1/2 in (69.85 x 49.53 cm), In the Collection of The Corcoran Gallery of Art, Gift of Frederick E. Church, (B) courtesy The James Madison Museum; **75:** (all) courtesy The James Madison Museum; **76:** (TL) courtesy The James Madison Museum, (TR & B) courtesy James Monroe Museum and Memorial Library; **77:** (T) Library of Congress, ref LCUSZ62 10253, (B) Library of Congress, ref LCUSZ62 16956; **78:** (TL) courtesy The Woodrow Wilson House, (TR) Library of Congress, ref LCUSZ62 32534, (B) courtesy James Monroe Museum and Memorial Library; **79:** (all) courtesy James Monroe Museum and Memorial Library; **80:** (both) courtesy James Monroe Museum and Memorial Library; **81:** George Peter Alexander Healy, John Quincy Adams, 1858, oil on canvas, 30 x 25 in (76.2 x 63.5 cm), In the Collection of The Corcoran Gallery of Art, Museum Purchase, Gallery Fund; **82:** Library of Congress, ref LCUSZ62 46804; **83:** (T) Thomas Sully, General Andrew Jackson, 1845, oil on canvas, 97 1/4 x 61 1/2 in (247.02 x 156.21 cm), In the Collection of The Corcoran Gallery of Art, Gift of William Wilson Corcoran, (B) Range/Bettmann/UPI, ref 10021715; **84:** (T) courtesy The Hermitage, (B) Collection of The New-York Historical Society, ref neg 42459; **85:** (main image, all) courtesy The Hermitage, (inset) courtesy Rutherford B. Hayes Presidential Center; **86:** (T) Library of Congress, ref LCUSZ62 22225, (B) courtesy James Monroe Museum and Memorial Library; **87:** (TL) courtesy Harry S. Truman Library, (TR) courtesy Mr and Mrs James A. Tyler, Jr., (B) Library of Congress, ref LCUSZ62 7567; **88:** (TL) Library of Congress, ref LCUSZ62 68952, (TR) courtesy James Monroe Museum and Memorial Library, (B) courtesy Mr and Mrs James A. Tyler, Jr.; **89:** (all) courtesy James K. Polk Ancestral Home; **90:** (TL) Library of Congress, ref LCUSZ62 91017, (TR & B) courtesy James K. Polk Ancestral Home; **91:** (T) courtesy James K. Polk Ancestral Home, (B) James K. Polk Memorial Association, Columbia, Tennessee, ref 1929.4.45; **92:** (TL) The National Portrait Gallery, Smithsonian Institute/Art Resource, New York, ref NPG.84.3, (TR & BL) courtesy James Monroe Museum and Memorial Library; **93:** (T) courtesy Harry S. Truman Library, (B) Library of Congress, ref LCUSZ62 29555; **94:** (T) courtesy James Monroe Museum and Memorial Library, (B) Library of Congress, ref LCUSZ62 24830; **95:** courtesy James Monroe Museum and Memorial Library; **96:** Library of Congress, ref B8184-10103; **97:** (both) courtesy James Monroe Museum and Memorial Library; **98:** (T) courtesy Lincoln Memorial University, (B) Library of Congress, ref LCUSZ62 48090; **99:** (T) courtesy Lincoln Memorial University, (BL) courtesy Harry S. Truman Library, (BR) National Archives N-B-3656; **100:** (T) courtesy Kevin Hoffman Collection, (B) Library of Congress, ref LCUSZ62 2070; **101:** (T) Library of Congress, ref 49-3461, (BL) courtesy Harry S. Truman Library, (BR) courtesy Lincoln Memorial University; **102:** (T) National Archives, ref 55-22151, (B, both) courtesy Lincoln Memorial University; **103:** (T) Library of Congress, ref LCUSZ62 35886, (BL) courtesy Rutherford B. Hayes Presidential Center, (BR) courtesy James Monroe Museum and Memorial Library; **104:** (main pcture) Salamander Books Ltd, (BL, both) courtesy Lincoln Memorial University; **105:** (T) Illinois State Historical Library, PG 104/105, (B) Library of Congress, no ref; **106:** (T) Library of Congress, ref LCUSZ62 22089, (B) courtesy James Monroe Museum and Memorial Library; **107:** Library of Congress, ref LCUSZ62 33270; **108:** US Naval Historical Center, ref NH 46775; **109:** (TR) courtesy Harry S. Truman Library, (BL) Library of Congress, ref LCUSZ62 5894, (BR) courtesy Rutherford B. Hayes Presidential Center; **110:** (T) Library of Congress, ref LCUSZ62 38251, (B) courtesy Rutherford B. Hayes Presidential Center; **111:** courtesy John G. Griffith; **112:** (TR) Library of Congress, ref LCBH832 30321A, (BL) courtesy Harry S. Truman Library; **113:** (all) courtesy Rutherford B. Hayes Presidential Center; **114:** Library of Congress, ref LCUSZ62 2247; **115:** (T) Library of Congress, ref LCUSZ62 22265, (B) Library of Congress, ref LCBH826 1484 B; **116:** (TL) Library of Congress, ref LCUSZ62 4915, (TR) Rutherford B. Hayes Presidential Center, (BR) courtesy Harry S. Truman Library; **117:** (TL) Library of Congress, ref LCUSZ62 13017, (BL) courtesy James Monroe Museum and Memorial Library, (BR) courtesy Harry S. Truman Library; **118:** (T) courtesy Rutherford B. Hayes Presidential Center, (BL) courtesy James Monroe Museum and Memorial Library, (BR) courtesy Harry S. Truman Library; **119:** (T) courtesy Harry S. Truman Library, (B) Library of Congress, ref LCBH836 188; **120:** (T) courtesy Dwight D. Eisenhower Library and Museum, (BL) courtesy Harry S. Truman Library, (BR) Salamander Books Ltd; **121:** courtesy Rutherford B. Hayes Presidential Center; **122:** Library of Congress, ref LCUSZ62 88102; **123:** Library of Congress, ref LCUSZ62 7756; **124:** (T) Library of Congress, ref LCUSZ62 39935, (B) courtesy Harry S. Truman Library; **125:** (T) US Signal Corps, neg 17608, (B) Salamander Books Ltd; **126:** (TL) courtesy Harry S. Truman Library, (TR) courtesy James Monroe Museum and Memorial Library, (B) Library of Congress, ref LCUSZ62 56945; **127:** (L) Library of Congress, ref LCUSZ62 48757, (R) courtesy Rutherford B. Hayes Presidential Center; **128:** (T) US Naval Historical Center, ref NH 1801, (B) Library of Congress, ref LCUSZ62 11390; **129:** Library of Congress, ref LCUSZ62 54111; **130:** (T) courtesy The Woodrow Wilson House, (B) Range/Bettmann/UPI, ref 10016647; **131:** (TL) courtesy Harry S. Truman Library, (TR) Range/Bettmann/UPI, ref 1001660, (BL) courtesy James Monroe Museum and Memorial Library; **132:** (T) Range/Bettmann/UPI, ref 10016651, (B) courtesy The Woodrow Wilson House; **133:** (all) courtesy The Woodrow Wilson House; **134:** (T) courtesy The Woodrow Wilson House, (BL) courtesy Harry S. Truman Library, (BR) Range/Bettmann/UPI, ref 10016643; **135:** The National Portrait Gallery, Smithsonian Institute/Art Resource, New York, ref NPG.66.21; **136:** (TL) Library of Congress, ref LCUSZ62 35155, (TR & BR) courtesy Harry S. Truman Library; **137:** (T) Range/Bettmann, ref 10015489, (B) Library of Congress, ref LCUSZ62 59666; **138:** (TL) Library of Congress, ref LCUSZ62 13031, (TR) courtesy Rutherford B. Hayes Presidential Center, (B) Range/Bettmann, ref 10016672; **139:** (T) James Monroe Museum and Memorial Library, (B) Range/Bettmann, ref 10016668; **140:** Don Eiler, Richmond, Virginia; **141:** Range/Bettmann, ref 10016659; **142:** Franklin D. Roosevelt Library, ref 83-7 (107); **143:** (TR) Library of Congress, ref LCUSZ62 16450, (BL) Library of Congress, ref LCUSZ62 68839; **144:** (T) Franklin D. Roosevelt Library, ref 53-227 (1754), (BL) Franklin D. Roosevelt Library, ref 53-227 (1733); **145:** (T) Franklin D. Roosevelt Library, ref 61-402 (1), (BL) Library of Congress, ref LCUSZ62 11427, (BR) courtesy Harry S. Truman Library; **146:** (T) US Signal Corps, neg 126975, (B) Franklin D. Roosevelt Library, ref 59–124; **147:** (T) Library of Congress, ref LCUSZ62 50932, (B) Library of Congress, ref LCUSZ62 67439; **148:** (T) courtesy Harry S. Truman Library, (B) MacArthur Arcgive, ref ph 3534; **149:** (TL) Salamander Books Ltd, (TR) US Signal Corps, neg 299276, (BL & BR) courtesy Harry S. Truman Library; **150:** (T) courtesy Harry S. Truman Library, (B) St Louis Mercantile Library Collection; **151:** (all) courtesy Harry S. Truman Library; **152:** (T) Salamander Books Ltd, (B) courtesy Dwight D. Eisenhower Library, ref 65–418 US Army; **153:** (T) courtesy Dwight D. Eisenhower Library, ref 68–352–1; (B) courtesy Dwight D. Eisenhower Library and Museum; **154:** (T) Range/Bettmann/UPI, ref 10023531, (B) courtesy Dwight D. Eisenhower Library and Museum; **155:** (all) courtesy Dwight D. Eisenhower Library and Museum; **156:** (T) courtesy Dwight D. Eisenhower Library, ref 72–2785–1 National Park Service, (B) courtesy Dwight D. Eisenhower Library and Museum; **157:** (T) courtesy Dwight D. Eisenhower Library, ref 62–2–1 US Navy, (B) Library of Congress, ref LCU9 5038; **158:** (TL) courtesy Harry S. Truman Library, (TR) courtesy Dwight D. Eisenhower Library and Museum, (B) Library of Congress, ref LCUSA7 25520; **159:** (T) Martin Luther King Library, Washington, D.C., neg 00773, (B) John F. Kennedy Library, ref PX 65-105:132; **160:** (T) John F. Kennedy Library, ref KN–24677, (B) Salamander Books Ltd; **161:** (T) Library of Congress, ref LCUSA7 25520, (B) LBJ Library Collection, Yoichi R. Okamoto, ref WH25–21; **162:** (T) courtesy Harry S. Truman Library, (B) LBJ Library Collection, Yoichi R. Okamoto, ref A2835.3a; **163:** (T) LBJ Library Collection, Yoichi R. Okamoto, ref A–3367–11, (B) LBJ Library Collection, Yoichi R. Okamoto, ref C7530.33a; **164:** (T) LBJ Library Collection, Yoichi R. Okamoto, ref C–9286–24, (B) LBJ Library Collection, Yoichi R. Okamoto, ref A–6016–12; **165:** LBJ Library Collection, Jack Kightlinger, ref B–1274–16; **166:** Salamander Books Ltd; **167:** (T) courtesy Dwight D. Eisenhower Library and Museum, (B) Library of Congress, ref LCU9 5038 9; **168:** (all) courtesy Dwight D. Eisenhower Library and Museum; **169:** (T) US Navy, ref K–97151, (B) Salamander Books Ltd; **170:** (T) The White House, ref 8528-02, (BL) Don Eiler, Richmond, Virginia, (BR) Gerald R. Ford Library, (BR, badge) courtesy Rutherford B. Hayes Presidential Center; **171:** (T) Gerald R. Ford Library, (B) Gerald R. Ford Library; **172:** (T) Salamander Books Ltd, (B) Jimmy Carter Library; **173:** (both) Jimmy Carter Library; **174:** (both) Jimmy Carter Library; **175:** (T) Jimmy Carter Library, (B) US Air Force, DF–SN–82–06713; **176:** (T) courtesy Rutherford B. Hayes Presidential Center, (B) Salamander Books Ltd; **177:** (T) courtesy James Monroe Museum and Memorial Library, (B) courtesy Ronald Reagan Library; **178:** (T) The White House, Karl Schumacher, (B) The White House,Bill Fitz-Patrick; **179:** (T) The White House, Karl Schumacher, (B) US Air Force, ref R–121–85; **180:** (T) The White House,Billie B. Shaddix, (B) Library of Congress, ref 71–967; **181:** (T) Bush Presidential Materials Project, no ref, (B) Bush Presidential Materials Project, ref P15234–22A; **182:** (T) Bush Presidential Materials Project, ref P8525–20, (B) Bush Presidential Materials Project, ref P17723–32; **183:** (T) Bush Presidential Materials Project, ref P17706–15, (B) Bush Presidential Materials Project, ref P28470–8A; **184:** (T) courtesy Tony Hall Collection, (B) Range/Reuter/Bettmann, ref 10016688; **185:** (T) Range/Reuter/Bettmann, ref 10016667, (B) courtesy James Monroe Museum and Memorial Library; **186:** Range/Reuter/Bettmann, ref 10023586; **187:** (T) Range/Bettmann, ref 10016675, (B) Range/Bettmann, ref 10023587; **188:** Salamander Books Ltd; **189:** The James K. Polk Memorial Association, Columbia, Tennessee, ref 1963.10.1; **190:** (TL) Library of Congress, ref LCUSZ62 1776, (TR) Library of Congress, ref LCUSZ62 91028; **191:** National Archives, ref 116992; **192:** Library of Congress, ref LCUSZ62 13493; **193:** Library of Congress, ref LCUSZ62 32924; **194:** Library of Congress, ref LCUSZ62 78051; **195:** (T) courtesy Franklin D. Roosevelt Library, ref 48–22:3724 (66), (B) used by permission of Temple University Urban Archives, courtesy of Harry S. Truman Library, ref 77–3546; **196:** (T) courtesy Dwight D. Eisenhower Library, ref 72–947–2, National Park Service, (C) courtesy of Harry S. Truman Library, (B) courtesy Dwight D. Eisenhower Library, ref 72–3646–3, National Park Service; **197:** (TL) courtesy of Harry S. Truman Library, (T) Range/Bettman/UPI, ref 10016970, (B) Salamander Books Ltd; **198:** (TR) courtesy Rutherford B. Hayes Presidential Center, (T) courtesy of Gerald R. Ford Library, (C) US Air Force, ref DF–SC–83–01261, (B) courtesy of Reagan Library; **199:** (T) Bush Presidential Materials Project, ref P13362–20, (B) Range/Reuter/Bettmann, ref 10016704; **200:** US Army, ref CC 122139; **201:** Range/Reuter/Bettmann, ref 10016663.

Editor's Note
Every effort has been made to contact original sources for permissions. The selection and captioning of all illustrations in this book have been the responsibility of Salamander Books Ltd and not of the individual contributors.

INDEX

Page numbers in bold indicate illustrations or mentions in captions. Artifacts (e.g. campaign ribbons) are indexed under the name of the president to whose term they refer.

207